Self-meditation

Self-meditation

3,299
tips, quotes,
reminders, and
wake-up calls for peace
and serenity

BARBARA ANN KIPFER

WORKMAN PUBLISHING • NEW YORK

Spine photograph courtesy Workman Publishing Co., Inc.

Library of Congress Cataloging-in-Publication Data is available.

ISBN: 978-0-7611-3928-7

Workman books are available at special discounts when purchased in bulk for premiums and sales promotions as well as for fund-raising or educational use. Special editions or book excerpts can also be created to specification. For details, contact the Special Sales Director at the address below, or send an email to specialmarkets@workman.com.

Workman Publishing Company, Inc.
225 Varick Street
New York, NY 10014-4381
workman.com

Printed in the United States of America
First printing July 2006

15 14 13 12 11

THANK YOU

Thank you to all the great meditation teachers whose work I drew upon by reading hundreds of books. I hope to try all of these myself!

Peter Workman, Susan Bolotin, and Jennifer Griffin welcomed the idea into the Workman family, and Mary Ellen O'Neill has been the champion of this revision. Thank you all.

Thank you to my colleague and friend, Bob Amsler, without whose technical help I would be lost. Most especially, I thank my family—my Sherpa and avid reviewer, Paul, and my sons, Kyle Kipfer and Keir Magoulas.

WELCOME

I was drawn to Buddhist studies and meditation by the theme of happiness that I found in so many of the books on the topic. The evidence of the positive effect of meditation on well-being is becoming quite impressive. Regular meditators have reduced levels of negative emotions, and mindfulness training and meditation have been shown to reduce stress, improve immune responses, and increase overall mental and physical health.

In general, meditation techniques teach people to become aware of the contents of their consciousnesses but at the same time to detach themselves from them. Thoughts can be seen in context for what they are—just thoughts. This increase in awareness can make an incredible difference in your life.

Self-Meditation is all about learning to listen to ourselves, be in the present moment, and not get caught up by attachment, aversion, fear, and suffering. These things are part of life, but by meditating you can find ways to notice them but not let them overwhelm you. Meditation teaches you to be mindful and honest, which makes your mind quieter and more open, your heart happier and more peaceful.

Namaste,
Barbara Ann Kipfer

WAKE UP!

Here you are, ready to self-meditate, and this section offers some simple guidelines and information for your practice.

MEDITATION CHECKLIST

Gather together

- ❑ regular time slot and amount of time
- ❑ quiet or peaceful place for your meditation
- ❑ meditation cushion, bench, or favorite chair
- ❑ distractions turned off (telephone and screens)
- ❑ comfortable attire
- ❑ comfortable sitting position
- ❑ meditation technique
- ❑ desire to meditate and diligence
- ❑ a smile

Options to consider

- ❑ stretching before sitting (yoga poses, Pilates, regular stretches)
- ❑ blanket, shawl, or sweater if you tend to feel chilled
- ❑ personalization objects or altar for the area

Creating a meditation space

It is great to have a regular spot (or maybe two) for meditation. The space should be quiet, pleasant, clean, naturally lit, and simple—an oasis from life's hustle and bustle. There will always be some noise, but do the best you can to find a quiet spot. Make a comfortable seat by choosing a cushion, bench, or favorite chair.

Choosing when to meditate

The best time to meditate depends upon your constitution and when you are alert and fresh—not worn out or over-stimulated. Consider: first thing in the morning, before bed, right after work, lunch hour or coffee break, waiting periods, or other predictably idle times.

Choosing how long to meditate

Short, regular sessions are better than infrequent longer sessions. You can start slowly (five minutes) and work up to twenty to sixty minutes. Remember not to pressure yourself, to meditate for the length of time that makes sense within your lifestyle. The most important thing is to practice regularly.

Positions for meditation

The position in which you sit or kneel should be comfortable. Your back should be straight, with the vertebrae stacked like blocks and your head being pulled up by an invisible string. Be a mountain or a tree. Your hands should be in a position that feels natural or is meaningful to you. Your eyes can be closed or half closed.

Focusing on the breath

The breath is always available and always simple, making it the best anchor for meditation. Focusing on the breath calms the mind and provides the stability necessary to cultivate concentration. You will be studying the nuances of your breathing and how it changes—and it will teach you awareness of the present moment.

Working with sounds
When sounds become dominant and call your attention away from breathing, focus all your awareness on the experience of the sound. Make a soft mental note of "hearing," but do not specifically call it "car" or "clock" or another concept. Attend to the sound, then let it go and return to the breath.

Working with sensations
When sensations in the body become dominant and call your attention away from breathing, focus all your mindfulness and attention on the sensation. Make a soft mental note of "sensation" or "feeling" or "ache" or "pain." Attend to the sensation, then let it go and return to the breath.

Working with thoughts and images
As soon as you become aware of thoughts or images arising in the mind, make a soft mental note of "thinking" or "wandering" or "seeing." Notice when you become aware of the thought or image—without judgment. Be mindful of where your mind has gone, then let the thoughts or images go and return to the breath.

Working with hindrances
When different mental states or emotions arise, especially the hindrances of desire, aversion, sleepiness, restlessness, and doubt, make note of them. As soon as you become aware of one of these, make a soft mental note. Do not get lost in the emotion. Observe it, then let it go and return to the breath.

MEDITATION TIPS

- ❑ Make sure your meditation space is well ventilated. An overheated or stuffy area will contribute to drowsiness. In nice weather, you may want to meditate outside in a peaceful spot.
- ❑ Tell others: Do not disturb during meditation! Seriously.
- ❑ It is a good idea to vary leg positions from one sitting to the next, especially as you are adjusting to sitting and developing your flexibility.
- ❑ Set a timer or use a meditation timer app or website. Peek at a clock after some time has passed and only when you do not have a timer available.
- ❑ Take three deep breaths to start your meditation.
- ❑ Relax your jaw and rest your tongue on the roof or bottom of your mouth.
- ❑ Breathe through your nose during meditation.
- ❑ To develop concentration, you can count your breaths, or note in/out or rise/fall to calm and train the mind. If you lose count or track, simply start again.
- ❑ If you are sleepy or restless, try walking meditation.
- ❑ Hindrances are guaranteed to come up. Accept this, observe them mindfully, then return to focusing on the breath. Think of this like bringing a puppy back to the newspaper to train it.
- ❑ Trust in your efforts to meditate. Do not waste time doubting or analyzing your practice, your "progress." Let go of expectations for results and just meditate!

- ❑ Keep meditating, day after day. Keep coming back to the breath, time after time. When you practice meditation, you develop mental muscles like awareness, concentration, and mindfulness. Many people exercise their physical body regularly—and meditation is the equivalent for your mind.
- ❑ At the end of your meditation, open your eyes gently and take three deep breaths to readjust.
- ❑ Dedicate the efforts of your meditation to benefit others. Try to carry the momentum of your mindfulness into whatever your next activity may be.

MEDITATIVE LIFE

- ❑ Drop any expectations but do take note of your intentions. Intention is the mental factor that directly precedes an action or movement. Meditation will help you become aware of your intention before you do or say something. Mindfulness of intention helps you live a life where you respond consciously instead of react.
- ❑ Reflect on impermanence and change in life. This will help you appreciate life's preciousness.
- ❑ Realize the limitations of success and stuff and wealth. Nothing outside of yourself gives you happiness.
- ❑ Practice not being attached. Let go of constant desire, grasping, and greed. Let go of constant aversion, dislike, and hate.
- ❑ Simplify your life.
- ❑ Cultivate patience, diligence, and perseverance.
- ❑ Practice Right Speech and Right Action. Live with honesty and integrity. Ask: Is what I am about to say or do beneficial to anyone?

Go to a garden and just stand in it. Absorb the fragrances, the light, the temperature, the music of the plants and birds and insects. Inhale the *prana* (cosmic energy) of these growing things. Recharge your inner batteries.

Take a minute to reflect on work as part of the spiritual dimension of the universe.

If you follow your bliss, you put yourself on a kind of track, which has been there all the while waiting for you, and the life that you ought to be living is the one you are living.—JOSEPH CAMPBELL

Let small chores serve as Stop signs for you: Breathe, relax, and experience peace.

EQUANIMITY MEDITATION: All beings are the owners of their karma. Their happiness and unhappiness depend upon their actions, not upon my wishes for them.

Use food wisely and appreciatively—it lifts your body and spirit.

Yoga and meditation are allies. Practice them together.

Though outer events may be difficult, the key to your happiness lies in how your mind responds to them.

Sit, stop, become a human still life. Do nothing, be nothing, except breathe.

It is very important to develop a state of mind called "immovable wisdom." It means having fluidity around an unmoving center, so that your mind is clear and ready to direct its attention wherever it may be needed.
—TAKUAN

Investigate your distractions: Focus on one for a little while, then return to your primary task.

Compose yourself in stillness, draw your attention inward and devote your mind to the Self. The wisdom you seek lies within.—BHAGAVAD GITA

Once you feel totally convinced of the preciousness and necessity of compassion and tolerance, you will experience a sense of being touched, a sense of being transformed from within.

Notice your attachments to food, clothes, and shelter. Can you be satisfied with less?

Laughter makes you grow more enlightened. It shrinks the exaggerated seriousness of your problems by making you relax your fixation on them.

Play spiritual music to soothe your soul—while you work, drive, clean, cook, bathe, pay bills, or relax. Harmonious sound can be magical.

When driving, concentrate on the experience. Feel the steering wheel, the pedals, the seat. Drive just to drive.

Breathing in, experience liberation. Breathing out, experience liberation.

A mantra should be one to three syllables and have a soothing sound.

If you see something on television or hear something on the radio that irritates you, change the channel, mute the sound, turn it off.

Before a performance, imagine yourself executing it perfectly from beginning to end. When you engage in fulfilling the needs of others, your own needs become fulfilled as well.

Practice virtue through mindful attention and nonattachment.

Think about a piece of music—some great symphony—we don't expect it to get better as it develops, or that its whole purpose is to reach the final crescendo. The joy is found in listening to the music in each moment.—ALAN WATTS

The art of mindful living requires keen interest and a lifetime of gentle and determined effort, remembering to wake up over and over again.

Think generous thoughts.

Instead of trying to plan everything out, dive into the present moment and tap into your wellspring of intuitive guidance.

Be aware of actions, emotional states, intentions, and mental and physical reactions. Then let them go.

If you work with creative awareness, are present in your thoughts and actions, and fully inhabit each moment, you will find a flow and rightness in whatever you do—every action will be as it should be.

AFFIRMATION: I am a fresh seed, sprouting anew.

Offer help.

Cultivate restraint through meditation. It gives you strength, energy, and composure of mind.

Is the situation dark or are you obscuring the light with your own ego? If you cease to worry about your own self-interest in a situation, you can simply let life unfold as it will.

Open the door to experiencing joy.

It is better to be useful over a long period and at a moderate pace than to make excessive efforts that are short-lived.

Cook with love—it's what separates good food from mere fuel.

In every situation and interaction today, remind yourself, "This is it!"

Add moments of conscious awareness to your day.

Love the people in your life. Act with integrity, bringing harmony to all.

When confronted by an angry person, simply observe his unhappiness and breathe in. Breathing out, try to understand and empathize.

As you prepare to start your day, envision a large, contented lion stretching and roaring. Raise your arms and spread them wide with palms forward. Stretch. Breathe. Leap forward into your day.

Be like a lotus, opening your heart to drink in the morning sun.

Can you love without interfering?

When you are in the middle of chaos, be aware that it will pass—so relax, breathe, and just accept it.

Know that you are worthy of grace. Receive every gift with gratitude and joy.

Moments of stillness and genuine simplicity offer glimpses of what it means to live in a spiritual and free way.

Be willing to be surprised.

Observing your opinions and harsh feelings, see them form and melt like snowflakes. Let go of the opinions and bad feelings.

Observe that all of the tumbling and rolling of this world comes from arguing over unimportant matters; calamity issues from the mouth.

The more you meditate, the more you get in touch with yourself. Breathing in, feel joyful. Breathing out, feel joyful.

Close your eyes and walk in the dark.

Send yourself *metta*. Sit quietly, then turn your attention to whatever aspect of your mind or body you feel most estranged from. Acknowledge and soothe it with warmth and acceptance. You can say the following (or whatever comes naturally to you): "May I accept this. May I be filled with loving-kindness toward this. May I use the pain of this experience for the welfare of all."

Take a few moments to contemplate something you are especially grateful for. Now remove the details of that experience and focus only on the essence that remains. Allow this essence to fill your body and expand through your entire being. Let it direct your life.

Meditation is not about escaping from life. Use your awareness to live with gusto.

Look. Stand still and really see.

Observe whether your mind is quiet or whether thoughts begin to flow. Are these creative thoughts or judgmental ones? Are you accepting the world as it is or are you somehow not satisfied?

Return to your breathing each time your mind wanders.

We should find perfect existence through imperfect existence.—SHUNRYU SUZUKI, *ZEN MIND, BEGINNER'S MIND*

Be mindful and let things take their course. Then your mind will become still like a forest pool. All kinds of animals will come to drink at your pool, and you will clearly see the nature of all things. You will see many strange and wonderful things, but you will be still. This is the happiness of the Buddha.

It is better to conquer yourself than to win a thousand battles. The victory is yours and it cannot be taken from you.

Exercise your sense of smell. Take something you want to explore—a flower, tea leaves, gingerbread cookies—and hold it near your nose. Be aware of the changes in the smell as you become saturated with the scent. Be aware of the sensations in your body as you breathe in and out. Stay alert to the fragrances around you.

Loving acts bear loving fruit.

AFFIRMATION: I rest in tranquility and grace. I am calm, fulfilled, and happy. I take refuge in my calm center.

At the end of the day, look for the stillness that underlies everything. Before you go to sleep, make a list of ten little things that made you happy.

If you want to eat everything in sight, stay with the experience and don't act on it. The feeling will take its course.

Remember the Golden Rule.

Create your own private world in a meditation. Give it a protective aura and make it calm, centered, quiet, and settled. Carry it with you even after your meditation.

Eat mindfully anywhere—even a fast-food restaurant.

Retrain your mind not to focus on the one bad thing but rather on the nine great things.

The more concerned you are about the happiness of others, the more you build your own happiness. Think only of what is good for the other person—do not expect anything in return.

Take slow, deep breaths while on the telephone, in the car, or simply waiting.

Meditate with sound. Play beautiful music and listen to each note with mindfulness.

Breathing in, be aware of your whole body. Breathing out, be aware of your whole body.

Take a step, then another. It might be the same step, but you have to take it.

Seek a "safe harbor" with your consciousness.

The practices of mindfulness and lovingkindness help us to understand that all things deserve care—that when you relate to all things with kindness, you are relating to yourself with kindness.

Each morning, ponder how you can devote the day to the good of all living beings.

See if you can drop everything for a moment.

If you catch yourself being paranoid or taking things too personally, question your logic. Are people really trying to hurt you? Or are they simply unaware of your feelings?

When you're angry, try this meditation: Breathing in, I calm my anger. Breathing out, I take care of my anger.

Eating a meal mindfully is an important practice.

Do one thing at a time.

As you begin to eat, notice the texture and taste of your food. Eat slowly and mindfully.

During the course of your day, try to send loving-kindness to strangers and associates. Note the difference between feeling isolated and feeling connected by means of your practice.

Blend the awareness of where you are with the awareness of where you are stepping.

Imagine that the way you walk through life is the way you will be walking through eternity. Think about how you want to live forever, and start to live that way now.

Most of life will unfold in accordance with forces far outside your control, regardless of what your mind says about it. Your thoughts have far less of an effect on this world than you would like to think.

Get up earlier—give yourself a time of stillness. Use it to cultivate awareness.

When you meditate more, you make better choices more often, and find better people and better opportunities.

Be willing to allow your preconceptions about yourself, your life, and everything else to fall away.

Each footstep should be regarded as a unique event in itself.

This may be the best moment of your life.

Every time you brush your teeth and rinse your mouth, remind yourself to speak purely and lovingly. Give your thoughts a chance to settle down.

The sound *om* is a very soothing, low-resonance tone. When you're feeling stressed, focus on your breathing and repeat the sound on every exhalation. Stretch it out for as long as you can. This will help dissolve your feelings of anxiety.

Whatever is not yours, abandon it.

Ask yourself, "What am I waiting for to make me happy? Why am I not happy right now?"

Visualize a place that heals and comforts you.

Learn with your whole body, not just your mind.

It feels much better to gently remove an insect from inside your home and put it outside than to kill it.

Being mindful means being aware of your breath and of where you are.

Limit your television time. Choose only programs you really want to watch and then turn off the TV.

Listen to both your intellect and your intuition.

Be a gardener of life.

AFFIRMATION: I can change.

Use mindfulness to see what is as it is.

One word that brings peace is better than a thousand spoken in vain.

Taming your mind is not a hobby or an extracurricular activity—it is the most important thing you could be doing. It can even help take the edge off a pressured situation because it gives you clarity, peace, and fortitude. You may need to simplify your life to meditate, but a benefit of meditation is that it will make your life simpler.

Every morning, when you wake up, resolve to keep a wide-open heart and mind.

Learn to touch the earth more gently.

Meditate while walking: pay attention to your feet as they leave the ground and touch the ground again.

AFFIRMATION: I select well-being and nourish joy.

At the end of a meal, allow the pleasant feelings of physical satisfaction to enter into your awareness.

See the perfectness of the present in every ordinary and difficult moment.

Omit needless words.

Make peace with the qualities you find unacceptable in others—these qualities exist within yourself too.

To listen well, you have to learn to be more empty, to set aside the complexity of your expectations, opinions, chatter, and the agitation that clouds your mind.

Imagine that you are an alien from another planet taking a trip through the human mind. As an alien, you would not take any of your observations personally; the thoughts and feelings you encounter would merely be fascinating. Think about that as you go about your day.

AFFIRMATION: My every thought, word, and action is permeated with divine love.

Meditation technique: Sit in a comfortable position and close your eyes. Let your breathing remain natural. Relax the root of your tongue and let it drop down. Release tension around the eyes by imagining them falling toward the back of the eye sockets, and allow the space between them to widen and soften. Let any sounds that come up fade away. Feel the air on your skin and notice your breath under your nose. Taste your own mouth. Stay steady and quiet within the changing world.

Don't expect big changes right away. Like piano and ballet, meditation takes daily practice.

Step humbly through each doorway with no expectations. Open door, open mind.

Be aware of our interdependence with everything and everyone. Even your smallest, least significant thought, word, or action ripples throughout the universe.

We can unlock the potential for happiness and satisfaction that lies within each of us by becoming aware of our mental processes and then applying discriminating wisdom to all our actions of body, speech, and mind.—KATHLEEN MCDONALD

Pay attention right now to what you are sensing and feeling. Notice how much resistance you have to shifting from the external to the internal. Whenever your mind flits away to another thought or image, relax and bring it back to yourself.

Bring mindfulness to the daily interactions between you and your partner.

If there is a place in your body that is sick or in pain, take this time to become aware of it and send it your love. Breathing in, allow this area to rest and, breathing out, smile at it with great tenderness and affection. Be aware that there are other parts of your body that are still strong and healthy. Allow these strong areas to send their strength and energy to the weak or sick area. Breathe in and affirm your own capacity to heal, breathe out and let go of the worry or fear you may be holding.

Remember that being generous is a blessing.

Practice walking meditation every time you go shopping.

Be just plain happy. Be happy in the being and the knowing.

Sit like a mountain or tree with a broad base extending deep into the earth and a trunk or peak that reaches toward the sky.

MEDITATION: Walk slowly back and forth down a long hallway in your home.

Set your plate in front of you and observe as minutely as possible the food you have chosen. Notice all of the colors and the smells.

Equanimity meditation: May I accept things as they are. May I be open and balanced. May I find equanimity and peace.

A good meditation can be as simple as doing something you love with mindful awareness.

Freedom is possible. It does not depend on having things, keeping things, and holding on to things.

Have the courage to let a thought slip by and not chase after it.

Use a mantra to find your own voice; they are a sacred source of great power and blessings.

Seize the novelty and uniqueness of every moment.

Do a breath and sound meditation: Focus on your breath and, at the same time, listen to the sounds around you.

Start eliminating the trivial.

Try *pranayama* (the balance of breath and its restraint): Inhale for four counts, exhale for four counts, and repeat for eight cycles.

Clean the kitchen mindfully.

Learn to live temperately. Too much pleasure, like good food that leads to indigestion, can lead to pain. Notice this change from pleasure to pain, and learn to curb your appetite.

Count the ways in which you are lucky. Remind yourself that every day you are getting stronger and things are getting better.

Let go of the battle.

If you regret a harmful action, word, or thought, write it down or confess it to someone you trust. Allow yourself to regret, and then let go of the past—focus on abstaining from it in the future.

Just by eating a little less, you will be healthier.

In meditation, be aware of the short space between the end of one thought and the start of another. Look for this momentary pause, no matter how brief. Try to rest in this space.

Consider each word carefully so that your speech is right in both form and content.

Each time you turn on the lights, remind yourself of your inner light, and bring your awareness to shine on all aspects of your life.

Remain a mere observer of your distractions. Do not try to identify or react to them. A distraction is just a distraction.

Eat natural, healthful, simple food. Try to stay away from meat, sugar, and highly processed foods.

If you stay with the moment, you will have enough time and materials to do what needs to be done.

Be sensitive to your entire body. Breathe in and out.

Work calmly and with a quiet mind. Even the simplest tasks embody great spiritual happiness.

Lie down in a comfortable position and focus on your breath. Imagine that you are a white skeleton lying on the earth. Scan the bones of each part of your body. Notice that your skeleton is not you; you are one with the atmosphere, everywhere at every moment.

Cow-face mudra: Interlock your fingers to form a cup, symbolizing unification of body and mind.

Get used to wiping the slate clean and never harboring grudges.

Count your breaths up to ten, and each time your mind wanders, go back to one.

It is good training to stay with the flow of sound; impermanence is very clear.

Equanimity meditation: May I be undisturbed by the comings and goings of all the events of this world.

See whether your actions are skillful or unskillful.

You can travel to sacred spots or create them in your own heart.

Pretend you are on a tropical beach. When you inhale, feel the warmth of the sun and the touch of the breeze. When you exhale, release tension from your body. Let your breathing ebb and flow like the waves of the ocean.

Your children are a part of your meditation.

Basic walking meditation is great after a busy day or on a lazy weekend morning. Choose a place where you can walk comfortably back and forth at least ten paces in length. Plant your feet firmly on the ground and let your arms and hands rest at your side. Close your eyes for a moment and center yourself, taking a few deep breaths. Feel your feet pressing on the ground. Now open your eyes and be aware of your surroundings. Walk slowly, with ease and dignity. Be mindful of each step. Notice all the sensations of lifting your foot from the earth and placing it back down again. Your mind will wander many times; simply acknowledge this and turn your attention to the next step you take. At each turning point, pause for a moment: Center yourself and focus on the first step of your return path. Walk for at least twenty minutes. At the very end, pause one final moment to internalize the mindfulness you've accumulated. Try to carry this momentum and concentration into the rest of your day.

Hone your awareness.

Take a moment's break and drop all doing—all thinking, all concentrating, and all contemplating. Just be at your center.

Sit alone. Travel alone. Do your practice alone. Enjoy your seclusion without desire.

Breathing in, see your parents in you. Breathing out, smile to the reflection of your parents.

The sooner a hindrance is noticed, the sooner it can be let go of. If we openly recognize and acknowledge strife as it's occurring, we stop feeding the fire. It burns out.

Picture yourself sitting on the bank of a river, and envision a log floating downstream. Follow the log, letting it float past you and out of sight.

What changes do you need to make to employ spiritual precepts in your life?

Stop chasing after things. Let mildew form on your mouth. Have no resistance, like perfect silk.
—SHIH-SHUANG

Are you taking full advantage of life's wondrous opportunities for growth and meaning?

By becoming aware of your negative energies and cultivating this awareness, you will make steady steps on the path.

Practice classic yoga postures to open the wonderful treasures contained in your body.

When you feel tired and angry, search for your "soft spot." Close your eyes, take a few deep breaths, and relax your body with each exhalation. Now think about someone you loved as a child and a time when you felt loved and nurtured by him or her. Focus on these warm, tender feelings and explore them without judgment. Allow the soothing feelings of love and security to overwhelm your entire being.

Transgressions are to be understood and corrected, not dwelt upon or agonized over.

Instead of being angry over nuisances, irritations, and frustrations, accept them with humor, serenity, or constructive efforts to improve the situation.

Can you let this go? Sit it out? Walk it out? Find your center? Make yourself tolerant?

When you feel trapped and bogged down, have some tea.

Be cheerful for no reason.

Helping yourself is the first condition for helping another.

Just remain in the center, watching. And then forget that you are there.—LAO TZU

INSIGHT MEDITATION: Close your eyes and concentrate for a few moments on the feeling or situation you want to explore. When you are ready, allow your subconscious to create an image that describes what you are trying to understand. At first, it may seem completely unrelated to what you have been asking. Be patient and study it; with practice, you will better understand the symbols of your mind. After a few minutes, end the meditation and open your eyes, reflecting on the insight you have gained.

Listen to your heart. Pay attention to your intuition.

Be mindful even during physical exercise. It can put you "in the zone" faster and keep you there longer.

Give your partner the freedom to follow his or her path. Open your heart and set the person free. Grow side by side.

To let go is to release the images and emotions, the grudges and fears, the clingings and disappointments of the past that bind your spirit.

Try dream mastery at bedtime. Center on your third eye; be attentive to the feeling between the eyebrows. Feel the *prana* flowing in; each out-breath should be empty. Be aware of your breaths and feel the *prana* coming into your heart. Sleep will overtake you and you will be awake during your dreams.

Have a beautiful vision. Look at something in a beautiful way.

Before a job interview or public speech, visualize yourself walking into the room and exuding self-confidence. You are very relaxed; you talk freely and your exchanges are very positive. The interviewer/ audience shows tremendous enthusiasm for what you have said and you feel happy that your performance has been so impressive. Keep this image in your mind for as long as possible. Reinforce the visualization by repeating affirmations like "I can handle this" and "I am very confident."

If you maintain mindfulness, nothing can upset you. You will not become angry or agitated. You will be able to stay patient, peaceful, and happy no matter what happens. This is because a negative state of mind cannot arise at the same time as a moment of mindfulness.

Pause and savor any insights, ideas, pictures, or sensations you gain while reading. Think of them as gifts, not distractions.

Alleluia! Adoramus te Domine!

Focus on doing just one very simple thing in the moment. Make each moment a single point of concentration.

To be awake is to be alive. Learn to reawaken and keep yourself awake, not by mechanical aids, but by an infinite expectation of the dawn.

What you do for yourself, you are doing for others, and what you do for others, you are doing for yourself. Any gesture of kindness, gentleness, and honesty toward yourself will affect how you experience and interact with the world.

Sit and breathe through your nose. Imagine that you are drawing in air through the base chakra, located at the base of your pelvis. When you breathe in, imagine your breath flowing upward until it reaches your heart. When you breathe out, visualize the air flowing down to join your next in-breath. Be aware of the feeling of inner energy flowing upward as it meets the out-breath to return into the body. You will be breathing low and deeply, and you may feel warmth or coolness in the chakra. Stay with this cycle of ebb and flow.

When you think about aging, don't forget the internal treasures that we accumulate with each year.

Do not move at all for a certain period of time. When desires arise, practice letting go of them.

Renounce one habit and replace it with open space. Be with whatever it had closed off for you. Practice with another habit each succeeding week.

Eat silently and mindfully during the first five minutes of each meal.

Why don't you invest 100 percent of yourself into the practice of making yourself and the people around you happy?

Think of each of the items you recycle as an offering to the community.

Awaken to the noble spirit of *bodhicitta*. Rejoice in all the good works of both others and yourself and share in all the good karma.

Try giving inspiring thoughts that occur during meditation a label as they arise, like "Einstein!"

OBJECT MEDITATION: Concentrate on a particular object, such as a crystal, candle flame, flower, or mandala. Feel its presence and simply focus on its texture, shape, color, and other features.

Be happy. Let both time and the world disappear. Nurture your mind with great literature.

Remember that each event and situation has a positive value.

Hold people in awareness: Honor them, wish them well, and open to their pain with acceptance and compassion.

Help children learn to be mindful. Recognize children's suffering and act with compassion to help them recognize anger, isolation, and fear. The energy of mindfulness can soothe and heal.

Breathe in and say, "What I have is enough." Breathe out and think, "What I am is enough." Breathe in and say, "What I do is enough." Breathe out and think, "What I have achieved is enough."

Focus your attention on something that normally bores you.

Love your questions, live your questions. Do not seek the answers; they will come if you just meditate.

Physical exercise is one of the best stress relievers, decreasing the body's production of stress hormones and increasing levels of feel-good endorphins. Unless you overdo it, you will feel better after a workout. Make a promise to yourself to move every day, vigorously enough to work up a sweat. You can walk slowly or run quickly with mindfulness.

Our enemy is not another person but the wrong perceptions and suffering within that person. The solution is not to hurt the person but to relieve him or her of their suffering.

Nourish your compassion so you can be a good listener.

SLEEPING MEDITATION: Imagine that with each breath you are melting into an ocean of light and space.

Whatever you are doing, just do it.

What is the prayer of your heart?

Slow down and enjoy life. It's not only the scenery you miss by going too fast—YOU ALSO MISS THE SENSE OF WHERE YOU'RE GOING AND WHY.—EDDIE CANTOR

Be in love with existence. Breathing in, absorb love and life. Breathing out, give love and life.

SKY MEDITATION: Lie down and imagine a clear summer sky with no clouds. Enter and become this clarity. Don't blink; just rest your gaze. Don't think; just observe the emptiness.

Work on Right Speech with patience and perseverance.

Admit that you do not know all the answers. Just say, "I do not know."

PILGRIMAGE MEDITATION: Choose a destination that has real significance to you and that would require enough time and effort to test your spiritual commitment. It could be a historic location, an archaeological site, an island, or any place you've always dreamed about. Take yourself through this journey, every step of the way—picture each step up the mountain or through the rain forest. Feel the satisfaction of patient accomplishment.

Remember that there are always plenty of things and people to love.

Let go of regret. Why reexperience something that went wrong? Wasn't it bad enough the first time?

When meditating, be aware of your mindfulness, investigation, concentration, tranquility, energy and effort, and equanimity and balance. Which qualities are present? Which are missing? See if you can enhance them at your next sitting.

Give yourself a beginner's mind, a nonjudgmental perspective, patience, trust, nonstriving, acceptance, and the ability to let go.

Listen to your inner voice and if you find that you are doing too much and are really tired, rest if necessary. Maybe after a good nap, you will want to meditate.

Sunset Meditation: When the sun goes down, surrender to the final moments of the day. Remind yourself that there will be a new day. Take strength from this process of renewal.

Tune in to positive healing qualities by breathing and receiving what you need. Rest in wholeness.

Be kind even to those you do not love. Be grateful to them for giving you the opportunity to do a kindness.

When you meditate, be aware of all the times you question whether you are doing it right or feeling what you're supposed to be feeling, or wondering what is supposed to happen. Don't try to answer your questions. Simply stay in the present moment, observing and accepting.

Breathing in, relinquish your needs. Breathing out, relinquish your needs.

Spend as much time in nature as you can. It can ground you and reaffirm your connection with the world.

Imagine never knowingly speaking a lie. Speaking the truth is at the heart of insight meditation practice.

What contributions have you made to the world? Which gives you the greatest satisfaction? Can you be of further service? Can you start now?

Go on a "media fast" for a few days: avoid television, movies, radio, music, and even reading. Just sit by yourself, doing nothing. Notice what you feel. These are the feelings you normally avoid by keeping yourself occupied.

Your expression is the most important thing you wear.

Act with kindness to act with kindness, not to fulfill your duty or earn brownie points.

Visualize a color in all of its depth and richness. Try to assume its positive qualities.

We are not as different from each other as we believe. We are not independent but interdependent.

Are you wondering? Are you questioning?

Try to draw courage and motivation from the achievements of others.

Eating is holy. Your meals should incorporate ritual and ceremony.

Even a few minutes in quiet meditation can calm your mind and open your heart, bringing you more deeply into the moment.

Scan your body with a beam of mindfulness.

Each time you check your watch, remind yourself that you cannot be anywhere other than where you are right now. Make the best of this moment.

How might the practice of mindfulness help you reduce a stressful problem?

Make your intentions pure and express yourself from the heart.

Be with things the way they are.

Keep the bigger perspective in mind, not getting caught in life's little whirlpools.

Focus on the sounds in your environment and accept whatever you hear.

Watch your actions; they become your habits.

Preface insight practices with some devotional chanting or bowing.

Make each activity of your day a meditation.

During meditation if you find it hard to count or follow your breath, just focus on your body as a whole or on a specific part of your body. When your mind wanders, simply come back to your body. Stick with this until you're ready to move on to your breath.

Do works that have no reward.

Focusing only on what you are doing frees you from thoughts of winning or losing, allowing you to execute tasks effectively. You are like an archer drawing the bow, but you are unattached to the outcome. Whether you hit your target is determined solely by your mindfulness and concentration.

Let past karma go—detach yourself and open up to something new.

If you expect your life to be up and down, your mind will be much more peaceful.

Travel well instead of thinking about the importance of arriving. Live life like a game. Give yourself goals, but remember that the true aim is to enjoy playing.

Go for a fast walk.

Remember to connect to what you are doing. With each moment you remember, you are on the path to freedom.

Let go of your frustrations and use your energy to create future fulfillment.

LIGHT-AND-DARK MEDITATION: Begin in a comfortable position. Close your eyes and picture the most loving and compassionate individuals you have ever known or heard about. They are gathered over your head and merge into one being that glows and radiates with warmth, love, and compassion. Now imagine that this being descends into your heart, where it takes the form of a sphere of infinitely radiant light that merges with your soft spot (where you keep your own warm, loving feelings). Breathing in, gather any negativity or darkness and bring them into this sphere. Breathing out, purify these negative feelings with the warmth of the light.

Be aware of how you end your meditations. Do not judge your meditaion, but observe it and simply see it for what it is.

Each time you vacuum your room, pretend that you are sweeping away your worldly attachments—let them go with the dust and dirt.

You can break the pattern and change the next moment: You can do something different, something enlightened, creative, imaginative, compassionate, wise, fresh.

With perseverance and self-discipline, you can learn to live mindfully almost all the time.

Merge with the sounds around you.

Become a master of every situation and you will always be in the right place.—LIN CHI

Read widely, think deeply, and retain your sense of discretion.

Don't be angry at yourself for feeling angry, or guilty for feeling guilty. Simply recognize and acknowledge your feelings—it is the first step toward changing them.

Mystic gaze (helps you transcend linear perception): First, select three points—you can even draw them on a piece of paper. Look from one point to another, concentrating on just one at a time. Go around the triangle three or four times. Be aware of your breathing as you shift your visual attention. Now focus on two points at a time. Finally, include all three points in your gaze.

If you want to recenter, just start saying, "Hello" inside, over and over. Then notice that you are aware of that. Don't think about being aware of it; that is just another thought. Relax and be aware that you hear "Hello" being repeated in your mind. That is the seat of your centered consciousness.

Before you go to sleep, lie down in bed and make your body as stiff as possible for two minutes, almost to the point of bursting. Then release for two minutes. Do this two or three times every night to ease into a relaxing sleep.

Appreciate, respond, and sense the bloom of each moment.

Be content to be nobody special. Be ordinary.

Candle Meditation: Place a candle in front of you and breathe naturally, focusing your gaze on the flame. Empty your mind and, whenever it wanders, refocus gently but firmly on the flame. Do this for as long as you feel comfortable.

Count the moments of awareness.

Try to imitate a plant's slow and confident growth.

Benefactor meditation: Begin by repeating phrases of lovingkindness. After about ten minutes, think of someone for whom you feel strong respect or gratitude: This is your benefactor. (Try to pick someone who is still alive and whom you are not sexually attracted to.) Now visualize your benefactor or say his or her name out loud. Recall all the ways in which he or she has helped you and allow yourself to acknowledge any feelings that arise from this. Now direct loving thoughts and phrases toward your benefactor. Repeat the phrases.

Forest-sunlight meditation: Imagine you are running through a dark forest. Now pause and take some deep breaths. You can see a clearing in the distance ahead. You reach the clearing and rest there momentarily. Then you find a path leading out of the clearing back into the forest. Follow this path until you emerge into the sunlight.

Act on your thoughts of generosity.

Remember that 90 percent of what you feel is simply your own interpretation.

It's more productive and a lot more fun to respond creatively than to react cantankerously.

Call a time-out whenever you sense your pulse or heartbeat increasing. Take slow, deep breaths and do whatever calms you down. Replace thoughts that reinforce anxiety with distress-reducing thoughts.

Clear your mind and open your eyes.

Throw yourself into life.

Instead of resisting your pain, see if you can open up to it. Notice how much better you feel when you stop denying it.

Direct your thoughts and energy toward realizing your dreams for the future. Visualize your success.

Stop and look deeply.

See suffering as part of the solution, not the problem.

The way to be happy is to make others happy.

Some foods "hum" and some foods "beckon." The former resonate with your body, whereas the latter tempt you but are not good for you. Eat "humming" foods and stay away from "beckoning" ones.

Can you continue to feel love and empathy even for those who have betrayed you?

Walk softly, live gently.

Exaggeration meditation: As you breathe in and out, use your imagination to exaggerate whatever it is you are feeling. This will help you see and go beyond the boundaries that have defined your life so far. Once you see that there is an infinity of feeling, you will be able to transcend limit after limit.

Stay content during the financial ups and downs of life. If you find yourself with less money, lower your wants. If you have more money, save or use what you have to benefit others.

Meditate on your weaknesses and deal with them bravely.

Pebble meditation: Hold a pebble in your hand and look at its texture and color. Feel its cool hardness on your skin. Now close your eyes and squeeze it. Imagine that the pebble is glowing in your hand, charged with energy. Think of a dream or goal and draw power and confidence from this energy. After the meditation, hold the pebble whenever you need to refocus.

Take a deep breath and count "one" when your lungs are full. Now breathe out completely, counting "two." Breathe and count up to "ten."

The quieter you are, the more you can hear.

Make a wish for all earthly beings.

Do your work with mastery.

Listen to your soul and to the energy of the universe. Seek inspiration or divine guidance to help you act in the most fruitful ways.

Steadying the mind, breathe in and out.

Respond with flexibility. In the face of anger, be compassionate. When faced with greed, be grateful. Confront a negative emotion with a positive one.

Rather than returning to old habits or fear-based responses, ask yourself, "How can I take care of myself at this moment? What would be the most helpful thing to focus my attention on right now?"

LIGHT-SHOWER MEDITATION: Check your entire body and release any tension you are holding. Now imagine you are standing under a shower of whitish-blue light. It enters through your head and flows through your entire body. Feel it washing away the impurities and toxins, one body part at a time. Let all the impurities flow out through the soles of your feet into the earth. Now imagine that the light is once again filling your body, flooding you with its healing power. Let it ascend through your head and out into the universe. Take some deep breaths and close the meditation.

When you're in trouble, think about what is useful, and stay with it.

Find opportunities to live away from the ticking of the clock.

BREATH-AND-SIGHT MEDITATION: Focus on your breath and, at the same time, observe the details of your surroundings.

Consider how mindful speech can serve as protection for the mind. Mindful speech keeps you in the present moment. If you are mindful with your words, you cut off an avenue for the expression of negativity.

Pause during the middle of your day to relax and review.

If you drift away from your meditation practice, do not be discouraged. Remember that the essence of meditation is to begin again and again. You can renew your practice any time.

Be quiet.

Meditate on the paradoxical relationship between mind and world. Your mind is in the world and, at the same time, the world is in your mind.

FULL-LOTUS POSTURE: Cross your legs at the calf and allow both knees to touch the floor. Each foot should rest on the opposite thigh, and both soles should be turned upward.

Caring for others is the best thing you can do.

Act as though it is impossible to fail.

Hold mindfulness like a cup of tea.

Rely on nothing until you want nothing.

Make a pact to meditate for one minute every hour of the day. Stop whatever you are doing and follow your breath with full attention.

Place an apple on a plate and close your eyes. Set aside all thoughts and preconceptions. Open your eyes and see the fruit as if for the first time. Touch it and begin to slice it, noticing its every aspect. Raise a section slowly to your lips and pause. Open your mouth, bite down, and feel the texture of the flesh and the taste of its juice. Continue to bite and chew slowly, pausing between swallowing and biting again. Be aware of your sensations from moment to moment. You can do this with other fruits such as oranges and pears.

Be one with your breathing, be one with the world.

DIAMOND MIND MEDITATION: Acknowledge all your unskillful actions and attitudes by imagining that a luminous nectar is flowing in front of you, washing away your negative tendencies.

Breathe, smile, relax.

Meditate without striving for a clearly defined outcome. Create a space to sit, quietly observing your feelings and thoughts and allowing yourself to just be.

Hold yourself to a higher standard than what others expect of you.

Whenever you cross a threshold, go through a doorway, or enter a room, see it as entering a temple and do so reverently.

How do you want to live this day?

MEDITATION: Bring your attention back to your breath each time your focus wanders. Working with, instead of struggling against, the resistance of your mind builds inner strength and deepens concentration. It also helps you develop patience and practice being nonjudgmental.

AFFIRMATION: I think, but I am not my thoughts.

Lie down on the grass and embrace the earth. Appreciate its support. Feel its energy and vibrations. Love the earth.

Know when to exercise restraint. It gives you control over your life.

Every time you smile away your irritation and anger, you achieve a victory for yourself and humanity.

MEDITATION: To feel more present in your body, sit comfortably and close your eyes. Bring your attention to what you are sitting on. Notice how it supports your bones. Then notice how your clothes touch your skin. Your body will feel simultaneously more connected and more distinct from your surroundings.

It takes only one conscious breath to be in touch with ourselves and the world around us.

Open your mail over the trash and throw away unnecessary items immediately.

Meditate on the open nature of reality.

Exchange self-awareness for awareness of others. Feel the joy that comes from deeply connecting with and helping others.

Walk slowly upon crunchy snow or autumn leaves, attending to the crackle of each step.

Turn off the TV, turn on life.

Toning meditation: Sing a vowel sound, like *oh*, *ee*, or *ah*, for four or five minutes. Play with it and feel it vibrate in your body. Go up and down your vocal range and make slow, long melodies with this sound. Give in to the toning and see where it takes you.

Stay centered.

When you are angry, do not focus on the person who has aroused your anger. Keep him or her on the periphery. Do not say that the other person has created the anger. Do not rationalize. Feel the anger and be grateful to the person for helping you recognize this. Your awareness will relieve you of your wound.

Cherish the simplicity and quiet of meditation. Nothing is missing.

Visualize the Buddha within.

Place your priorities in a sacred circle. Promise to do your best to protect that circle from harm.

Think of yourself as a cat, completely relaxed in front of a warm fire. Feel your muscles flex and yield without resistance to touch. Breathe in and out at least fifteen times.

Let your thoughts pass through your consciousness like clouds through the sky.

MEDITATION: When your breathing becomes so refined that you cannot notice any separation between inhalation and exhalation, you should stop counting. Counting is useful only when you are training your mind to concentrate.

AFFIRMATION: I am open and receptive.

Finding beauty in the ordinary and the ordinary in beauty is Zen living in action.

Awaken to the knowledge that you have hands to perform the most intricate movements, feet to take you to the farthest places, and ears and eyes that allow you to enjoy this amazing world.

Choose one or two meditations and make them your core practice.

Whenever you hear the quiet voice of intuition, pay attention to its advice.

AFFIRMATION: I am a mountain.

Shift around in your seat and see how different postures change your breathing and meditation.

Many people are afraid of empty time and fill it with television, talking, reading magazines, anything they can think of not to be "alone" with time. "Empty" time can become meditation, relaxation, and breathing time.

Sit quietly, eyes closed, one hand resting lightly on the other. Do you get a mental image of your hands? Are you aware of various sensations? Investigate and distinguish between the different levels of your experience.

What a gift to give others: to allow them to make mistakes—even big mistakes—and still hold them in your heart with kindness.

Following the path means living each hour of the day in awareness, letting your mind and body dwell in the present moment.

Scan your body bottom to top, visualizing all your negativities rising and evaporating away. Feel completely cleansed, purified, and charged with blissful energy.

Focusing your mind on just one object reduces the number of signals to your brain, so that you can settle into a deeply relaxed yet highly alert state.

Rhythmic exercise—like tai chi, swimming, yoga, and walking—can focus the mind and be even more energizing than meditation.

Ring a bell and listen to its wonderful resonance.

AFFIRMATION: I love myself just as I am.

Tranquility is fostered by time alone and time in nature.

When you are going through a difficult time with a loved one or friend, do a brief meditation to cultivate compassion. Sit, looking beyond the conflict, and reflect on the fact that this person is a human being like you. This person has the same desire for happiness and well-being, the same fear of suffering, and the same need for love. Note how this meditation softens your feelings toward this person.

When you find yourself in a slump, keep your eyes open. Refocus with increasing precision by noting the beginning and end of each breath.

Doing nothing requires vital energy and is not the same as laziness or passivity.

Live with less clutter.

Remain within the freshness of the present instant.

Pay attention to all the tiny balancing movements your body makes when you sit or stand.

Make a list of the things you have faith and trust in. Carry the list in your wallet or purse. When you are feeling sad or lost, pull it out and read it until you feel better.

When you give, expect nothing in return.

Open your heart to what is in front of you. Where you are is the path and the goal. Remember that where you are going is right here, right now.

Stay simple.

MEDITATION ON THE FOUR DIVINE ABODES: 1) lovingkindness and friendliness, 2) compassion and empathy, 3) joy and rejoicing, and 4) equanimity and peace of mind.

When you get ready for bed, remove your cares and responsibilities just as you would remove your clothes. Imagine that you are growing lighter, more relaxed, and more spacious. Let your mind be emptied, and let there be a glow in the center of your heart.

For one week, keep a journal of the thoughts that predominate in your mind. Notice the emotional and physical qualities associated with these thoughts. See if you would like to let go of unskillful thoughts and cultivate skillful ones in a particular area. Use this insight for a week to remind yourself of these positive intentions.

Do you become consumed by objects of momentary desire?

String moments of mindfulness together, breath by breath.

Talk yourself into relaxing. Say, "Please relax."

Give a gesture of appreciation to someone who has set aside time for you.

Meditate upon death by dying a little with each exhalation. Melt into the present moment. Let go of whatever sensations you feel and of any attempts to control your mind. Breath by breath, forgive others and forgive yourself. Accept others for what they are, and accept yourself totally. Make peace with the world. Let go and let be. Soar into the freedom of desirelessness.

To attain true inner freedom, you must be able to objectively watch your problems instead of being lost in them. Start by watching, just being aware that you are aware of what is going on.

Pretend there is a butterfly inside your heart. Watch it gently open its wings. Breathe deeply and slowly, imagining your breath flowing into the butterfly. Feel its wings spread with compassion and love. Now let it fly into the world filled with light and warmth.

Force yourself to be patient.

Repeat the mantra "filter" to stop and ask yourself whether what you are about to say is beneficial to anyone.

Focus on an activity that you perform automatically. Attend closely to its details, listening to your body and being sensitive to the quality of your mind. Be wholeheartedly there.

Always choose the way that seems best, no matter how rough it may be.

To have peace, you must first have understanding, and understanding is not possible without gentle, loving communication.

The key to healthy living is learning how to change your state of mind.

Give whenever, however, and to whomever you can.

Control the menu of thoughts and images that flash through your mind. Dwell on the positive and let them inspire you.

When in doubt, shut up.

Observe free of preference or dislike.

OM MUDRA: This hand position helps you connect with divine energy. Bring the tips of your thumbs and index fingers together, each hand separately, to form circles. Then place your hands palms up on your knees.

Can you respond to what others really need?

Do not lean on anything or anyone.

Be aware of your body when you get up in the morning and when you get ready for bed at night.

Affirmation: I am happy just as I am. I am peaceful with whatever is happening.

Jump in a pile of leaves.

In Buddhism, *ah* is the sound of openness and the source of all speech. Let it come out naturally with your breath. Enjoy this peaceful sound and fill the world with it. Use it to remove all feelings of imperfection, guilt, and negative energy. Feel pure, healthy, and strong. Relax in the experience and be one with the sound.

Whirling is an extremely powerful way to merge with the divine. Start with your weight on your left foot and rotate counterclockwise on the ball of that foot. Use your right foot to push off and maintain balance. Your eyes should gaze softly ahead, without a focus. Slowly raise your arms to shoulder level, with the palm of the right hand turned up and the palm of the left hand turned down. If you get dizzy, focus on the knuckle of your left index finger. When you are ready to stop, pick a spot on the wall, then stand still, and stare at the spot until the room stops spinning and your body comes to rest.

- Verbalize the positive.

You can search the entire universe for someone who is more deserving of your love than yourself, and that person will not be found.

It takes less energy to do an unpleasant task now than to worry about it all day.

Notice the motivations of your speech and the effect of your comments and responses. When you speak with intention, what kind of response do you get? Now try to speak naturally and mindlessly. What is the response now?

Every day, when you return home from work, rejoice. Stand in front of your door and appreciate this moment. Breathe in and out three times. Be there.

- Speak and act with a pure mind. Happiness will follow.

With meditation central to your being, your life is free from suffering.

- Be quiet, loving, and fearless.

Tape-record a list of qualities you would like to possess. (Try saying them as affirmations.) When you need a reminder, play the tape and really listen.

Paint, sing, dance, or do whatever you feel like to make this world a little more beautiful.

Appreciate the effort of all those who labored to put the food on your table.

When you feel stressed or disturbed, rather than trying to find the root of the problem, just give it up and let it go. Don't analyze or try to figure it out. You don't need to understand it. Just forget about it.

With generosity, overcome meanness.

AFFIRMATION: I see things clearly.

When your mind is completely open and "unfurnished," you will have plenty of space for creative thoughts.

Refrain from gossip, falsity, slander, and harmful speech.

LION BREATH: Inhale through both nostrils for four counts. While holding in your breath, curl your tongue backward until it hits the roof of your mouth, and let out a deep growl!

NAMASTE MUDRA: *Namaste* means "I recognize the light in you" or "I honor the divinity in you" and indicates respect and humility. Place your palms together with fingers extended, thumbs and fingers parallel. Your arms should be bent, elbows down. Bring your hands to your chest.

Only by starting where you are can you ever get anywhere.

Forgive yourself.

Pick an object, such as a seashell, and look at it actively, alertly, and dynamically, as if you were feeling it with your hands.

Sit back and relax into the richness of what is.

When it rains, look for the rainbow.

Nod to your computer before you turn it on, as the samurai bow to their swords. Silently thank those who made it. Be aware of your interconnectedness—of the oneness of all things.

VERSE FOR GOING TO SLEEP: Falling asleep at last I vow with all beings to enjoy the dark and the silence, and rest in the vast unknown.

Speak little and softly, aware of the pointlessness of unnecessary words.

Follow your breaths while talking, making them long, light, and even.

Be aware of your mind and of the spontaneity of life in each moment.

With mindfulness and awareness, you pry your mind away from fantasies, chatter, and subtle whispers of thoughts. You place it here and now.

Exercise a disinterested acceptance at all times.

Hold your friend's hand with alertness. Watch your energy grow.

Hot pepper meditation: This is a good way to practice fortitude and self-restraint. Clear your mind and eat some hot pepper or hot sauce—a bit more than you would actually enjoy. Focus on the pain, then try to relax and soften the sensations in your mouth and throat. If you want, repeat this exercise to push your limits, maintaining a clear, focused mind.

This breathing exercise is useful for clearing your mind. Begin by inhaling slowly and smoothly. Then exhale forcefully, contracting your abdominal muscles sharply, raising your diaphragm, and forcing the air out. Inhale again, this time relaxing your muscles, allowing your lungs to fill with air. Exhale sharply once more. Repeat this twenty times. Now breathe the same way, but hold your breath between the inhalation and exhalation for as long as you can. The exhalation should be short and active, the inhalation long and passive; inhale for eight counts and exhale for one. Again, repeat twenty times.

Train yourself to focus on stopping or pausing between breaths.

When you are restless, be restless. Don't make a fuss about what you feel. It's like the weather—what can you really do about it? When it's hot, be hot and sweat. When it's cold, be cold and shiver.

If you want to add clarity to your thinking, use the color yellow in your meditations.

Affirmation: I am a creative, sexual, emotional being.

Keep your word.

Say "yes," be open, and love.

Allow your wakefulness to simply be. Do not try to improve on its freshness. Remain unoccupied by memories of the past or plans for the future.

Reflect on how your attitudes and principles are a result of outside events and conditions.

When you become your activity, the "I" is forgotten.

Make taking out the trash a walking meditation.

Sit in front of a blank, white wall and focus on it. Allow the reflected light to fill your consciousness.

You do not need to leave your room. Remain sitting at your table and listen. Do not even listen, simply wait. Do not even wait, be quite still and solitary. The world will freely offer itself to you unmasked, it has no choice, it will roll in ecstasy at your feet.—FRANZ KAFKA

Life is an art, and like perfect art it should be self-forgetting; there ought not to be any trace of effort or painful feeling.—DAISETZ TEITARO SUZUKI, *AN INTRODUCTION TO ZEN BUDDHISM*

Beginning, be aware of beginning.

Focus on your own actions and take responsibility for them.

Desire the best for everyone, even those who have wronged you.

Make your transitions conscious decisions.

Open a window and see how wondrous life is. Be attentive to each moment, letting your mind be clear like a calm river.

Say a little prayer to a figure of mercy, kindness, and infinite love.

When a relationship ends, let it go and move forward.

Refrain from outrageous conduct.

Put all the happiness you can into each moment.

Treat meditation as an ongoing experiment, not a short-term process. Take an active interest in it without getting distracted by your expectations about the results.

For one week, do not take anything you are not sure you have permission to take, even a glass of water. Observe what happens.

Be aware that your empty plate will soon be filled with precious food.

Know you are breathing in. Know you are breathing out.

When you're in physical pain, pay attention. Maybe there is an underlying physical or emotional cause.

Let go of the "I've got to/need to/have to/love to/hate to/want to/don't want to" feelings that lie at the heart of suffering and emotional hunger and attach you to objects of desire.

When eating and reading the newspaper, just eat and read the newspaper.

Sit, eyes closed, and focus on your palms or your belly about two inches below your navel. Stabilize your attention.

Recall the moments when you have done good things for others. Remember how good it felt, and feel it now as vividly as possible. See yourself as a giving, kind, compassionate person who radiates lovingkindness. Now cultivate these sensations toward yourself.

Wait and trust, and you will be shown the solution.

MINDFULNESS VOW: Aware of the suffering caused by exploitation, social injustice, stealing, and oppression, I am committed to cultivating loving-kindness and to working for the well-being of all people, animals, plants, and every other precious thing on earth. I am committed to practicing generosity by sharing my time, energy, and resources with those in need.

Look and listen, focusing on the experience itself rather than on what you perceive.

Find friends who share your goals.

When judgments arise during meditation, just be aware of them, avoiding the temptation to judge them as well.

Basic relaxation meditation: Lie down on a comfortable surface and close your eyes. Let your arms rest slightly apart, palms up. Your legs should be spread apart and relaxed as well. Now sense your whole body, especially where it touches the surface you are lying on. Start the body-scan by following your breath and bringing your awareness to your feet. Wiggle your toes, and then flex and relax them, letting go of any tension there. Now bring your awareness to your lower legs, slightly tensing the muscles and then relaxing them. Do the same for your thighs, and then for your hips. Continue for the rest of your body, bringing your awareness to your abdomen, rib cage, chest, shoulders, arms, fingers, neck, throat, and head. Feel their heaviness melting into the ground. Feel the calm in each part of your body. Wherever you sense tension, let that area relax. When you have scanned and relaxed your entire body, go back to your breath. When you're ready, slowly wriggle your fingers and toes. Stretch your arms and legs. Open your eyes and gradually come to a sitting position. Try to carry your mindfulness into the rest of your day.

Recognize illusions as illusions, projections as projections, and fantasies as fantasies.

With one conscious breath, you can be back in contact with yourself and everything else.

When you turn on the water faucet, see the larger picture. See the water flowing down from the glaciers and mountains, running deep into the earth, sustaining you and all life.

I AM HAPPY/I AM SAD MEDITATION: Pick one of these statements and visualize it as clearly as possible. Picture yourself feeling that way mentally and physically. Now focus on the other statement. Go back and forth between the two and try to feel how neither is very "true." Then just say, "I am" to yourself, sinking deeply into it and experiencing how "true" that seems. You can also perform this meditation using other contradictory statements, such as "I am tired/I am alert."

Spend ten to twenty minutes trying to be fully aware of the complexity of each moment. Whenever your mind tries to wander, bring it back to the sights, sounds, smells, tastes, and touch you experience.

Love your life.

Meditate each morning and evening for five minutes.

Don't put the blame on others—it gives them power over you.

Becoming intimate with how it feels to peacefully ride the trail is like going to your room to be alone in a house full of people.

Take frequent relaxation breaks.

Every little thing—traffic lights, a smile, a flower, your cup of coffee—can serve as a bell to stop, breathe, let go, and be mindful.

Tensing holds on to pain. Instead, relax around the sensation. Let the pain be there. Go right into the area where the pain is with a concentrated, investigative mind.

While working, do a conscious slump. Let your spine curl forward and drop your head slowly. Feel the weight of your shoulders as they slump forward. Stay with the gentle stretch and breathe. You are allowing your upper body to give in to gravity. Then, slowly, sit up. Savor the sensations of coming back to a sitting position. You can do this as many times as you like, and you can even add it to the beginning and end of every meditation.

For once, do nothing. Don't be so single-minded about keeping your life moving. How about a huge silence?

Take a walk and imagine you are hiking through a foreign land.

Meditation on the five remembrances (this meditation asks us to reflect on the nature of reality and our actions): 1) There is no way to escape aging. I too will grow old. 2) There is no way to escape physical degeneration. My body too will weaken. 3) There is no way to escape death. I too will die. 4) Everything and everyone changes. We must part even from loved ones. 5) My deeds are always with me as propensities. Only my karma accompanies me when I die. My karma is the ground on which I stand.

Focus on one of the judgments you carry about yourself or about the world. Look deeply at it and smile with compassion at all the suffering it caused.

See work as integral to your spiritual practice, and approach it as a way to elevate your spirit.

Visualize your whole body and mind as being filled with total darkness. Feel the sadness without being overwhelmed by it. Now imagine a healing light coming from within you, in front of you, or above you. See the beams of light—bright, warm, joyful. Let them fill your entire body, penetrating each and every cell. Now imagine the light shining beyond your body, lighting the whole world and universe. Feel the nature of this healing light: It is not solid and cannot be held—it is just light.

Know that this is a wonderful moment.

With a compassionate state of mind, your actions will always carry a tone of kindness and softness, which is very useful in overcoming difficulty with anyone.

SWEEPING MEDITATION: You can do this either sitting or standing, eyes either open or closed. Focus on a specific part of your body, such as the belly. Really concentrate on the flesh, the warmth, and any feelings there, and consciously relax and direct positive thoughts or energy to that area. Repeat this exercise for other parts of your body. Once you have become familiar with your internal body, you can "sweep" through, starting from the top of your head and passing over all your organs and muscles, replacing irregularities with positive energy.

Treat difficulties like struggling plants. Give them compassion and unconditional love.

Think of your attachments as boxes stored in an attic. Go to the attic and remove each box, one by one, throwing them all into a big garbage bin. Feel a sense of lightness as you let go of your attachments.

Are you a habitual planner?

One day, you will find the source of your energy.

Each day, spend some time quietly appreciating your wealth of talent and knowledge.

Focus on your breath, then transfer your awareness to your right arm, from the fingers to the shoulder. Now do the same for your left arm. While remaining aware of your arms, become conscious of your torso, and then your neck, head, and face. You are now aware of your entire upper body. Without losing this awareness, become progressively aware of each part of your lower body. Embrace the whole of your physical presence and sit in this embrace for the rest of your meditation.

Meditation changes your response to stress and reduces your response to yourself because you begin to see things the way they really are. You start to appreciate the beauty and wonder of the mundane.

Do something you truly enjoy, like cooking, gardening, or painting.

You have feelings, but you are not those feelings. You have thoughts, but you are not those thoughts.

Do everything like it's the last thing you'll ever do.

Be diligent today.

Say to someone important to you: "Thank you for playing a part in my life. I wish you peace and happiness in your life."

Rest in the dreamlike, infinite nature of mind.

Every now and then, speak as you are thinking. It can add intimacy and spontaneity to your relationships.

What is this true meditation? It is to make everything: coughing, swallowing, waving, the arms' motion, stillness, words, actions, the evil and the good, prosperity and shame, gain and loss, right and wrong into one single koan.—HAKUIN EKAKU

Walk barefoot and savor each sensation in your toes and the soles of your feet.

Treat discursive thinking and obsessive thoughts like old audiotapes that you are now bored with. When they start, ignore them and return to the present moment.

Sit in the cave of the heart and find freedom.

Label your pain and other difficult emotions. Speak them out loud.

Children want respect for their needs and fears. With respect, you can offer children protection and wholehearted nurturance.

Put all you are into the smallest thing you do.

Work stress can be greatly reduced simply by an intentional commitment to cultivate calmness and awareness in the domain of work and by letting mindfulness guide your actions and responses.

Before meditating, say this to center yourself: "Entering the meditation space, I see my true mind. I vow that once I sit down, all disturbances will stop."

Watch the way you walk, breathe, smile, and react.

What do your temporary acquisitions fulfill for you?

Washing the dishes is like bathing a baby Buddha.

Be whole. Exclude nothing.

When you meditate, just focus on transforming your mind. The effects will manifest themselves after your meditation.

Delight in your time alone. Don't call it loneliness; call it aloneness or solitude. Once you accept and embrace it, you will find that it provides an expanse of blissfulness, and that the happiness that comes from it can be even deeper than that found by being with other people.

Each day's commute is a once-in-a-lifetime experience. No two trips are ever the same.

As you sit in meditation, become aware of a space opening inside your breath. See what happens to your awareness of the sounds in your surroundings. Allow your breathing to lead you into awareness of your thoughts and feelings. See if you can hold the question, "What is this?" about everything you encounter.

Resolve to no longer react negatively to the things that happen around you.

Adapt yourself to circumstances, like water in a vessel.

As you meditate, imagine yourself opening a door that leads to a higher level of awareness. When you open the door, light floods in. See yourself walking into this bright, heavenly room.

Look for the good in everything. The trick is to see every situation in both a realistic and a positive light. Hope for the best, shoot for the best, but be perfectly content with whatever comes.

Meditation is nourishment for your spirit and for your body.

Daydreaming is a good way to pay attention to your needs and desires. Give yourself ten minutes a day to indulge in this meditation.

Labyrinths can be good practice for building concentration. When you're lost, or feel like you're going in the wrong direction, you may feel worried or confused. But as you walk on, you train yourself to refocus and drop negative thoughts. You can find labyrinths in some churches and cathedrals, or you can purchase canvas labyrinth walks for your backyard or "finger" labyrinths for your home or desk. You can even create your own labyrinth by carving a simple walkway in your backyard or outlining a path with stones.

When nothing is yearned for, you are free to enjoy what you do, free to see the patterns, free to hear the music in all things.

The next time you shake hands with someone, offer an open hand, open heart, and open mind.

Every moment of meditation is an opportunity for a fuller, happier life.

When you open up and note just what's happening in each moment, without holding on, without pushing away, without struggle, then you find inner rhythm, an ease and effortlessness that can be practiced.

Hear the traffic.

Visualize a favorite place until you are transported there and have become one with nature.

Disregard whatever you think of yourself, and act as if you were absolutely perfect. You just need courage. Behave in accordance with your own best standards and do what you think you should. Do not be afraid of mistakes; you can always correct them. Only intentions matter.

The everyday mind is Buddha's mind, and the profane is also the sacred.

One-point meditation: Choose an involuntary body rhythm, such as your heartbeat, and contemplate (one-point) this rhythm.

Who is the hungry ghost within you?

Hold it all in until you have figured out how to say it in a useful way.

Meditation gives you a chance to find your center at the end of a hectic day. Just as rest stops help birds reorient themselves during migration, meditation helps you stay on your path through life.

Choose a routine activity such as opening a door, brushing your teeth, or making coffee. For one week, do it completely mindfully, noting the intentions before your actions.

Use gentleness and a sense of humor to stay in the present moment.

Witnessing is enough—you do not need to act.

Gnana MUDRA: Join the tip of your index finger to the first joint of the thumb. Then place your hands palms up on your knees. The *gnana* mudra symbolizes enlightened individuality.

Reciting a mantra instinctively opens your mind to supernormal powers and insights.

Imagine that all your negativities are being flushed out by light and nectar flowing through your body, and that negative karma is leaving you in the form of a dirty liquid. Feel with certainty that your negativities no longer exist and that you are completely purified and filled with blissful energy.

Live each season as it passes; breathe the air, drink the drink, taste the fruit, and resign yourself to the influences of each.—HENRY DAVID THOREAU

Allow experiences of life to come in and pass through your being. When you see a couple together and you feel jealousy, just smile. Be happy that a blocked feeling stored deep inside of you now has a chance to pass through. Open and relax.

Meditate on an attachment you would like to get rid of such as an addiction or dependence. Visualize yourself walking across a landscape to a place of hope and peace. There is a rope tied to you on one end, and on the other, a box carrying that attachment. Make a conscious decision to let go, and then cut the rope and continue on your journey.

Accept the anxieties and difficulties of this life.

Meditation is the balance of awareness, concentration, and energy—a moment-to-moment balancing.

Listen to the sounds around you. Notice that even the loudest sounds are impermanent, passing away into silence. Just listen . . . do not scan for sounds, wait for them. Be aware of their presence and absence.

Make your religion kindness.

Focus on the way you move and carry out simple tasks. Notice any awkwardness or unnecessary effort in basic actions like sitting and standing. Try to slow down and be conscious of moving easily through space. Do everything smoothly and gracefully.

Choose love over fear in every situation.

Wisdom replaces ignorance when you realize that happiness does not lie in the accumulation of more and more pleasant feelings.

If you exercise in the morning, build in an extra five to twenty minutes at the end for deep relaxation and meditation.

Notice that your wrong perceptions are rooted in anger, and breathe in. Smile to your ignorance, and breathe out.

AFFIRMATION: My heart is open to receiving healing help.

Mentally bow to three people you are having difficulties with. Keep doing this until the difficulties are gone.

Sit silently and absorb the fact that the whole world is a dream. Nothing is of lasting significance. Everything will disappear, including you. So when things go wrong, just relax.

Whether there is or is not a way to overcome suffering, there is no use in worrying.

Come back to your breathing, come back to the world.

If you are in a dilemma, imagine a dialogue between the two sides. Explain each of the positions until there is nothing left. You might just see which one has more force, or even mediate between the two.

Give thanks for the morning light.

Sun breath: Start your meditation with these basic movements. Stand tall, with your hands at your sides. Breathe into your belly while stretching your arms. Breathe in and bring your hands to *namaste*, prayer position at your heart. Stretch your hands out and exhale, then inhale lifting your hands over your head. Exhale and lower your hands to your sides.

Don't just do something. Sit there.—SYLVIA BOORSTEIN

Slow down and look around you.

Go jogging or walking, and time your breath to your steps. How far can you go before you lose track?

Allow yourself to be exactly what you are, and allow this moment to be exactly what it is.

Give thanks for your life and strength.

Prune the garden of your mind. Each weed you pull up makes room for green grass.

Affirmation: I know who I am.

Eat when hungry, sleep when tired. Listen to the rhythms of your body.

Before you open your mouth, learn to pause and listen to yourself.

Practice right mindfulness while sitting, standing, and walking.

Become more loving and you will become more joyful. Choose something to love; it does not matter if it is a person, an animal, or even a rock. The rock may not be able to return your love, but that is not the point. You will become joyful because you have loved.

Notice your thoughts and feelings—and question them.

When you feel your spirits sagging, form a half smile. Maintain it for at least ten minutes.

Find something enjoyable about each morning.

Zen is just picking up your coat from the floor and hanging it up.

While meditating, do not be bothered by the various images in your mind. Let them come and go. Your only job is to remain calm.

Lovingkindness is a practice that directs your awareness toward healing. Breathing in, take in negativity and suffering; breathing out, radiate love and peace. It might seem counterintuitive, even scary, to open yourself up to pain, but it actually helps you to overcome fear and self-absorption while developing your capacity for compassion. This technique can be practiced in sitting meditation or whenever you face negativity such as dealing with a grumpy salesclerk or arguing with a friend.

Be aware of your body as you seat yourself for meditation, and as you stand up afterward. If you move any part of your body during the meditation, try to do it slowly and with complete awareness of each aspect of the movement.

When your cup runneth over, make offerings.

Let light become your companion.

INNER-THOUGHT MUDRA: This hand position restores balance to body and mind. Clasp your hands together and place them at the level of your solar plexus. Then release your middle fingers, extending and bringing them together to form a point.

Stop waiting. You have waited long enough, longer than was necessary. The only time to start living is now.

Meditate on emptiness, impermanence, and nonself.

Do yoga poses and forward bends to calm your nervous system.

Tune in to your breath when you're lying down. Feel it move through your entire body. Note its ebb and flow—the constant process of change.

Mantras can be used as therapy for the sick.

Practice making friends with yourself and accepting yourself fully, softening and opening your heart. This will ultimately lead you to do the same for others.

Place a small handful of raisins or nuts in front of you. Observe their appearance and smell. Pick up one, feeling the sensations of lifting your arm. Now bring the piece to your mouth and begin to chew it. Notice the impulse to take another before the first is chewed and swallowed. Be with every aspect of this experience.

Pay attention.

Are you aware of each step you take? What are all the different sensations involved in walking? Distinguish concept from experience in both your meditation practice and everyday life.

Stop buying into the idea that you have to have more things in order to be a valuable human being.

One essential thing you can give to yourself and to others is time.

In the shower, feel the energy of the water as you rid yourself of impurities. Let it take you back to your birth, and feel a deep-seated sense of renewal. As the water cascades down your body, let it carry away discomfort and distress, leaving you refreshed and invigorated.

Imagine that you are a fetus in your mother's womb. You feel weightless, surrounded by warm fluid. You feel safe, soothed by your mother's heartbeat. Feel yourself growing and developing, supported by your mother's love.

Breathing in, liberate your mind. Breathing out, liberate your mind.

Stop thinking and talking about it, and there is nothing you will not be able to know.

If something interferes during meditation—such as a buzzing fly or a barking dog—simply become aware of the sound. The buzzing or barking is not really an interruption unless you allow it to be by becoming overly involved with it.

Sitting to meditate is hard work and takes effort, as does the cultivation of any productive habit.

Make homage to Shakyamuni Buddha, surrounded by innumerable bodhisattvas. Imagine them filling the sky above you.

Next time you feel upset or angry—pounding heartbeat, knotted stomach—ask yourself if what you are about to say will be harmful. If yes, don't say it. Simply become aware of your body's reactions and the physical sensations of anger. Applying meditation in action ensures that your brain is in gear and that nobody gets hurt.

Do good, even when you are alone.

Sit quietly. Allow your concerns to surface. Ask, "What is the truth?" You will feel a mental "click" when you reach the truth.

Inhale pure love. Exhale pure peace.

See everyone as a Buddha.

Keep good company.

Include everything. Make it a lifestyle to be aware of your joy, your pain, your desires, your regrets. Do not divide or compartmentalize. The more you include, the more you will expand, and the more perceived boundaries will recede.

Eat a good breakfast.

Stay with the nakedness of your present-moment experience.

You become what you think about all day long.—RALPH WALDO EMERSON

Imagine yourself in a tower that is full of books containing all the wisdom you have acquired and all the wisdom you hope to gain. Draw strength from your accomplishments.

NO-MIND MEDITATION: Perform this meditation once each day for seven days. Stand with your eyes closed and make nonsense sounds, uttering any gibberish that comes to mind. You can sing, shout, mumble, or make any sound that is not an actual word. After twenty minutes, stop speaking, sit down, and be silent. Relax. Do this for twenty minutes. Complete your meditation by lying on the ground, letting go of any remaining negativity.

VERSE FOR TURNING ON A LIGHT: Ancient trees, water, and wind, join my hand to bring light to this moment.

Imagine that you are a surfer preparing to ride a big wave. You paddle out, see the wave coming, and position yourself on your board. As the water swells up beneath you, you sense the wave's momentum and align the surfboard with its direction, paddling yourself into the sweet spot of this perfect wave. You glide through the tunnel of water and arrive safely on the beach.

Are you paying attention to what you are doing?

Settle into your everyday breath. After it has slowed down and smoothed out, inhale, exhale, then pause. Rest in the stillness. After a few seconds, you will feel a little ripple—the swell of your next inhalation. Allow it to gather for a few more seconds before you inhale again. Continue to pause between your exhalation and inhalation, and try to lengthen the pauses. After ten to fifteen breaths, pause after each inhalation as well. Try to stretch these pauses too for another ten to fifteen breaths.

When you take a shower, are you really in the shower? Feel the water. Be mindful.

Maintain silence for a whole day.

Unhook your mind once it is caught in a reactive state.

SHIVA DANCE MEDITATION: In this practice, dance is total meditation. First, dance with your eyes closed, as if possessed. Let your unconscious take over. Do not control your movements or think about what is happening. Just be totally in the dance. Do this for twenty to forty minutes. Then, for twenty minutes, lie down with your eyes closed and just be still. Finally, for five minutes, dance in celebration and joy.

Acknowledge your dependence on the kindness of others.

Be aware of suffering. Don't trivialize or ignore it.

Experiment with opening up when you want to close down.

Meditate on Jupiter when you need creativity, expansion, growth, and spontaneity.

Be serious yet lighthearted, alert yet relaxed, spontaneous yet restrained, engaged yet dispassionate.

Have the ambition to live mindfully and completely in the present moment.

Sit down and close your eyes. Set aside thoughts, concerns, and worries. Search for the place inside where you feel happy or joyful. Merge with that feeling and let it permeate your whole being. Continue for as long as you can. Then open your eyes and carry this feeling with you.

Notice how you appear to exist in and of yourself, not as the product of a mind and body.

With loved ones, the best approach is to simply stop for a moment, breathe, and come into an awareness of precisely what is taking place, and then to act more skillfully, more appropriately, and with consideration to all parties involved.

Break out of your box! Drop the limiting image of yourself as a separate, fixed entity. Meditation will help you let down the walls and let go of the fear. You will see that no one is attacking you and that there is nothing to defend.

There is no teacher like your own experience.

The moment one gives close attention to any thing, even a blade of grass, it becomes a mysterious, awesome, indescribably magnificent world in itself.—
HENRY MILLER

See if you can simply listen without interrupting. Can you listen without judging or even reacting to what is being said?

Don't just meditate; enjoy the beauty of meditation.

Find friends who love truth.

As you get ready to leave your home in the morning, take three deep breaths. Walk out the door and enter the world with your eyes wide open and a smile on your face.

When you feel an attack of sluggishness, make the mind more alive by directing it to the present moment.

There is a big difference between drinking a cup of tea while being there completely—and drinking a cup of tea while thinking about five other things. There is a big difference between taking a walk in the woods and really being there—and taking a walk while planning dinner or imagining the stories you will have about your walk. It is only by being fully in the moment that the fundamental questions of the heart can be answered.

What is right under your own feet?

Listen to the voices of your soul, and form a prayer to gain truth and vision.

When your mind is burning up with thinking, don't feed the fire with fresh thoughts. Let it burn out naturally through your meditation.

In the chaos of daily life, we need to be mindful of many things, and we need mindfulness to perceive our body, speech, and mind. However, it is awareness that bridges the gap between our own mindfulness and our everyday life. It helps us to pay attention to how we are using our body, speech, and mind as we move through the day.

Are you able to open your heart to suffering? Can you recognize its ever-changing nature?

In yearning for nothing, you will be free to enjoy what you do, free to see the patterns, free to hear the music in all things.

Contemplate the variety of life in this universe. Look at the stars in the sky and consider the innumerable dimensions of life beyond this galaxy. With this immense vision in mind, think about how and why you ended up in human form, on this particular planet, and in your unique circumstances.

Every little thing you do, from making your bed to mowing your lawn, takes you on a spiritual path toward discovering the pulse and sacred essence of man and nature.

Make a commitment to a more healthful lifestyle.

Unlearn your concern with thoughts.

Be aware of what you are saying while you say it. You may express anxiety and discomfort in social situations through mindless speech. You may ramble and prattle on without any real awareness of what you are saying. You are filling up space, filling the void of your fear and anxiety with words.

When a dog is chasing after you, whistle for him.—
RALPH WALDO EMERSON

Read slowly and calmly; let the very act of reading be peace.

Seed-thought meditation: Start by choosing a seed thought (a word or phrase to focus your meditation on). Now imagine that you are surrounded by the protective white light of your creator, the source of all. Breathing in, absorb this light, feeling the unconditional love of your creator. The more you breathe in and out, the more relaxed you will become. Now say to yourself, "My lower self is aligned to my higher self. I am my higher self." Feel that connection—that you are indeed your higher self. Now say to yourself, "My higher self is aligned to my God self. I am my God self." Feel that you are indeed your God self. Finally, say, "My God self is aligned to the Most High God, the Great I AM. My will and the will of God are one. I will to will thy will." Now ask the unconditional love of the Most High God to flow through you. Relax in this love, feeling lighter and lighter. Let it radiate from you, filling and expanding your aura. After some time, imagine that you are standing in a beautiful garden. Spend some time walking around. Then see yourself coming to a very large, old tree, with a seat beneath it. Sit on this seat and relax in its shade. Sensing the wisdom emanating from the tree, ask to be shown what your seed thought means for you at this time. Just let the knowledge, insight, and wisdom flow into you. When you have received all that there is to receive, give thanks. Slowly walk through the garden until you come to a gate set in the garden wall. As you go through the gate, come back to the consciousness of the room you are in and slowly open your eyes.

Are you looking for what you need in the places where it can be found?

Turn within for guidance.

Walk *kinhin* clockwise around a room while holding one hand in a loose fist, keeping your thumb on the inside. Wrap the other hand around this fist, resting your thumb in the slight indentation at the top of the first hand. Hold the hands together at the upper part of your stomach, near the base of the ribs. Take one step after each full breath.

Whatever you do in the morning sets the tone for the entire day. If you lash out in anger, then that begins a chain of angry moments. Laughter is the best way to start out. Keep it up throughout the day!

Use common sense. Put on your oxygen mask first, then help others.

Be like a tree. Open your palms to the sky and spread your arms like branches. Be open and patient wherever you are.

If someone hits you, do not strike back.

Do any complaints—even those tempered with humor—serve any purpose? Wouldn't a more direct request or suggestion alleviate a problem?

Drink your coffee mindfully.

Be uninterruptedly aware.

Affirmation: To boost self-esteem and remind you of your intrinsic value, make simple, positive statements like, "I am a good person." The affirmation can be about qualities you already have or those you hope to have. Repeat each affirmation like a mantra, one hundred times a day.

Remember.

To be in the line of your third eye (the source of inner vision), simply fix both your eyes on the tip of the nose.

Rest your fork or spoon between bites, don't put more food into your mouth before you finish chewing and swallowing what you have eaten already, and notice how you become aware of each act of eating.

Whenever you take a bath or shower, look at your body and see that it is a gift from your parents and their parents and all of the ancestors before you. Wash each part with care and appreciation. Stop, sit down, and become aware of your breathing. Fully accept the present moment, including what you are feeling and what you perceive to be happening. Do not try to change anything at all. Just breathe and let go. Breathe and let be. Allow this moment to be exactly as it is, and allow yourself to be exactly as you are. When you are ready, move in the direction of your heart, mindfully and with resolution.

Choose to live.

Do you obsessively go over the past? Let it go, let it be. Just say, "I'm mulling over it again," leave it aside, and return to your breath and the present moment.

When you pick up a magazine, the articles and ads are food for your consciousness. Ads that stimulate your craving for possessions, sex, and food can be toxic. If after reading a magazine or newspaper you feel anxious or worn out, it means you have been in contact with toxins.

Consider what really matters to you. What would you need to do and say to feel complete before you die, to feel that you are not leaving any loose ends, and that you could die in peace? If you had only one more year to live, how would you change your life, beginning right now?

Focus on reality itself rather than on your intellectual and emotional reactions to reality.

Respect happiness. Respect happy people. Make happiness the goal of your life.

Visiting an art gallery can be a meditation. Go during a quiet time when you can sit and contemplate a work of art without being disturbed.

Gardening is soothing for the soul, releasing tension and reducing stress hormones in the body.

Learn to "touch and go"—not to hold on but to allow each moment to arise with freshness.

Ask yourself whether what you are about to say or do will be useful.

A drink of water can become a mindfulness bell that helps bring your awareness to exactly where you are.

Be aware of your food. Recognize that although it is so fragrant and appetizing, it also contains much suffering—the death of the animal and the toil of the farmer. See that this balance of pleasure and suffering reflects all of life.

Silence is the bridge.

Surrender everything—your body, your life, your inner self—and you will experience peace, ease, non-doing, and inexpressible happiness.—YUAN-WU

Breathe and smile.

Imagine that you are a pebble sinking into a lake—effortless and detached—finally reaching the bottom and finding perfect rest.

Know where you are going.

If you are a parent, invite your children to share in your meditative experiences.

Visualize a tiny spark of hope as a pinpoint of light piercing the darkness you are in now. Move toward this light and watch it grow brighter and more powerful. Reinforce your faith that, in time, things will get better.

Write it on your heart that every day is the best day in the year.—RALPH WALDO EMERSON

Choose to be everybody's friend, whether they like you or not.

Enjoy whatever you're doing right now.

Be cautious among the worldly.

For one day, detach yourself from your opinions, and resolve to let go of judgments and conclusions. Pay attention to your emotional responses as you strive for complete objectivity.

Realizing that there is nothing to hold on to that can offer lasting satisfaction shows us there is nowhere to go and nothing to have and nothing to be. This is freedom.

Reflect on all the times you opened your mouth and spoke empty words to fill a silence. Do not be afraid of silence.

Let yourself feel good about giving to others.

When it is cold, be cold. When it is hot, be hot. Be one with the environment. Accept it.

Find joy in the sweetness of surrender, the stillness of meditation.

All the unconscious tensions waste energy that you could better apply to consciousness. Attention eliminates tension.

When you are not attached to anything, all things are as they are.

Accept everything about yourself and your life. Embrace your moment-to-moment experience with wakefulness and care.

Relax each muscle of your body as though it were a soft piece of silk drying in the breeze.

Walk mindfully on your way to work.

Meditation lets you work on your attitude. It lets you be without opinion, judgment, or expectation.

Be balanced in everything you do.

Are your communications sensitive, healing, and harmonizing?

Look into your partner's eyes. Look into your children's eyes.

Go confidently in the direction of your dreams!
Live the life you've imagined. As you simplify
your life, the laws of the universe will be simpler.
—HENRY DAVID THOREAU

Write a poem or personal narrative about a spiritual experience you've had.

Reflect on the benefits of *metta* meditation. You are increasing kindness, self-respect, and respect for others, and living in harmony with all. Be confident that, over time, these benefits will accrue.

Stop for a moment. Be aware of your breath and of where you are.

Do not take what is not yours.

Be completely open and receptive to whatever comes into your field of awareness. Let it all come and go. Watch in stillness.

Meditate on the beautiful aurora borealis (northern lights).

Be with whatever is happening in the moment, and your sense of completeness will be present. You don't have to do anything about it.

Help bag your own groceries, mindfully separating cans, bottles, and fragile items like eggs, and keeping chemical items away from food.

Learn to speak the words that you wish to hear, to speak words that you do not regret. Learn to speak simply and wisely.

Spend a few minutes reviewing all the good things that have happened to you in the past twenty-four hours as well as all the good things you did during that time. Allow yourself to feel appreciation and gratitude for them. Extend this meditation to the previous week, the previous month, and even the previous year. Allow these feelings of appreciation to fill your heart.

For one week, act on every generous urge.

Can you stay committed to an awakened heart and not be swept up by your ego when everything is going well?

Slow down and relax.

Watch your breath as you would watch a visitor. At the same time, awaken your mind. Eventually the breath disappears altogether, and all that remains is the feeling of wakefulness. This is called "meeting the Buddha."

Step peacefully.

Feel happy when coming back to the breath. Don't worry that you're going to have to do it a thousand times. That is why it is called practice.

Remember that worrying is pointless—it only adds to your suffering.

Reflect on yourself and on your life. How are you living? How could you simplify things? Do you create problems for yourself? Use meditation to help you with your reflections.

During charged or touchy discussions, be mindful of the words you are using, and guard against defensiveness, belligerence, hostility, and superiority.

Wake up early to meditate or do yoga.

In a calm frame of mind, imagine another version of yourself, one who is egotistical and self-centered. Imagine also a group of poor people, unrelated to you, who are needy and suffering. Now visualize this other version of yourself transforming, softening, and bending to help this group of poor people. Notice how much warmer, more connected, and more alive you feel.

Go outside on a peaceful night and scan the sky for one star that you find particularly appealing. Listen to that star, and to the entire universe. Close your eyes and hold their messages inside you.

Meditation is being aware of each feeling. Recognize it, smile at it, look deeply into it, and embrace it with all your heart.

When you're feeling stuck, meditate. Settle into a comfortable position. Then ask yourself, "How am I doing? What does not feel quite right? What do I need to pay attention to right now?" Set aside whatever answer surfaces. Do this a few times until you have three or four answers to consider. Now choose one and simply ask, "What is the crux of this problem?" Do not try to analyze, understand, or reach a conclusion. Wait for a revelation—a word, an image, or a feeling. Then ask, "Is this right?" When you have hit upon something that feels right, sit with it in silence for a few moments.

When you start to feel drowsy, acknowledge this. Then move on and find a different object to focus on.

MEDITATION: Once your concentration has been well established, drop the noting, labeling, and breath-counting. At that point, simply be directly aware.

Take a long breath, and when your lungs are full, silently count "one." Breathe out completely until your lungs are empty, counting "two." Count up to "ten," then count backward to "one." Continue to breathe and count for as long as you like.

See the whole person.

What do you feel you cannot live without? What price do you pay for it? What kind of fulfillment does this item or service provide? Look at your cravings gently, without judging. Make room for change.

Keep a journal of your meditative experiences. Reflect on the insight you have gained and the obstacles you have overcome.

"TOWARD THE ONE" SUFI PRACTICE: Start by walking casually. Then synchronize your breathing with your pace, four steps per inhalation and four steps per exhalation. Say "toward the one," one word per step, and just be silent on the fourth step. Walk like this, with complete attention, for as long as you wish.

Open to the effortlessness of being rather than doing.

Natural-light energy meditation: Sit facing the sun. Then breathe in the sun's energy through all the pores of your body. Let it be an inexhaustible fountain of energy.

Next time you find yourself at a lake, pond, river, or ocean, listen to the "white sound" of the water. Enter into the flow of the water and let it wash everything away. Let the sound of the water wash over you and through you. Let all your thoughts fall into the water and dissolve. Watch and listen until you become one with the waves.

Are you open to constructive criticism? Do you learn even from hostile opinions?

Bathe in the center of a sound. Feel the sound as if it were the entire universe. Feel as if every sound is moving toward you and that you are the center of all these sounds.

When you feel embarrassed, recognize that it is your own ego, rather than the situation itself, that is the cause of your embarrassment. See the humor in the difference between your pretensions and your performance. Laugh at the part of your ego that was wounded by the experience. Then, gently, let it go.

Unlearn your concern with things.

Look at life's difficulties as valuable training for your character and future endeavors.

To feel more balanced, first stand with all your weight on your right foot. Then stand with all your weight on your left foot. Shift back and forth four or five times. Feel the change in energy. Finally, just try to be in the middle.

Connect with all that is good and positive.

Think of the center of your being as the center of a cyclone or tornado. Whatever happens around it does not affect it. It is eternally calm. Follow this silence, and truth, love, and blessings will come to you.

Take two to three days to carefully notice the intentions that motivate your speech. Direct your attention to the state of mind that precedes talking—the motivation for your comments, responses, and observations. Try to be particularly aware of whether your speech is even subtly motivated by boredom, concern, irritation, loneliness, compassion, fear, love, competitiveness, greed, hate, or something else. Be aware of the general mood or state of your heart and mind and how it may be influencing your speech. Try to observe without any judgment. Notice the motivations in your mind and the speech that flows from them.

Think about all the ways in which impermanence manifests itself in activities as simple as eating breakfast. Before you eat, you are hungry. After you eat, you are not hungry anymore. Before, the plate is filled with food. After, it is all gone.

Ride the moving breath.

Pick one activity that you do every day and do it mindfully.

Instead of fighting, bow.

Think through what your day would have been like if you had not thought that some of it should have been different.

Turn a source of irritation into an opportunity to be mindful.

Hold your seat. Stay centered—not moving, not reacting. Allow your thoughts and impulses to come and go. Release your illusions.

Just breathe.

Notice your need for control, whether it be over people, politics, your body, your mind, your past, your future, or even the weather. Try to observe this desire, rather than getting caught up in it. Note any thoughts you have about what you believe "should be." Soften and relax negative feelings about not being in control.

What would it mean to eat only food that didn't cause harm to you or anyone else?

Counting your breath occupies your mind so that your mind doesn't occupy you.

See opinions for what they are; don't cling or become attached to them.

Just because something is no longer useful to you doesn't mean it's useless. Pay attention even to your garbage. Notice not only what you discard, but also how you throw it away.

Close your eyes and imagine the sound of silver bells ringing. They are thoughts to open the door to the spiritual world.

Look for the source of your thoughts.

When you see a friend and suddenly feel joy in your heart, concentrate on this joy. Feel it, become it, and remain centered in your happiness. You can also do this when you see the sun rising or the snow falling—whenever your heart rises.

Determine to increase your mindfulness from moment to moment.

For a period of time, pay close attention to your motivations and intentions. Before you turn on the television, ask why. Before you take your first sip of coffee, ask why. If you do something you feel ashamed of, ask why. If you do something you feel proud of, ask why.

To be born again is to let go of the past and look without condemnation upon the present.

Breathing in, be aware of your mind. Breathing out, be aware of your mind.

Complete what you have begun.

Infinite patience creates instant results.

See yourself in others.

Try to go to bed earlier so you can meditate just before or at sunrise.

From the moment you get up, be mindful, making your whole day a meditation.

Everything you hate in others is something you hate in yourself.

As your feelings of equanimity grow stronger, fear and dislike will decrease.

When cooking, clean as you go.

Purchase a kneeling bench for your meditation practice, folding your legs back and under.

Sit in the center of life and open yourself to awareness of its dance, noting that everything that arises will also pass away.

Stop and allow yourself to fully grasp the situation you're in. Realize that you have the ultimate choice about what to do or not to do.

Meditate on your children and your parents.

Make the most of what comes and the least of what goes.

Learn to be centered enough to just watch internal disturbances come up. Do not fight the release of stored energy. See the feeling or thought, let it happen, then release and let go. Let your body and mind purge an internal disturbance.

Take a sip of water. Taste it little by little. Notice how it affects the senses in your mouth. Scan your body for all the sensations generated by drinking water. After a couple of minutes, drink as much as you want. Take note of your new sensations.

Pretend you're walking into a spiral maze of massive stones. With each step, you feel lighter and more connected to your spirit. By the time you reach the center, you are fully in touch with your intuition. Know that all the wisdom you need lies deep within you.

You must be the change you wish to see in the world.
—MAHATMA GANDHI

At the end of your out-breath, let go of your thoughts. It is like moving a boulder out of the bed of a stream so that the water can keep flowing. Allow your energy and life force to evolve and move forward.

By paying attention to your experience from moment to moment, you will wake up from your worries and daydreams and return to the simplicity and clarity of the present.

Polish your path.

Many Hindu meditations combine deep breathing with the chanting of mantras. For example, the mantra for Ganesha, the elephant god, is *Gam*, and the mantra for Krishna is *Klim*. The deity's qualities are invoked through the repetition of the mantras, giving the chanter a transcendental awareness that moves beyond ordinary perception.

Breathing in, observe the impermanent nature of all. Breathing out, observe the impermanent nature of all.

Morning meditation: Mindfully shower, get dressed, and prepare your breakfast.

Be soft when you feel harsh.

Half-bow: Hold your hands, palm to palm, at chest level and bow from the waist.

At the beginning of each week, choose a simple activity that you usually do on autopilot. It can be as simple as putting on your makeup, shaving, washing your hands, making tea or coffee, or getting into your car. Pause for a few seconds before you begin the activity. Then, perform it with full attention, as though it were a formal meditation. Build on your mindfulness and power of attention week after week.

When you rise from bed, feel your feet making contact with the floor. Be aware of their weight, the floor supporting your body, and the motion of your feet and legs as you begin to walk.

Wash your brain.

If just one person on the boat is calm and maintains equanimity, the rest of the people will calm down too.

During television commercials, hit the mute button and take some mindful breaths.

Imbue each act and moment with mindful attention.

If you feel confused, tangled, or bent out of shape, meditate. As you become more centered, you will feel less overwhelmed, more effective, and more relaxed. Your heart and mind will gently release.

Don't grasp for compliments, reject blame, or tune out. Remember that things always change. Keep the larger perspective in mind.

A mind beyond judgments watches and understands.

Let the discerning person guard his mind, so difficult to detect and extremely subtle, wandering wherever it desires. A guarded mind brings happiness.—BUDDHA

Instead of judging or condemning, do a compassion meditation for someone who is causing pain or harm. Use healing phrases like "May you be free of your pain and sorrow" or "May you find peace." Investigate and contemplate, right here, right now.

Note how your mind creates stress. Gently ignore its fabrications and return to mindful attention.

Set a timer for every hour, on the hour, reminding you to wake up and appreciate the miracle of every moment. Say, "[Your name], wake up!"

When an impulse arises, simply meditate on it. Do not do anything until it has arisen three times. You will discover a center of balance and understanding in the midst of the forces within your life.

If you do not try, you will not know.

If you can just stand still and let go, you have pure awareness.

Release anxiety by lengthening your exhalations deliberately and gradually. If your regular exhalation lasts six counts, draw it out to seven for a few cycles, then to eight for the next few cycles, until you find the optimal length for your exhalations.

Reality is ever-changing, ever-growing, indefinable.

Expand your understanding of who you are.

Make a list of the most important activities you need to complete each day. Close your eyes and see yourself entering into a state of mindfulness as you undertake and complete these projects.

When you find yourself losing interest, just pick one thing to focus on—one sentence, one step, one breath. Your mindfulness will take you back into the present moment and carry you back into your activity or surroundings.

Meditation washes away the dust of desire and protects you from temptation.

When you feel conflict with others, understanding their suffering is the first step in being able to communicate, forgive, and begin again.

Overtones meditation: Sit comfortably with your eyes closed. Shape your lips as though you had a straw between them. Inhale, then exhale vowel sounds like *ooo, ou, eee.*

Prostration: Start in a standing position. Raise your arms in salutation and then lower them, first to your forehead, then to your throat, then to your heart. Now lower your knees to the floor. Finally, lower your whole body, placing your forehead on the floor. Repeat three times.

Chant *ah* on the out-breath. Dissolve, rest, just be.

Four steps to expand your understanding of spiritual truths:

1) Study—read or listen to spiritual teachings about the truth.

2) Reflect—contemplate the deeper meaning of the words.

3) Apply—use the teachings in your life.

4) Integrate—become one with the knowledge.

Are you trying to release your self-absorption and egotism?

Develop your motivation and sense of responsibility. Your self-confidence will increase and your fear will decrease.

Eat a piece of fruit with care and attention.

Get rid of the false and you will automatically realize the truth.

Create an island of being on the sea of constant doing in which your life is usually immersed.

Stop from time to time and pay attention to your inner dialogue. You are not your thoughts. Feel comfortable with *not* believing them.

Each morning, be aware of your transition from sleeping to waking.

Zen is a way of being happy.—TAO SHAN

If your act is motivated by true kindness, it will naturally bring a positive result.

Even the simplest acts can bring a powerful sense of presence and grace to your life.

True patience manifests itself as a nongrasping openness to whatever comes next. It is a calm willingness to be present.

Make a weekly list for your inner self, just as you would keep a shopping list for your trips to the grocery.

When you are angry, see that you're like a burning house, and breathe in. Put out the fire and breathe out. Go back to your true self.

When eating, chew each mouthful thoroughly, enjoying the richness of the moment.

Use different colored lights in meditation to unlock different energies.

Before picking up the phone, pause for a moment and think about the purpose of the call.

Stretch your arms above your head and give praise to the sky.

See your thoughts as balloons floating by.

SEA-TUMBLING RELAXATION: Lie down in a comfortable place, with your arms and legs extended. Imagine lying at the edge of the sea on an empty beach. The tide is coming in. Gentle waves lap at your feet and ankles and very slowly move up your body until you are immersed in shallow water. As the water rises, feel yourself floating; let the rhythmic currents draw you out to sea. Feel the waves beneath you as you glide up and down. When you're ready, roll over onto your stomach, and ride the crest of a wave back to shore, landing on the smooth, warm sand. Stay there and relax in the profound calm.

You don't have to be mindful of everything at the same time. Just focus on what you find to be most meaningful.

Accept that your ego is an illusion.

Be alert among the apathetic.

We mistake pleasure for happiness even though we know pleasure doesn't make us happy. Pleasure is pleasure, a temporary gratification of desire. Happiness is a deeper satisfaction, a feeling of wholeness, of non-neediness.

Break your meditation into smaller sessions if you find yourself frequently distracted. As soon as you start to lose focus, take a break and relax for fifteen to twenty seconds. Over time, you will develop stability and increase the depth and duration of your concentration.

Five contemplations before eating:

1) This food is the gift of the whole universe—the earth, the sky, and much hard work.

2) May I be aware of the quality of my deeds as I receive this food.

3) May I practice mindfulness to transform greed, hatred, and ignorance.

4) May this food nourish me and prevent illness.

5) In gratitude, I accept this food so that I may realize the path of love, compassion, and peace.

Try to understand the difficulties of your parents and determine to work for their release from suffering.

Breathing in, see and let go. Breathing out, see and let go.

Do not permit your mind to wander aimlessly. Always be mindful of your thoughts.

Let the force of gravity center you. Sit and become aware of how it holds you to your chair. Stand and feel it pull you toward the earth. Walk and feel it grab you with each step. Notice how the objects around you are all held in place by gravity. Stay aware of this invisible force as you go about your day.

When you're reading, do a five-second mini-breathing meditation at the end of each paragraph. Just pause and take a conscious breath. Then read on.

Rejoice whenever you hear about someone else's success.

Take a bath in an imaginary rainbow. Let its colors and light rejuvenate you.

Walk away from situations that are harmful or not in your best interest.

Breathing in, satisfy the mind. Breathing out, satisfy the mind.

Being totally focused on your work brings you powerfully into the present moment.

Notice the silence between sounds and the space between thoughts.

Only if you keep the peace within yourself can you bring peace to others.

Practice losing your self-consciousness so that you can be open to unencumbered awareness.

Why be angry with anyone?

Touch someone with true caring—without any automatic or mindless movement.

Remember that you will one day die. Let the impermanence of life help you see the pointlessness of ego, pride, and materialism. Appreciate the preciousness of every moment.

MOVEMENT MEDITATION: Gather a group of people and clasp your hands to form a circle. Slowly lean backward with your face to the sky and hands held up, using a simple chant like "*Ya hai.*" Bring your body and head forward and swing your arms down and back, saying the simple chant, "*Ya huk.*" Repeat until your speed and rhythm are coordinated and the circle opens and closes like a flower.

Life responds when we take a risk.

When you enter your meditation area, see your true mind. Vow that once you sit down, all disturbances will stop.

Say this in meditation: "I know I am breathing in. I know I am breathing out. I am aware of the hair on the top of my head. I smile to the hair on my head. I am aware of the soles of my feet. I smile to the soles of my feet. I dwell in the present moment. I am aware that this is the only moment in which I am alive."

PREPARATION MEDITATION: Sit, arrange your legs, lengthen your spine, rock side to side and front to back on your seat bones, tilt your pelvis slightly forward, soften your belly, tuck in your chin, rest your tongue and position its tip on the roof of your mouth, breathe through your nose, rest your hands in a comfortable position, and just relax.

The first step in growth is to do what you love and be aware of doing it.

Thoughts are not the enemy.

Take a long walk and appreciate your freedom.

LUCID DREAMING EXERCISE: When you wake from a dream, go over all the details until you have them fixed in your mind. Before you go back to sleep, tell yourself firmly several times, "The next time I am dreaming, I will recognize that I am dreaming." Visualize yourself as being aware that you are dreaming inside each dream you recall. With patience and practice, you will be able to converse with those you meet in your dreams, control the course of the dreams, and even change to different dreams.

Absorb yourself in this moment.

See the cause-and-effect relationship between intention in the mind and movement in the body.

Gaze deeply at something until thoughts disappear.

Why rush through some moments to get to other, "better" ones? You don't have to fill your moments with activity and more thinking in order for them to be rich; quite the opposite is true. Be completely open to each moment, accepting it in its fullness, knowing that, like the butterfly, things unfold in their own time.

When you grab something to eat, make sure it is for hunger, not for emotional or spiritual sustenance.

Think of what does not think, such as rocks, the color gray, or the rainbow in the sky.

Think about the damage that anger causes to yourself and to others, and breathe in. See that it burns and destroys happiness, and breathe out.

Imagine yourself sitting in a very quiet place. You attempt to speak words of wisdom, but they will not come out. Each time the words stay inside, you gain spiritual energy. Let the wisdom build up—you are learning the wisdom of silence. Stop trying to speak and just sit—you are becoming wiser.

Push on with all your determination, and just when you feel defeated and blocked, throw yourself into the gaping abyss before you—into the ever-burning flame of your true nature. All illusionary thoughts, feelings, and perceptions will die with your Me, and your Self-nature will appear. You will feel resurrected, truly healthy, and filled with joy and peace.—BASSUI TOKUSHO

Play with children.

Cleanse yourself of the dust of the world.

Be "awake" even when you are asleep.

See your own difficulties as divine messengers expanding your consciousness. Real blessings often appear through disappointment, loss, and pain.

Drop the constant compulsion to look somewhere else for something more.

LIGHT MEDITATION: Visualize a white light—pure, transparent, formless—in the space above your head. See this light as universal goodness, love, and wisdom—the fulfillment of your highest potential. Let it descend through your head into your heart, where it expands to fill your body, turning you into itself. You are now in a state of wholeness, perfection, serenity, and joyfulness. Stay here for as long as you like.

Have an ease and openness of mind that receives with interest every kind of circumstance and asks what you can learn from each experience.

Breathe out a long *ah,* pausing when you need to. Enjoy the sound of your voice and imagine that the whole world is filled with the peaceful sound. Feel healthy and purified. Be at one with the sound. Relax in the experience.

Thumb Meditation: Sit with your arms extended straight in front of you, slightly below shoulder level and parallel to the ground. Close your right hand into a fist. Wrap your left hand around your right hand with your left-hand fingers over your right-hand knuckles. The heels of your hands should touch. Straighten the thumbs, extending them up so that the sides are touching. Now gaze at the thumbs. Inhale for five seconds, exhale for five seconds, and pause for fifteen seconds. Start by doing this for three to five minutes, working up to eleven minutes.

Recharge yourself. Imagine lowering a bucket into a well of energy that never runs dry.

Walk the perimeter of a peaceful room.

Work with an attitude of true service. See if you can add volunteering to your schedule.

First, establish yourself in the Way. Then, teach the Way.

Take delight in your surroundings. Be interested in everything—the trees, the clouds, the cars, and the people—around you.

Your breath is a spiritual lighthouse guiding you back to the present moment. Use it to get back to where you are.

Quiet your mind and open your heart.

Pause every half hour to come back to your breath.

Do a sitting meditation for five minutes in the morning and five minutes in the evening, either right after dinner or just before bedtime. See if you are a morning or evening sitter—or both.

Your words will come out right if you speak from lovingkindness.

The joy of meditation is daily food.

Happiness comes not from reaching out, but from letting go and opening to what is true.

Visualize a mountain lake with a smooth, glass like surface. Imagine that a breeze sends ripples across the water. As the breeze subsides, so do the ripples, and the water is smooth again. Come back to this vision whenever something ruffles you. Feel the ripples and then let them settle.

Make a list of the qualities you admire in other people. Each day, meditate and practice one of these qualities.

Many eyes go through the meadow, but few see the flowers in it.—RALPH WALDO EMERSON

Look within your own mind.

Don't mindlessly snack throughout the day. Notice the moment right before you reach for a snack. Be aware of whether you really want it. If you do, enjoy it mindfully.

While in the car put on some soft, mellow music.

It does not matter what others do or think or say, unless you decide that it matters to you. Something happens and you feel your energy change. At that moment, relax and let go of the sense of being bothered.

LAST-LOOK MEDITATION: Let your current thoughts, feelings, and preoccupations disappear. Breathe deeply, eyes closed. Now open your eyes and look at everything as if it were your last moment on earth. Consider the beauty and preciousness of this moment—the only one you have left. Recognize that every moment is like this one.

If you learn from current challenges, you will not have to repeat the same difficulties.

Without clinging or pushing away, without seeking or rejecting, do what needs to be done.

Meditation can be a difficult practice to get into. Be patient.

Before you can learn, you must admit that you are a student.

Stop chasing the noises around you. Just let them be.

Try to live so that whenever you stop and look back at the footprints you have made, you see a happy path, one that you will want to continue to follow.

Eat with moderation, never to the point of oversatiation.

Think of a person or situation that has made you angry or bitter. Hold that image and look at it from every angle. Focus on your role: Where were you wrong, thoughtless, or mistaken? Imagine how you would feel if you were no longer angry or upset. Make amends, offer forgiveness, and let go. Resolve not to harbor resentments in the future.

Cultivate a spacious mind.

Take mental notes. Name your experiences as they unfold.

Look at the open sky. Dream about the possible, rather than trying to pin down the permanent.

Why be unhappy about something if you can do something about it? If nothing can be done, what does being unhappy help?

Be accommodating: Make room for the small, moment-to-moment disappointments of everyday life. Don't forget where your preferences lie, but remain spacious and relaxed when they are not met.

Apply the mindfulness of meditation to daily life.

Live each day with freedom, strength, and wisdom.

Don't gobble down your food. Eating is a holy act that requires your full presence.

When you realize in your own experience that happiness comes not from reaching out but from letting go, not from seeking pleasurable experience but from seeking what is true, the transformation of energy frees the compassion within you. Your mind is no longer bound up in pushing away pain or holding on to pleasure. Compassion is the natural response of an open heart. When you settle back and open to what's happening in each moment, without attachment or aversion, you are experience. From this attitude that you develop in your practice, you can begin to manifest true compassionate action in the world.

Give up yourself to others. Give up yourself to life. Give up struggling to make sense of it all. Simply, give up.—TAO SHAN

Approach life with a loving heart, and it will open and flow more easily.

Your "luck" is your exertion.

If you have trouble speaking with truth or eloquence, try to imagine what the Buddha would say if he were in your situation.

You can't control other people. But they can't control you, either!

Join or start a meditation group.

Lovingkindness practice: Whenever you feel resentment, breathe in the negativity, and breathe out love and peace. Do it whenever you need to, even in minor situations.

Peace is a daily, a weekly, a monthly process, gradually changing opinions, slowly eroding old barriers, quietly building new structures.—JOHN F. KENNEDY

Hug a tree.

To lessen your ego attachment, meditate on the emptiness of our existence—that we are controlled by causes, conditions, and external circumstances.

Trust your inner goodness.

Water the seeds of life through mindful living.

All-senses Meditation: Each time you become aware of using one of your five senses, say to yourself, "Now I am aware of smelling, tasting, seeing, hearing, touching."

Arrive early.

Tarot meditation: Take a deck of tarot cards. Pick one card per day. Meditate on the Seed Thought on your card.

Stop grasping, and you will be free.

Rather than identify with your thoughts, take a step back and observe them.

Relaxation exercise: Bring your attention to your breathing. When you feel ready, repeat the word *relax* to yourself, either silently or out loud. Say the first syllable, "re," as you breathe in, and the second syllable, "lax," as you breathe out. Do not try to force your breathing into a rhythm or pattern; just breathe normally and match the speed of the affirmation to the breathing. When your mind wanders, gently bring it back to your breath and continue to repeat the word *relax*.

If you are nervous or on edge, follow your breath.

Attend to the moment-to-moment unfolding of the present.

With fear, you can recognize that you have it and work to release it. Decide not to fight with life. Face the fear that causes you to feel like fighting.

When your body and mind are at peace, they are attuned to each other—there is a bridge between them.

Let your mind move beyond the limitations of time and expand into eternal presence.

Stay centered in the midst of external appeals to desire.

Does the thought that you're having now create suffering or well-being?

Choiceless, open awareness allows everything to unfold as it must.

When you laugh, laugh through your whole body, from the soles of your feet.

Cleaning out your home creates space and clears mental clutter too.

Move in the direction your heart tells you, mindfully and with resolution.

Meditate on the suffering that arises from lack of wisdom. Try to see it from the point of view of a specific person, family, or society, and resolve to help that person or group by the most unpretentious means possible.

Make peace with each breath you take.

Instead of pushing toward your next destination, just enjoy the process of getting there.

Forgive.

LOCKED-THUMBS MUDRA: This is very useful in insight meditation. Open your left palm and rest it just below the navel. Interlock your thumbs.

Find simplicity by paying attention to the roots of your complexity and then letting go.

It is as important to have a formal meditation practice each day as it is to eat.

Look for the small things; you will see more of the details of life.

See the world as a movie—evanescent, insubstantial—nothing more than a continuous series of ever-changing pictures. Like the figures on the screen, recognize that what we call the self is not real, and that it also dissolves upon analysis.

When you feel dissatisfied, just sit down, close your eyes, and focus on your breathing.

Attend a spiritual workshop or retreat.

Watch the clouds and the moving water.

Equanimity is the power of mind to experience changes and yet remain centered and unmoved.

HOLLOW-BODY MEDITATION: Imagine that your body is open and filled with clear space. Let your feelings come and go.

When you're confused, return to your immediate experience.

Try to stay with one complete in-breath and one complete out-breath. Gradually increase your cycles.

Add nothing, subtract nothing.

If your mind is calm and constant, you can keep yourself away from the noisy world even though you are in the midst of it. Your mind will be quiet and stable.

Take deep, slow breaths while on the phone, in the car, or simply waiting.

Add a few drops of essential oil to your bath and meditate while you soak in the warm water.

When you are no longer absorbed in your melodrama, you will find you are in a state of awareness with a flow of energy emanating from within. This awareness gives you freedom.

Upon greeting someone, put your palms together and bow.

Imagine that you are a kite soaring in the sky. Surrender to the wind, but be aware of the string that anchors you to the ground and keeps you safe.

Instead of fearing change, see it as an opportunity for growth.

Spoon breath: Form the syllable *oo* with your lips as you inhale through your mouth in seven small bursts. Swallow the seven breaths. Exhale through your nose, counting to seven. Repeat twenty-four times both in the morning and the evening for one week.

Let your life be a story of understanding. Let go of your fear, anger, and other negative feelings—they are all hindrances to understanding.

Close your eyes and imagine the calming feel of an animal's soft fur.

Eat and be merry.

Breath walk: Start by walking slowly and leisurely. Count the number of steps you take per breath (inhalation and exhalation). Continue for a few minutes, then lengthen your exhalation by one step. Let it be natural. Do this for ten breaths. Now lengthen it by one more step. If you're comfortable, you can also lengthen your inhalation. Continue for about twenty breaths. Breathe normally for the duration of the walk.

Read the *Tao Te Ching* by Lao Tzu.

Start each day by reminding yourself that you attract the positive—good people, good outcomes, good opportunities. Repeat a positive mantra.

During meditation, you may find yourself recalling unpleasant events and feeling upset, angry, or unhappy. Do not worry. Your feelings are natural responses to negative experiences. Just acknowledge them and smile. Let them go without getting caught up in them. Rest your attention on the sensations in your body.

If you are married, meditate on your wedding ring and reaffirm your commitment to your partner and your relationship.

Go to a local park and swing on the swings.

Practice doing one thing at a time. Do it consciously, slowly, and with awareness and respect.

Change your routines.

See perfection in imperfection.

Before you prepare breakfast, close your eyes and see what you really want. Do not think about what is available; think only about your desire. Then go and find that food.

Your inner growth is dependent upon the realization that the only way to find peace and contentment is to stop thinking about yourself.

Instead of viewing your life in terms of what you are not getting, open your heart with joy to all of the things you are continually receiving from the world.

Take the first step of your day mindfully.

Mindfulness protects you from negative habits, such as grasping and condemning, that create pain and confusion in your life.

For a day, catch every negative thought that passes through your mind. See them, but don't judge them, and then let them go. Neutralize each negative thought with a positive one, remembering that everything happens for the best.

Mantras are a combination of prayer and meditation.

Breathe in "one, one, one, one" until your lungs are full, and breathe out "two, two, two, two" until they are empty. Do this for ten counts.

A sense of wonder and delight is present in every moment, every breath, every step of ordinary life.

Be patient with yourself. A calm and peaceful mind is the only way to overcome failure.

Be gentle with all things.

Your goal in meditation is not to accumulate knowledge or learn something new. It is simply to cultivate a fresh, uncluttered perspective—a beginner's mind.

Be at one with darkness. Turn off the lights and open your eyes wide. At first, you may find them straining to find light. However, you will eventually find the darkness to be soothing and harmless.

See the limitations of worldly success.

Be sensitive to your body. Listen to what it tells you. Whenever there is a conflict between your mind and body, trust your body.

Be a student of truth.

Lie down and breathe in and out. Feel your body touch the surface you are lying on. With each out-breath, sink deeper and deeper into the surface, letting go of any tension or worry. Send love and compassion to your whole body. Be grateful toward all the cells in your body.

Each wakeful step and each mindful act is the path of life.

Let your feelings and thoughts pass by like clouds in the sky.

Watching thought is letting go of the content as we become aware of the process, seeing the space around each object of the mind.

GLOBAL-AWARENESS MEDITATION: Sit quietly and contemplate all the things that are happening around the world. Let your thoughts lead you to a deep awareness of where you are. Offer blessings to the whole world. Become aware of the different emotions and physical and mental states of everything out there, including animals and plants. Realize that all of this is the play of the divine.

Each time you open a door, take a few mindful breaths.

Think about ways in which you could change your day.

If you find yourself repeatedly angered by similar things, see if you can detect a pattern. What expectations were you holding? Would you still react that way if you had none? You will find that once you accept things for what they are, you will become less angry and more effective at influencing them.

When the phone rings, pause for a moment to let it ring. Listen to it. Relax before you pick it up.

Shed your past like a snake's skin.

The wisdom of the heart is here, now, at any moment. It has always been here, and it is never too late to find it. The wholeness and freedom you seek is your own true nature, who you really are. Whenever you start a spiritual practice, read a spiritual book, or contemplate what it means to live well, you have begun to open to this truth.

Take a day, or a few days, to just be silent. Turn off the TV, the radio, the telephone, even the thoughts in your head. Do not read, write, or surf the Internet. Take refuge in the calm and peace of a quiet mind. Keep still.

Hear yourself talk.

See your internal body, your external body, and both together.

Just sit—not trying to accomplish anything, not trying to change anything.

Take a moment to appreciate what you have mindfully accomplished each day. Build on that mindfulness the following day.

Your mind is like a swinging door. Thoughts and feelings come in and out, like people. Be the door, not the doorman.

Simplify.

Be conscious of yourself as a presence, as occupying space, as part of creation. Be aware of your life history. (Do not think about the history; just be aware of its existence.) Now be aware of yourself as a being with a future. Finally, recognize that you have no real boundaries, that you are unlimited by past and future, and that you do not have to be affected by the opinions of those around you.

When you help others, let it be as natural and unaffected as if you were helping yourself.

Bring what you have learned during meditation into your daily life.

Accept the good and run with it.

Feel the ground beneath you. Settle into the gravity as it pulls you toward the earth's center.

Close your eyes for a moment. Relax in the sensation of slow blinking.

Walk away from what is bad for you.

Give positive energy to others while expecting nothing in return.

Intellect mudra: Place both hands together—knuckles touching—against your lower abdomen. This enlightenment gesture reminds us of the divinity within.

Recognize that you are free. Rejoice in the freedom of your spirit.

Include sensations, thoughts, and feelings in your meditation to widen your awareness. Welcome whatever arises without judgment or resistance. Imagine that your mind is like the sky and that your experiences are floating through it like clouds.

You must learn to be still in the midst of activity and to be vibrantly alive in repose.—INDIRA GANDHI

EQUANIMITY MEDITATION: May I be balanced and at peace. May I learn to see the growth and passing of nature with openness and acceptance. May I bring compassion and equanimity to the world.

Use your mindfulness to notice and stop bad habits.

Go to sleep with a tranquil mind. Meditate for a few minutes on an image that you associate with happiness or peace.

Have faith.

Remember that any and every room can be a place of spiritual practice.

Bring your attention to your breath whenever you're stuck waiting in line or watching commercials on TV.

Eat slowly, moderately, and respectfully. Listen to your body.

Remember that anger makes you suffer. Stay away from it.

Let your words be coherent and controlled, clear and pleasant, calm and gentle.

By releasing the beliefs and concepts that hold your sense of self solid, you soften the ground of basic goodness so that love and compassion can break through.

Are you tired after a busy week? Have you been pushing yourself too hard? Stop!

Take breaks throughout the day to recharge your spiritual batteries.

STRESS RELIEF AT WORK: Look away from the computer screen, breathe out, let your mind decompress, and simply be. Relax in the moment.

Keep learning, keep adapting.

Use bells, chimes, and gongs to dispel negative energy.

Bow to the morning sun.

When you fully do something, there is just the doing.

We should all strive to gain some measure of control over our basic muscle movements and body functions. Fidgeting, nail biting, scratching, and other nervous habits should come under the control of our minds.

Praise someone sincerely in your mind and heart, and you will take on his or her good karma. Seeing the best in others also increases your own good qualities; acknowledging the good in another elicits the best in yourself.

Trust your breath. It will give you the freedom to accept the experience of meditation, without the need to constantly monitor whether everything is okay.

Keep a pebble in your pocket and, each time your mind wanders, squeeze it as a reminder to return to your breathing.

Give whatever you do your wholehearted attention.

Do something each day that gives you energy . . . something just for you.

Stand with your arms at your side and feet spread apart. Take a deep breath and push air through your mouth to make a sound. Do not choose any sound in particular; just let your life force express itself. Keep doing this for as long as you want to.

Break your work and activities into increments. Set a timer for thirty minutes and focus only on that activity. When you get distracted, note the distraction, but continue to focus on the task at hand.

Beginning is easy; continuing is hard.

Imagine that you are going to die in the next minute. It will push you into the present moment, and you can stop needing, stop wanting, stop fighting, stop struggling, stop maintaining.

When you feel dissatisfied, turn inward and see if you can capture the negative energy. Now turn it into positive energy by using it to focus on your breathing. Just sit and center. Let go. Let be.

Let things take their natural course. Your mind will become still, undisturbed by the events in your life.

Be audacious. Do not let a single opportunity pass you by.

Send a love note to someone you are thinking about today.

Practice mindfulness and nonattachment even when you are with your family. It will help you avoid falling into repeated arguments.

Stop, sit, breathe. Look, listen, feel.

Let your words be in harmony with your thoughts and intentions.

Make your own miniature Zen garden. Use items from nature and place them in sand in a shallow dish. Create wavelike patterns in the sand around the objects.

Pay closer attention to your thoughts and actions, and give deep consideration to signs that you may be making errors in judgment.

When facing a crucial exam or test, visualize yourself feeling at ease and speaking or writing the correct answers with total confidence. You are relaxed and happy, secure in your knowledge. See yourself feeling extremely pleased with your efforts and confident that you are going to receive the highest accolades. Keep this in mind for as long as possible. Reinforce the visualization by repeating an affirmation like "I can handle this" or "I am very confident."

Look within to your fountain of goodness. It will bubble up as long as you dig for it.

Remember not to be anxious for results from your meditation practice.

Listen—or your tongue will keep you deaf.

Practice moderation and restraint.

Meditation can be done anywhere, even at your desk.

Reside at the center of the circle. Reside at the center of the world.

You can come away from or dissolve a negative mind state just by counting your breath.

Balancing Meditation: Sit and watch your breath until you are calm. If you are right-handed, concentrate on the left side of your body, particularly your left hand and foot. (If you are left-handed, concentrate on your right side. In the visualization exercise that follows when it says "right" substitute "left" and vice versa.) Imagine that you are walking toward a door. Reach out with your left hand and turn the handle. Begin to walk through the doorway, taking the first step with your left foot. As you pass through, turn toward the left and close the door with your left hand. Now imagine a wave of energy coursing up the left side of your body. Bring this increased awareness into your life.

Begin your morning with something warm: a cup of tea, decaffeinated coffee, or hot chocolate.

Remind yourself to be happy.

Take time to be alone on a regular basis so that you can listen to your heart, consider your intentions, and reevaluate your goals and activities.

Be silent. Just listen. Existence will take care of you.

Carry a sense of openness and wholeness within you. Use your breath to help you renew this feeling.

Embrace the adage that prayer is speaking and meditation is listening.

Once you have your mind under control, you can leave your mindfulness techniques behind and progress to the next level: just sitting. Sit in full awareness, noticing thoughts and feelings, not engaging, not judging, simply being.

Be aware of everything that you love unconditionally.

Cultivate gratitude for even the smallest wonders.

Sleeping meditation: Imagine that your bed is in the middle of a luminous lotus bud, a small temple, or a pavilion of light. Let it resonate with a healing and regenerating light that infuses you with sleep. Rest in the assurance that it will protect you from harm.

Clean your house. It not only gets rid of dust and clutter but cleanses you within as well.

Gently bring yourself back to your center. Let your breath connect and quiet your body and mind.

Listen to a CD of rain forest sounds.

Affirmation: My every thought, word, and action is a mirror of the spirit's presence within me.

Harmonize your thoughts, intentions, and speech.

When you wake up in the morning, stretch your arms to the sky and breathe deeply, filling your spirit with the emptiness around you.

Your breath is the string that will guide you through the labyrinth, the bread crumbs that will lead you through the forest.

Study yourself. Paradoxically, the more you do so, the more you will forget yourself.

Watch your mind as it moves between opposites. Look for the moment in which it is still.

Do what is beneficial. Send forth positive energy.

Do not be worried about distractions during meditation. All you have to do is recognize your distractions to bring your mind back to concentration. For instance, if you start thinking about lunch in the middle of your breathing exercises, just notice the thought and say, "I am breathing in and thinking about tomato soup." By noticing your distractions, you have already brought your mind back to mindfulness.

Be independent; don't cling to anything.

THOUGHT-LABELING MEDITATION: Breathing in and out, notice your thoughts. Which ones tend to occur together?

Give yourself thirty to forty-five minutes for a bath. Do not hurry. Let every movement be thoughtful. Be aware of each part of your body and of the water. Follow your breath.

By learning to stop resisting reality, what used to look like problems will start to look like helpful stepping-stones in your spiritual journey.

Chew your food so that you can savor its sweetness, bitterness, sourness, saltiness, and mildness or hotness.

When you are calm within, you can better see the order in the chaos. When you are completely attentive, you are grounded.

Aromatherapy: Use chamomile and neroli to soothe and comfort, frankincense to relax, lavender to heal, and jasmine and ylang-ylang to lift your mood.

Sit out in the open air in an upright, relaxed posture. Choose a random object in front of you and look at it steadily. See it purely as a form occupying space, not naming it or judging it. Each time your mind tries to think about the object, let the thought go. Be present, and just see.

When in doubt, listen to your inner voice.

Do not lie unless it is for the good of others.

Serenity prayer: God, grant me the serenity to accept the things I cannot change; the courage to change the things I can; and the wisdom to know the difference.

Meditate to enrich your life and to bring joy to your existence.

The art of relaxation is a gift that only you can offer yourself.

Bring attention to all the things you have taken for granted.

Meditate on happiness. Let any thoughts or images that make you happy come into your mind. When they trail off, turn to your senses and meditate on what real happiness is for you. You will feel a deep, ecstatic, inner glow when you find it. Let this glow carry you throughout your day.

Sitting back and noticing your thoughts helps you see habitual patterns. Use the insight of meditation to change them.

Share the best of yourself through your words: your joy, your love. Try to avoid sharing the worst of yourself: your blaming, criticizing, judgmental words. Use your words to support, not tear down.

Life is like sound; it is ephemeral.

Experience each moment mindfully, without attachment, striving, grasping, or involvement, but with full appreciation for the essence of the moment. How great to simply be yourself.

Be joyful.

Work on your emotions, but also remember to relax and be mindful of external sensations.

Sometimes the best way to be in touch with your feelings or thoughts is to stop feeling and stop thinking for a moment. Give yourself the gift of silence. Give space to your feelings and thoughts.

You already have what you need to transform your life.

All you can control is your reaction to the circumstances in your life.

CENTERING PRAYER: Choose a sacred word as a symbol of your devotion. It can be a religious word, a word from a poem or song, or anything that feels sacred to you. Sit quietly and repeat the word to yourself. When your mind wanders, gently come back to the centering prayer.

Whenever objects of attraction or aversion arise, meditate on the emptiness of both; view them as illusions and emanations.

Think about the meaning of friendship. What do you value most in a friend? What would you like to give to others as a friend? Good friends are a great source of happiness and freedom.

Use the color orange to break down barriers, gain energy, and add zest to your life.

Are your hands on the steering wheel?

Notice that when your mind drifts to another place or time, you become lost in imagination or worry. Try to stay in the here and now. It is the safest place to be.

Every moment is eternal.

Notice the veining of a slab of marble or the grain of a piece of wood. Be aware of the life in everything.

What can you do today to serve others selflessly?

Repeat this focus sentence during meditation: "I have a body, but I am not my body."

Start by following your breath and then become your breath. At that point, you disappear; there is no technique—no deliberate watching of breath, no koan, no mantra, no noting—just pure awareness.

Speak mindful words. Don't ramble; say only what is important.

Contemplate the rapid changes of your body. Your cells are completely renewed after seven or eight years. Your brain also changes over this period. Are you this changing body and mind?

If an angry driver wants to zoom past you, let him. Flow with the traffic instead of fighting it. You will have a calm heart, whereas he will still be angry.

On a clear night, sit outside and look at the stars.

Accept and appreciate all the help you get.

Drop what you are doing and listen, as if you are hearing sound for the first time.

Touch an object, gently and with sensitivity. Feel its beauty and wholeness.

Visualize yourself performing well at your favorite sport or exercise. See that you are totally absorbed in the activity and feel how natural your success is.

Be honest, loyal, and disciplined.

Imagine that there is a glob of warm honey on top of your head. As it melts, it runs down your face and neck, covering your shoulders, chest, and arms. It gradually moves down your whole body to your toes. Let the sensuous wave of warm honey take away all your tension and stress, leaving you relaxed and renewed.

Let life flow.

Watch your body: Be alert to every gesture, every movement. Over time, bad habits and nervous behaviors will disappear, and you will experience a sense of deep peace.

Like a Sufi, live in your breath twenty-four hours a day.

When someone says something harsh, simply notice the words and count to ten before responding. Do the same when someone says something flattering.

Be aware of the tendency of your mind to busy itself with external stimuli, searching for things to watch or think about. It's just a habit. Each time you notice it, you lessen the likelihood of its happening again.

Think of one person that you take for granted. How might the practice of mindfulness bring new vitality to your relationship?

Think about how much energy is wasted resisting or rehashing what has already happened and grasping or pushing away thoughts about the future. You are struggling with yourself. You cannot do anything about the past and most of the things you think may happen, never do.

Remind yourself from time to time that this is it.

The way out of a trap is to study the trap and see how it was built. Take it apart piece by piece. A trap cannot confine you if it has been taken apart.

When you walk, what are you aware of? Are you carrying an image of your foot or leg? Can you feel different sensations within the movement? Is there an overlap between the image and the sensations? Practice distinguishing between concept and experience.

If you feel like dancing, dance. If you feel like swaying, sway.

Love is the fuel of life.

Allocate more time for your chores.

Breathing in, make your mind happy and at peace. Breathing out, make your mind happy and at peace.

Do your tasks with your whole being. Do not do them just to get them done, even if you are in a rush.

When meditating, open yourself to the universe.

Take a walk or do some type of exercise during your lunch break.

Anything can be a meditation. Just de-automatize. If you do each activity—taking a shower, eating a meal, talking to someone—as though for the first time, then your whole life becomes a meditation.

Imagine that there is a small ball of light shining over your head. Turn all your attention toward this light. Imagine that all the energy in your body is being drawn upward through your spine and into your head, as if this light had magnetic force. Return to the light whenever your mind wanders.

When you say, "I don't know," you see the world with fresh eyes, with openness, as having new possibilities.

There is nothing to achieve and there is nothing to become. You are already that which you have been seeking.

Breathing in, concentrate your mind. Breathing out, concentrate your mind.

One minute of practice is one minute of generating the energy of mindfulness.

The smile you send out returns to you.

Compassion is the best healer.

AFFIRMATION: I am more than these feelings.

Do not suffer from your own anger. The person who has harmed you has already moved on, so why still feel the burn, the persecution, and the constriction of anger?

Be mindful during your commute. As you seat yourself in the car, bus, or train, take three breaths. Notice the environment. Participate in the journey.

We all like to tell ourselves stories—to make up facts or reasons—to feel more comfortable with our lives. But this comfort is only momentary. If you sense a story starting in your mind, say, "Not now." It will compose you and place you back in reality, where you can actually form a genuine insight or solution to your problems. Vow not to tell yourself stories.

Slow down. Haste makes remorse.

Acceptance and understanding of change is a deep spiritual insight that can transform your life.

QUARTER-LOTUS POSITION: Let both knees touch the floor while crossing your legs in front of you in a basic cross-legged position.

In the Sanskrit word *mantra*, the root word, *man*, means "to think," and the suffix, *tra*, means "tool." *Mantra* literally means "tool for thinking." The repetition of sacred phrases has been used since ancient times to aid in meditation—to purify and focus the mind, offer devotion and thanks, and protect and nurture spiritual activity.

Close your eyes and imagine pristine spring water pouring through you from the top of your head down to your feet. Let the water purify your body and wash out any negative energy you may be carrying.

Don't let your fear swallow you. Label it. Observe it. Take control of it.

Treat everything as though it were a dream.

Change and spice up your activities.

Divide the day and night into three periods each, and during those periods, take a little time out to meditate.

Do you know who you are?

Curl up with your favorite item—a book, CD, stuffed animal—in a special spot.

Whichever seeds you water will blossom and grow into plants. If you repeatedly act out of anger, you are watering the seeds of anger. If you meet your anger with kindness, then the anger seeds cannot grow, but a loving plant will come in its place.

Look at each morning as a rebirth and understand that only this one day exists.

PRAYER: Help me to be patient and generous.

For each thought and feeling ask, "Does this create well-being or suffering?"

Disappear in the dance.

Wherever you are, listen. Bathe in the sounds around you and find a point of silence within.

Cultivate lovingkindness and mindfulness until they become a way of life.

If you want a more active type of meditation, try chakra meditations. You will visualize focal points of consciousness, breathe beautiful colors (each chakra has an assigned color), and get acquainted with your amazing body. Chakra meditations also help you develop concentration, since you will have to listen to an instructor.

Remember that unpleasant feelings will pass. Notice rather than react.

Look for what is, rather than what is not.

Whatever happens in a meditation session arises from daily life.

Cooking is not just food preparation—it is an expression of yourself. Give yourself plenty of time to do a good and enjoyable job.

Contemplate the experience of suffering in your life. Choose one painful incident and think or write about it. Can you trace the energy you've expended in wanting this experience to be different? Can you see your desire or craving? Contemplate letting go of this desire or clinging. Do you think you have the capacity to find this freedom? Can you give yourself this possibility?

Act on your desire to contribute to the world.

Sit quietly, and look slowly around you. Take in each sight and object as it presents itself. Try not to label or think about what you see. Gain only a sense of shape, color, and presence. Acknowledge that everything you see is taking place, moment by moment, inside your own mind. Be aware of yourself also as a presence in the here and now, experiencing the play of your own mind and the fact that you are alive. End the meditation by offering gratitude for what you have experienced.

Begin your practice of generosity with giving away material things.

Pretend that you are at the center of a thousand-petaled lotus. Sitting, let a "centering word" (a word that brings a sense of balance and wholeness—such as *home, love, light, peace*) come to you. Now let an associated word come to you. Stay with the new word for a few seconds, then return to the centering word and wait for the next association.

Affirmation: I trust myself and others.

Visualize something wild, like a unicorn or Frankenstein's monster. Be as outlandish and original as you can. See what you can do with your mind.

Live your life now instead of waiting for the future.

Know your faults. Then move on and forget about them.

Ride the ups and downs of your life as you would a wild horse. You cannot tame the laws of nature. Just stay in the saddle.

Do you appreciate, respect, and attend to your mentors, teachers, and other guides?

Whenever you change your position—whether it's sitting down after standing or standing up after sitting—appreciate the moment of change, of freedom.

Wherever you go, there you are.

If someone irritates you in some way, try to overlook it and see the person from another angle. Avoid situations that cause you to clash.

Hug wholeheartedly.

Let your attention be with your surroundings.

To be uncertain is to be uncomfortable, but to be certain is to be ridiculous.

THREE-PART CONTEMPLATION:

1) Imagine what it may be like to have no fear, no worry, no stress, no confusion, no one to be angry at, no pressing matters, and nothing to wish or wait for.

2) Invoke an image of yourself as a baby—innocent and carefree.

3) Bring that image and feeling into your life. Look at your life and the people in it without any worry.

Imagine that you are as happy as happy could be. (Your ability to imagine this is proof of this dormant capacity within you.) Do this daily, and you will soon start feeling happy for no reason at all.

AFFIRMATION: I give love and service.

Sit as under the *bodhi* tree, being mindfulness itself, free from distraction.

Eat and drink mindfully. Consume only items that give your body and mind well-being and joy.

The chores of daily life can be as beautiful as the sunset.

Practice dharma (cherishing others and establishing inner peace and happiness) twenty-four hours a day.

In the midst of tension and struggle, ask yourself where calm and peace lie.

REMEMBERING-YOUR-GOODNESS MEDITATION: Sit and close your eyes. Do not analyze or expect anything. Bring to mind something you have done or said that you feel was good or kind. Be with the happiness that comes with the memory. If nothing comes to mind, then focus on a quality you like about yourself. Be with your thoughts, but do not involve feelings of desire or aversion. Just concentrate on your goodness and happiness. Let go and begin again whenever you get distracted.

It's traditional to recite mantras 108 times, but you can recite them for as long, or as briefly, as you want. Just be sure to end with a dedication to fellow beings to lock in your meditation.

As you prepare for sleep, take a few mindful breaths, feel the support of the bed, and smile. Let your muscles relax as you sink into the bed.

Remember that no matter where you are or what you face, within your heart peace is possible.

Be aware that you're breathing in. Be aware that you're breathing out. Be aware of each thought as it crosses your mind. Smile to it. Be aware of each thought as it leaves your mind. Smile to it. Be aware of the space between your thoughts. Do not be caught up in your thinking. Dwell in the present moment.

If you try hard enough, you might just surprise yourself.

Before you meditate, bow three times, then bow to your cushion or seat.

Write down your thoughts and feelings, and contemplate the events of the day. Regard your life as an amazing play; it is a great story, and you should be thankful for it.

CENTERING PRAYER: Put yourself in a reverent frame of mind by using a prayer deeply familiar to you, such as the Lord's Prayer. Contemplate the image of God dwelling in the depths of your soul. When you feel centered by your love for God and God's love for you, meditate on a simple word like *love* or *father*.

Think about how your breathing changes when you drink coffee, eat lamb, exercise, or nap.

Overcome anger with gentleness.

When in pain, soften rather than resist. Expand your awareness to include it rather than tightening, contracting, and wishing it away. Welcome the pain—make friends with it.

Undertake each task with spirit, and you will eventually find that every act is an expression of the Buddha-mind.

See yourself as you are, remove the obstacles that lock you up, do your best to help others, and leave the rest to the powers that be.

To practice moving meditation (meditation in motion), you must first accept where you are. Be erect and attentive. Divest yourself of all expectations. Let go of any standards—of technique and comparison. Be clear, observant, and unobstructed. Simply observe and experience. If negative feelings arise, acknowledge them and return to your awareness of your surroundings. Be intimately involved in the action. Everything changes and each situation requires a different response. Keep your mind, body, and senses awake.

If you don't have any control, then all you can do is go along for the ride, maybe even relax and enjoy it.

Think your thoughts after the meditation.

Look deeply at someone you care about. Accept this person completely in this moment.

Take a few mindful breaths before you start eating. During the meal, try to be aware of the sensation of chewing your food.

Receptive meditations (just sitting and releasing) help you to embrace the flow of all experience—pleasant and unpleasant, internal and external—opening you to the dynamism, subtlety, complexity, and totality of your life.

Use the power of fragrance to create an atmosphere for your meditation.

Writing really helps to heal toxic memories. First, take twenty to sixty minutes to write the basic outline and description of your memory. Then, rewrite it, adding what you have learned from the experience. Finally, write it one last time, not as a personal story, but as a lesson that others might benefit from.

Patience is the mark of true love.

Investigate your distractions and mind clutter. Be an observer. Do not try to name them or react or judge. A distraction is just a distraction. If a thought or series of them bombards you, acknowledge this and then let it/them go.

Each moment you are awake is an expansion of your knowledge.

When you cannot stop thinking about something, just think about the best-case scenario. Then think about the worst-case scenario. Find peace in your middle ground.

On a clear day, look at the sky. Contemplate its vastness. Let your mind expand. Become the sky.

Walk each step without paying attention to the one before it or the one to come.

Is there something you are resisting deeply? Are you resisting this resistance? Feel it. Embrace it. Now allow it all to disappear. If you stop resisting, something wonderful just might happen.

INHALE-EXHALE WALKING MEDITATION: Be aware of your natural breathing rhythm as you start out on your walk. Once you have settled into your pace, whisper "rechaka" as you exhale, and whisper "puraka" on the inhale. Then expand your awareness to include the sensations in your feet. This effectively quiets the thoughts flowing through your mind and moves you into a clear state of consciousness. You will be aware of your whole body and spiritual presence, without any thoughts.

Lavender and flaxseed eye pillows can be very relaxing. Lavender calms and restores, and flaxseed molds to your face, relieving tension.

Ponder your koan even outside of meditation. Think of koans as friends that accompany you throughout the day. "Speak" to them as often as you can.

Scatter joy.—RALPH WALDO EMERSON

Do your work with peace, kindness, and humility.

In meditation, putting distance between yourself and your thoughts allows your mind to become relaxed, flexible, workable, and pliable, and you have more clarity about your direction in life.

Catch yourself each time you want something to be other than it is. This is the cause of suffering—and each time you catch it, you save yourself from it.

Walk, run, exercise.

The awakened mind is free flowing, natural, and well rounded, and as with Teflon, nothing sticks.

Don't eat standing up.

Volunteer at a soup kitchen, literacy program, or help hotline. Give clothes and food to shelters, find homes for abandoned animals, and help conserve the planet.

Feel the intensity of your own drive for success. See that intensity in your opponent too. Know you are the same. Knowing this, relax.

Through *zazen*, you can channel energy that is normally squandered in compulsive and purposeless action into focused achievement. Your nervous system will feel relaxed and soothed, inner tension will be eliminated, and even your organs will be strengthened.

AFFIRMATION: I accept the world just as it is.

Watch every action, every thought, every desire, even the smallest gestures. The more watchful you become, the more graceful you can become. Your chattering mind will grow quiet.

You don't have to figure anything out or make anything happen. Just sit, be aware of your breathing, and your concentration and mindfulness will penetrate whatever comes along.

Do just one thing at a time, keeping your mind in the present. Practice doing it more slowly, with more intention, and more awareness and respect.

Arrive where you are.

Try not to focus your mind on anything in particular; rather, let it spread and fill your body. Let it flow through your whole being. You will become more efficient, using your eyes, hands, and legs only when necessary.

Mindfulness keeps you in the present moment and makes life more interesting.

We are immersed in a world of constant doing. To get back in touch with being is not that difficult. We remind ourselves to be mindful. Moments of mindfulness are moments of peace and stillness, even in the midst of activity.

If you're in the right spirit, any and every room can be a place of meditation.

Understanding is the essence of love and forgiveness. Love and forgiveness are the essence of happiness.

Whatever the day's weather, accept it. To complain about the rain, or lack of it, shows a mind out of tune with nature.

Meditate on Saturn when you need self-discipline and temperance.

Combine yoga and walking.

Be absorbed.

Find a photograph from your childhood and try to experience again your thoughts, feelings, and perceptions at that time.

When you wake up every morning, stretch like a cat, without opening your eyes. After three or four minutes, with your eyes still closed, begin to laugh. At first, it may seem strange and forced, but your attempt will soon cause genuine laughter. Lose yourself in it for five minutes. It may take a few days to get used to this meditation, but before long, it will become spontaneous and will change the nature of your whole day.

There is nothing more important to true growth than realizing that you are not the voice of the mind. You are the one who hears it. Much of what the voice says is meaningless, a waste of time and energy.

Affirmation: I act, but I am not my actions.

Verse for turning on the water: As I turn on the water, my body's essence pours before me. Clouds, oceans, rivers, and deep wells all support my life.

Organize a nature or labyrinth walk with a group.

No matter how much we worry or fret over something, it never helps the situation.

Are you living according to your deepest values, or are you just reacting to the fluctuations of the moment?

Before going off to sleep, meditate, imagining that you are resting your head in the lap of a protector.

Focus on a sound or image to stop the chatter of your mind. Repeat a mantra, or gaze at a candle flame or mandala.

Take *metta* breaks throughout the day. See if you can offer *metta* to someone who irritates or upsets you. Try to listen to him or her with *metta* intentions—with your heart and mind, not just your ears.

When you notice desire, you can try to let it go by switching your attention to something else.

Be mindful of the very process of thinking. It will help you catch inaccuracies and prevent self-sabotaging behaviors.

After meditation, realize that everything is pliable, open, and workable. Nothing is heavy and solid.

When you live with the awareness that questions are more important than answers, that encountering things as they are is more beneficial than just accepting your old stories about them, a huge burden falls by the wayside and you can transform your life.

Be grateful throughout your meals.

Share your pleasure, and hope that none will feel your pain.

Create a personal support system.

Visualize yourself in an overgrown garden. See yourself clearing the weeds and creating something beautiful in their place.

Prepare for each day by imagining the energy of the cosmos flooding into your whole being. During every interaction meditate on giving your energy, attention, kindness, and appreciation without seeking anything in return.

Each human action can be an exercise toward enlightenment.

Whatever you set out to make—a bed, a meal, a knitted scarf, a work of art—make as well as you can, boldly and energetically.

Accept your unenlightened state and let life unfold as it will. You will gain enlightenment only when all desire to arrive somewhere is completely abandoned.

In that moment when story and judgment do not interfere, you discover the rich silence of listening.

Metta PHRASES: May I be filled with lovingkindness. May I be well. May I be peaceful and at ease. May I be happy.

What now appears to you as the most alien and difficult will become your most intimate and trusted experience.

Energy mudra: Palms up, touch the tips of your thumbs to the the tips of your middle and ring fingers. Let your index and little fingers extend forward. Hold this mudra for five minutes during each meditation.

Ask yourself if what you are about to say is true, kind, and beneficial. Is this the right time to say it?

Live responsively, consciously, and intentionally—directing your life from within, not by the demands of the clock or external agendas, or as mere reactions to external events. Listen to the music of the moment.

Go deeply into *no* by conducting a very negative meditation, allowing yourself to feel upset, depressed, dead. After twenty to forty minutes, jump out of the negativity to *yes*. Repeat the mantra "yes, yes, yes" until you feel cleansed and well again. Going so deeply into *no* gives you a purifying catharsis, helping you attain the peak of *yes*.

Breathe in and out, calming the bodily processes.

Are you able to differentiate between the "commercials" and the "main story"?

See.

Be a lighthouse rather than a lifeboat. Guide by example, and let others find their own way.

Before a performance, recall a similar one you successfully executed in the past. Feel it with as much detail as possible. When your positive feelings reach their peak, make a physical gesture that underscores these feelings, such as a nod or a smile. Gradually, let go of the memory and open your eyes. Use your physical gesture during the performance to reinforce your confidence and success.

Shake off all worries and anxieties, not thinking of the future, not thinking of the past, just enjoying the present moment.

Before going to bed, meditate on your place in the universe. Feel that you are safe and loved. Think about what the night can teach you.

Before getting out of bed in the morning, write down your dreams and create something from them—a poem, a story, or a drawing.

What is vital is not thinking about the present but actually being in that present moment.

Be friendly to those around you. Kindness is uncomplicated. You can practice it anytime, anywhere.

Nothing is fixed, everything flows.

Let go of the habit of clinging to people, things, beliefs, ideas, and opinions.

Take time to wag your tail a little.

Close your eyes and imagine that you are in the presence of the wisest person in the world. Picture that person vividly. Ask him or her a question concerning a problem you have. You may be surprised at the accuracy of your answer(s). Sometimes you'll answer your question with another question, which can help you see the problem in a different light.

Are you living with the consciousness of your own mortality, valuing each day, hour, and minute?

Listen to Gregorian chants.

Be alive through your daily activities, and peace will bloom.

Welcome your meditative experience without judgment or aversion.

Avoid extremes. Too much or too little both cause illness.

Begin again.

Let the entire game happen on its own without changing or manipulating anything.

Simply allow the mind to go free. Tell yourself you don't have to do anything. When there is no sense of having a task to do, the mind relaxes. Allow this to become the basis of your meditation.

Spend at least thirty minutes each day on stimulating, mind-stretching activities.

Keep your back straight at all times.

Go and explore this perfectly ordinary day.

There is a simple way to stay open. You stay open by never closing. How much love do you want to feel? How much enthusiasm do you want to have for the things you do? If you want to feel love, enthusiasm, and joy, then don't ever close.

Carefully review your current life—your schedule, finances, work, relationships, family life, home, leisure activities, possessions, goals, and spiritual pursuits. See if you can simplify each of these areas. Would you feel happier if you could?

Notice acts of beauty in yourself and others, and use them for inspiration.

MEDITATION: Sit comfortably, with your palms facing. Curl your left hand into a fist and wrap your right hand around it, heels touching. Bring your thumbs together, resting them on the left index finger without touching the right index finger. Hold your hands at mouth level, eight to ten inches away from your face. Now inhale deeply through your nose and exhale through your mouth, directing air through the opening created by your hand position. Do this for as long as you wish, perhaps even until you fall asleep.

Enjoy the spectacle.

Condone the faults of others.

A wholehearted mindful embrace of everything that arises in your mind is the only path to true freedom.

Feel the simple joy of being alive and share it with everyone you meet today.

Repeat a calming mantra when you are on the phone with someone who annoys you.

Observe your body with clinical detachment, as if you were a doctor or scientist. Notice one aspect about yourself, such as a gesture you regularly make. Be conscious of this aspect throughout the day. See if you can change it or use it more effectively.

Understand that you are a continuum. Even a piece of fruit is a continuum. Like it, you are a fusion of many things and many moments.
Allow your continuum to unfold in balance, joy, and peace.

Simply sitting for twenty minutes is a victory.

For seven days, become like a watcher on a hill, just witnessing whatever passes by. Remember not to identify with or lose yourself in external events.

If you keep doing what you've always been doing, then you'll keep getting what you've always been getting.

When stuck in a frustrating situation, ask yourself, "What would it mean to be patient right now?"

Most of the time, we "leave our bodies" to meet the sounds of the world. This time, relax into your breath and let the sounds fall inside you, resting in the space between your ears. Let them come to you.

Follow your breath as far as it goes, noting "in" and "out," or counting "one" and "two."

Set the table with care.

Early in the morning, go outside and look—really look—at the stars, the fading moon, and the sun coming up. Feel the air, the temperature, the moisture.

Do not waste time in thought, judgment, fantasy, daydreams.

The more you reconnect with your essential wholeness and well-being, the more you suffuse your body and mind with life energy and love.

In this moment, choose to sow seeds for health and happiness.

Cooking is not just preparing food; it is an expression. Allow plenty of time, and work on it with nothing in your mind and without expecting anything. Just cook!

Play some mellow background music during meditations.

Mindfulness creates a gap between impulse and action. It opens space for you to dip into your heart and come up with a pearl of kindness.

Let your effort be relaxed and steady.

When driving, turn off the radio and just concentrate on the experience. Feel the steering wheel, the pedals under your feet, and the seat supporting your torso. Watch the world pass.

Wish for everything to come to pass exactly as it does.

Do something with your mind to get it out of the way. This is the function of meditation practice. It gets the mind out of the way so that you can be one with your experience.

Examine and analyze.

Whatever you do, direct your intention to benefiting others.

Give yourself wake-up cues that you can easily see—on the bathroom mirror, bedroom door, or stair banister.

Cultivate your own spirit. Do not look for something outside yourself.

Hug mindfully.

Breathe in, focusing on inconstancy. Breathe out, focusing on constant change.

To eat in the Zen way, appreciate every bite and crumb. Taste everything fully and completely. It'll prevent bingeing (if you savor every bite of chocolate, you won't need much) and may even help you find more enjoyment in healthful foods.

Leave earlier than you think necessary.

Today, moment by moment, realize that each person you encounter and each event that occurs is life for you. Life is not somewhere else.

Bow to the sunset.

Meditating while working makes clear the most fundamental Zen principle: that meditation is not merely a matter of focusing and concentrating during sitting practice, but is about living in that state every minute of your life.

What will people think if you don't put on that act of being in control?

Feel the cosmos as a translucent, ever-living presence, and your mind will become completely silent. You will understand that you are just one part of this vast universe, and your worries, fears, and frustrations will begin to lose importance.

When working at the computer, pause every now and then to follow your breathing and notice how you are sitting. Stretch your neck, straighten your spine, and relax your body.

Prepare a long-term strategy to improve the world.

You do not need to squeeze so tightly.

Use Stop signs and stoplights to remind yourself to slow down, take a break, and look around.

Recite a mantra or prayer to steady yourself on your way to work.

Open your heart to others.

Appreciate each moment as a vehicle for developing wisdom.

Often in forgetting your destiny, you get overinvolved in collecting things, in attachments and possessions, in wanting to become someone special. You get involved in many of the activities of little mind, taking your ambitions, your desires, and yourself very seriously. You lose the perspective of big mind and of death.

Be grateful for even the smallest wonders.

Take a breath; take a break. Cultivate the power of the moment. Let everything else subside.

Do not underestimate the power of feeling the simple movements of your body throughout the day.

No matter how difficult the past, you can always begin again today.

VERSE FOR STARTING SITTING MEDITATION: Each thought, each feeling creates the world. I hold joy and suffering tenderly in each breath.

Meditate on your root and navel chakras to strengthen your visualization skills and unleash your inner power. Start with the root chakra, which is at the base of your spine. Feel the vibrant energy of the color red revitalizing this chakra. Move up to the navel chakra, which is in the abdomen, lower back, and sex organs; feel the joyful color orange flowing there and awakening it. When you're finished, take some deep breaths and open your eyes.

Imagine that you are a single drop of water, forming an ocean with billions of other drops. Meditate upon your spirit—one among many, but part of One.

Reduce your urge to overeat by resting your fork between bites, and waiting until you have finished chewing and swallowing before you put more food in your mouth.

Don't worry about having to repeatedly remind yourself to come back to your breath. That's what practice is.

You will find both your questions and answers right where you are.

When you're stuck in a constant internal dialogue, be aware of it and say, "Stop talking" each time it starts.

Like an oyster cultivating a pearl, cultivate something that is special to you.

Do a walking meditation on a trip to the bathroom.

AFFIRMATION: It is all connected.

Retreats and workshops can be valuable components of your spiritual practice. However, be careful not to use them as substitutes for your day-to-day efforts.

Let your fears exist. Face them to master them.

Where does the power of your breath come from?

Look at the world through your heart, rather than through your head. Pretend that you're headless. Walk around, feeling free and empty above your shoulders. Eventually, you will settle into your heart. At that point, sit down to meditate, close your eyes, and fully experience your headlessness. Let your center remain in your heart.

Imagine a pool deep in the earth that is a source of vitality and energy. Breathe in and feel this energy as liquid light passing into your legs and up into your spine. Feel it rising like a fountain through the top of your head. As you breathe out, feel this energy cascading back to the ground to be reabsorbed into the pool. On each in-breath, feel invigorated; on each out-breath, feel cleansed. Do this meditation for a cycle of three complete breaths.

Train yourself to be free.

To stop the song in your head that stubbornly refuses to leave, go back to the breath and let go of the song. Intentionally practice letting go of each thought.

Be very watchful of your thoughts, for they are subtle and potentially dangerous. Luckily, the very act of watching changes them. After you've become aware of your thoughts, watch your emotions, feelings, and moods as well.

Waiting means patience and silence. It means not being driven to action by your desires. Waiting means stillness of mind, whatever the activity.

The more fluid you are, the more alive you are. Learn to surf the waves.

Each day, view your life as a process and mindfully embrace each stage.

Be pure of heart.

Make conscious breathing your anchor.

Always look at the cause; do not be caught up in the symptoms.

As you bring your trash to the curb, meditate on the value of throwing out what you no longer need, and take this opportunity to throw away beliefs and thought patterns that no longer work. Imagine your mental garbage being carted away, just as your real garbage will be.

Walk on the edge of a beach, where the water meets the sand, with your eyes closed, feeling your way, totally attentive.

Use what might otherwise be wasted time—in your car, standing in line, waiting for an appointment—to focus on your immediate experience. Concentrate on your breath and expand your meditation practice into daily life.

Whenever you can find time for just being, drop all doing. This is a moment of utter relaxation and concentration.

Relax with a minimeditation and then focus on one or more of your most common "control-needing" situations. Visualize it clearly, feeling the pain of powerlessness and needing to be in control. Then ask yourself to have compassion. Treat your vulnerability with tenderness.

For every minute you are angry, you lose sixty seconds of happiness.—RALPH WALDO EMERSON

Constant mindfulness brings tranquility and insight, sustaining wisdom even in the midst of humdrum activities or distractions.

Accept the noise.

Be spontaneous and childlike, opening to the wonders around you.

Quiet chronic worries and judgments. Focus on the present moment rather than on the future, and don't be afraid to see yourself honestly and clearly. Choose love rather than fear.

No one can make us angry if we have no seeds of anger inside.

Concentrate on the solution rather than on the problem.

Hold an object that you use frequently, such as a cup or a pen, in your hands. Close your eyes and feel the object, becoming as fully aware of it as possible. Investigate it with your fingers, gently and reverently. Now open your eyes and absorb all of its details. Think about all the moments you've spent with it, and be grateful for all the use you've gotten out of it.

Walk step by step, pressing your feet to the ground.

Healing begins with a single breath.

ENERGIZING MEDITATION: Sit and clasp your hands several inches away from your diaphragm, with the index fingers up at a 60-degree angle. Chant the mantra *ong* starting from the back of your palate and extending through your nasal passages. Repeat for as long as you wish.

Without holding or pushing away, without accepting or rejecting, move along with daily work, doing what needs to be done, helping wherever you can.

Let go of each thought, one by one.

Don't block out the world with sunglasses or headphones.

THE FIST: Curl your left hand into a fist and place it on top of your open right palm. Rest your hands against the area just below the navel.

Depend on yourself.

Take lovingkindness breaks throughout the day. Incorporate the intention of lovingkindness into mindful speech and deep listening. See what a difference you can make simply by intending to heal the other person and by listening with attentiveness.

Stop for a moment to find your center and remind yourself of what is important, who you are, where you are, what you are doing, what you can and can't control, and what is really happening now.

Count backward. Visualize yourself rowing a boat toward an island. Feel each pull of the oars and let your breath grow slower and longer. At "zero," see yourself arriving at the shore. Begin a silent meditation.

Seek beauty.

Do something serene. Go for a walk, light some candles, take a bubble bath, or just sit and meditate. Release the day's cares.

Be happy, not just for your own sake but for others. Happy people make others happy, whereas unhappy people say or do things that hurt others.

Make a point to pause and notice the world around you and inside you for one minute on the hour, every hour.

Only when you leave the amusement park of your mind can you enter reality.

COLD-SHOWER MEDITATION: This is a good way to practice softening and accepting uncomfortable feelings. Make the water a bit colder than usual. Clear your mind and be compassionate. Gradually lower the setting and see how long you can stay centered and focused. Push your limits without becoming self-punishing.

Watch your mind with a gentle, open attitude, allowing it to settle and come to rest.

Imagine inner peace.

Are you including the welfare of all beings in your spiritual practice?

The mind is all the basic equipment you need to achieve happiness.

Regular practice of mindful breathing will disentangle you from the compulsive, habitual hold of the mind's preoccupations.

Flower arranging can be a meditation in itself. Arrange your flowers based on the Zen "Principle of Three" (heaven, earth, human world). Cut a Y-shaped fork from pliable wood and wedge it horizontally one inch down into the mouth of a vase. Carefully select three main branches, and bunch them together as you insert them into one side of the Y-shaped fork. The effect should be of a single branch unfolding into a triangular shape. Add other flowers to your arrangement, placing each flower into the vase individually. Keep the arrangement open and do not obscure any of the other flowers.

When thoughts or melodies run through your head, be glad. Then bring your attention back to what you were doing.

Leave your body at rest, like an unmovable mountain. Leave your speech at rest, like an unstrung guitar. Leave your mind at rest, like a shepherd who has brought home his flock and sits contentedly by the fire.

Stop trying to have the right opinion about everything. It's okay to simply say, "I don't know." You'll find that in acknowledging this, the clouds of confusion will dissipate, and your intuition will lead you to your true feelings.

The antidote to restlessness is concentration: Count your breathing up to ten, then start again.

TASK-FOCUSING MEDITATION: When you feel overwhelmed with work, take a few seconds to relax and breathe deeply. Accept that you cannot do everything at once. You can do only one thing at a time. Decide to focus on just one task and clear your mind of everything else. Whenever your mind veers toward other things, gently bring it back to the task at hand. Be aware of everything about it and mindfully use all of your senses. Calmly watch yourself performing the task until you've completed it.

You would have peace if you did not concern yourself with the sayings and doings of others.

Sitting, feel that you are at the center of the universe. Imagine spheres of energy and awareness expanding from within you to infuse the space around you. Sit serenely at the center.

Notice all that you're asking for in every situation. Each day, select one situation in which you ask nothing. Observe what you are receiving. Observe what you are giving.

When you feel anger brewing inside you, say, "No anger."

Choose a word or brief phrase that has deep spiritual or personal significance to you. Then close your eyes and softly repeat this word or phrase.

Make a list of things that you are very attached to. What purpose do they serve? What would happen if you let go of one of them? Each day this week, let go of one of these attachments, just for the day. See how this feels; you may be surprised.

Everything has implications: Every thought, word, and deed has an effect; absolutely everything we think, say, or do makes a difference.

If you have trouble sleeping, focus on your breathing. Sink deeper into sleep with each breath.

Examine your motives as often as you can. Before getting out of bed, establish a nonviolent outlook for the day. At night, examine what you did during the day, and whether your motives fulfilled your intentions.

Let a long breath be long and a short breath be short.

Everything you do—positive or negative—trains your mind. So be sure to watch your mind. Pause and become quiet for a few moments so that you can see whether it's going in the right direction.

Are you sensitive to what others are experiencing?

SHANTI (PEACE) MUDRA: Place your middle finger over your index finger and touch an object, such as food, while saying, "Om Shanti Shanti Shanti."

Put a chair in the center of a room. Open the doors and windows and sit on this chair. See what comes to your mind, both externally and internally. Just stay in your seat. Gain wisdom and understanding.

Meditate on your belly button as a cord that goes back to the origin of life, connecting you to all who have come before you.

Look not only at your actions but also at their repercussions. Every mental and physical action has an important effect.

An important part of your practice is that you exercise restraint. If you don't have any restraint, you don't have any control over where your life is going.

Sit comfortably and take a few deep breaths, focusing on the in-breath and out-breath. Note your thoughts and feelings, especially any attempts to avoid or push away what you do not like. Welcome these thoughts and accept them. In doing so, you will begin to get a feel for accepting and letting go.

Shalom meditation: Breathing in, silently say, "Sha," the first syllable of *Shalom*. Breathing out, silently say, "lom," completing the word of peace.

When you stand up after a meditation, do so mindfully.

Pray for others to receive what they need most at this time. Do so for yourself as well.

Feel that life likes you just the way you are; otherwise, it would have made you differently.

Zen is not some kind of excitement, but concentration on our usual everyday routine.—SHUNRYU SUZUKI

If you consistently cultivate generosity and lovingkindness to all, you'll make lots of friends, many will love you, and you'll feel relaxed and peaceful.

Do you have the patience to wait until your mind settles and the water is clear? Can you be quiet until the right words appear?

Keep the promises you have made.

If there's anything lying around, unattended, in your home or life, pick it up and put it in its rightful place.

Choiceless awareness is simply being receptive to whatever unfolds each moment.

Partake of healthful food at regular intervals.

If a problem can be solved, there is no need to worry about it. If a problem cannot be solved, there is no reason to worry about it.

The time that you give to meditation will be given back to you, with interest.

Visualize a loaf of bread baking in the oven. See the heat expand the pale dough and turn it brown. Feel its warmth and smell the aromas. Imagine removing it and setting it on a rack to cool. Then envision eating the warm, fragrant, comforting bread. Let it replenish your body and soul.

Imagine yourself five years from now as the person you would like to be, having accomplished and contributed all that you wanted to. Coming back into the present, contemplate how to begin the process of becoming that person.

There is only one moment in which you are alive: right now. Accept each moment as an unrepeatable miracle.

Bring awareness to your walking. Slow down a bit, centering yourself in the present moment, in your body. Appreciate the fact that you are able to walk; do not take it for granted. Walk with dignity and confidence.

Each time you think of helping someone else, you are planting seeds of love and generosity in your mind.

Imagine wading into a river, and feel its power coursing through your body. It is a source of strength, running deep inside you.

Whenever you see something that sparks love or compassion, close your eyes, meditate on the experience, and allow it to deepen.

Use any opportunity to relax and revitalize.

Sit alone in a dark room or outside at night. Watch your breath. Say, "I will use my finger to point at myself," and then point away from yourself. See yourself in the trees, the water, the universe. Maintain a half smile. Watch your breath for ten to twenty minutes.

Speak only when it is useful to do so. Talking unnecessarily is like allowing weeds to grow in a garden.

When eating, notice the thought, return to eating, notice the thought, return to eating.

Imagine yourself as a child lying on your back, gazing into a cloudless sky and blowing soap bubbles through a plastic ring. As a bubble drifts up into the sky, you watch it rise, and this brings your attention to the sky. While you are looking at the bubble, it pops, and you keep your attention right where the bubble had been. Your awareness now lies in empty space.—B. ALAN WALLACE

Wake up to energetic music instead of a jarring alarm.

The clean house isn't the goal. The process of cleaning is the goal.

Are you scrutinizing all your thoughts and actions, and plucking out any trace of unwholesome motivation?

Be aware of the blissful state between waking and sleeping.

Make your responsibilities labors of love. Don't turn your work into an escape from life, substitute for love, or a way to make yourself more important than others are. Don't resist, question, or focus on the negative. Simply do your best and complete your work in full awareness of the present.

Let go of the battles in your life by opening to them and being present with them.

Whenever you feel stuck or tired, find something to love. Love is life. Your energy will start flowing again.

Let your mind be like a gatekeeper. A gatekeeper does not take into account all the details of each visitor; he simply notices their entering and leaving. Similarly, when you meditate, do not take into account all the details of each experience. Simply notice the feeling of inhaling and exhaling, letting your breath go in and out at the edge of your nostrils. Eventually, your mind and body will become so light that you will feel as though you are floating. This is a sign of deep concentration.

Watch your thoughts; they become your words.

Before entering into a yoga posture, see yourself performing it perfectly. Move into the pose with focus and control.

Mindfulness is knowing what is happening while it is happening, no matter what it is.

Creative awareness is about waking up to life—to all the choices and possibilities for change. The basis of creative awareness is acceptance.

Be grateful for all the care you have been given.

Don't just watch TV out of habit or boredom; ask yourself if what you're watching is worthy of your attention. If not, read a book or run some errands.

Always choose quality over quantity.

To learn more about Buddhism, pick up a book by Thich Nhat Hanh.

Create a computer background or screensaver that encourages mindfulness.

Be awake to the continually changing tones of your breath. Be aware of the blessing of the air flowing in and out. Feel a sense of beginning on each in-breath. Let go on each out-breath.

Embrace the wonders of life both within and around you. Allow beautiful and healing elements to penetrate you.

Write down a timetable of your week to help pinpoint times for meditation.

Share good books with others to double the pleasure of reading.

By learning to "lose track of time" through focusing on the present, you begin to discover hidden dimensions to everyday experience that have always been there for you but have been veiled by your being time bound.

Keep your mind still. Treat the outside world with serene acceptance. Remain absolutely calm and empty.

Rise up with courage.

Let there be no desire, no turmoil, no past, no future. Just be contented in the present moment. See what happens.

Dance like a tree in the wind.

Personify your pain as an upset child. Imagine holding this child lovingly, soothing him or her until the pain subsides.

Bring your full self to everything you observe and feel.

Are you remaining steadfast in your aspiration to a higher, deeper, more meaningful life?

Meditate on the image of Blind Justice to remind yourself that reality will ultimately bring about justice and that everything happens for a reason. Accept things as they are, rather than looking for something or someone to blame.

If it is false, harmful, or cruel, do not say it.

Keep your mind clear like a mirror.

Pretend you are a rock.

Remember that everything in the world is the substance of illusion.

When in shock, stay in touch with your breath.

Before you watch television, drink alcohol, or do anything else that distracts you from reality, pay close attention to your motivations and intentions—asking yourself "why?"

If at any time something doesn't feel right to you, why not honor your feelings? An attitude of trusting yourself and your own basic wisdom and goodness is very important. The more you cultivate this trust in your own being, the easier it will be to trust other people more and to see their basic goodness as well.

Find enjoyment in perseverance. Perform a difficult or tedious activity for a designated amount of time every day for one week. When the time is up, put it down. Pick it up the next day. See what happens to you and your mastery of the activity.

By eliminating desire, you can eliminate suffering. If you remove the cause, the effect will stop. It means you give up futile grasping, painful longing, that feeling that you have to have something you don't have.

There is good and bad, and that is good. There is perfect and imperfection, and that is perfect.
—TAO SHAN

Like resting before a journey, quiet your mind and ready yourself for the practice of insight meditation.

Doing anything with mindful awareness can be an effective meditation.

Sit, close your eyes, relax, breathe. Imagine that your death is approaching. Replay your life as though it were a movie. Pick two accomplishments that you are proud of. Look at what makes these experiences memorable, and consider the qualities of mind and heart that you brought to them. Note how the memories affect you. Consider how you might live differently if you could live your life over again.

Read a holy book and discuss favorite passages with other seekers.

Do not walk and eat at the same time.

Listen to the meditation tapes of Jack Kornfield—Buddhist monk, meditation teacher, author, and psychotherapist.

Smiling makes you happy and attractive.

Treat simple, repetitive work like knitting, needlepoint, and even washing your face as meditation in action.

Read or listen to a tape of the *Tibetan Book of the Dead.*

Compassion meditation: Think about someone you hate or despise. Sit, breathe, and half-smile. Bring to mind the qualities you hate or despise most. Try to examine what makes this person suffer, and what makes him or her happy. Try to see this person's motivations and thought patterns. Consider whether his/her consciousness, views, and insights are open and free, or influenced by prejudice, narrow-mindedness, anger, or hatred. Is this person his or her own master? Continue until you feel some compassion in your heart. Repeat this exercise many times, focusing again and again on the same person.

Voyages are accomplished inwardly.

Nourish mindfulness by taking care of your body.

Be patient with yourself and do not lose your sense of perspective.

As soon as you pay attention to what's happening now and see that everything that rises also passes, your grasping impulses will decrease. You will find that there's nothing to hold on to.

When you are aware of every mental and bodily activity—of all your thoughts and feelings, both secret and open, conscious and unconscious—then you will attain genuine clarity.

Before you eat, close your eyes and bless the meal with a gesture of thanks or a purifying mantra.

Be aware of the nondoer in the doing, the nonmover in the moving.

Try life force energy healing therapies, such as Reiki, acupuncture, biofeedback, and therapeutic touch.

Spend part of a day observing the discomfort and pain in your life. Observe your reactions without judgment or attempt to change.

If you start to think, "This is silly," or "I don't want to do this," simply observe the thought and let it go. It is natural for these thoughts to arise, but you do not have to indulge them.

For seven days, begin each day by shouting "Yahoo!" a few times, then just laugh for twenty minutes for no reason at all, sitting or lying down. Then just sit and let go, silently watching.

Make a promise to enjoy every minute of every day.

Give yourself some silent time each day, for in moments of emptiness, the spirit enters. Float in the silence. Let it fill your body and mind.

Listen to the birds, the wind, the traffic, or some music—just listen and do nothing. Let your ear be like a door, allowing sound to enter, but not engaging in any activity. Relax in the peace around you.

Take pleasure in reaching out and giving to others.

Listen to your heart, maintain a sense of humor, and follow the middle way.

Improve your karma by reframing your response to difficult situations. See if you had instigated your problems in any way; bad karma is often the universe's attempt to balance your actions. Resolve not to make the same mistakes in the future, and just allow the situation to pass. If you fight your karma, you will only create more bad karma. Patience is meditation.

Look at situations dispassionately so you can apply reason and common sense. When you do so, you will drop negative emotions because you will clearly see that they never benefit you.

Attachments are inexhaustible; vow to put an end to them.

The next time you exercise, make a point of following your breath as much as you can. Be mindful of your body as you move. Note what takes you away from the present. Then return to your experience.

When the bell rings, listen to the bell.

Sit with dignity. Stand with dignity. Walk with dignity.

Rather than counting breaths, whisper, "Inhale, exhale, inhale, exhale . . ."

Rest your attention in your current experience. Stop yourself from looking ahead to what may happen next. Remind yourself that this is it!

As you pursue your inner journey of meditation and mindfulness, you will come to see yourself with more understanding and compassion. You will feel more in touch with your purpose, passions, and meaning in life.

Feel the simple loving presence in each moment.

Rather than trying to create your spiritual life from scratch, think about the tools and spare parts you already possess. Are there prayers that you already know? How about mantras, hymns, and songs?

MOVEMENT MEDITATION: Lie down on the floor. Breathe and relax. Starting with your head, move whichever way seems natural. Then bring it back to rest. Go through each body part down to your toes. Before ending this meditation, acknowledge and appreciate your efforts.

Drop those thoughts!

Celebrate mind, body, and spirit. Use reason constructively and creatively. Be aware of your kinship with all beings. Revere the infinite mystery of life.

Identify your happy colors.

Find a toy that you have enjoyed in the past but that you can part with now. Give it away. See what it's like to be without it. When you're ready, do the same with yet another toy. Note how you feel and what your life is without them.

Answer letters and emails the day they arrive.

By waking up fully to each moment, you can learn to be awake and alive in ordinary life. Then ordinary life becomes something extraordinary.

Read *The Prophet* by Kahlil Gibran (nineteenth-century poet, philosopher, artist, prophet, and writer), poems by Rumi (thirteenth-century Muslim mystic and poet), and the *Yoga Philosophy of Patanjali* by Swami Hariharananda Aranya.

AUTOMATIC DRAWING MEDITATION: For ten to twenty minutes each day, sit down, look around, and draw something you see. Don't worry about the subject or how good the drawing is. Just draw from within your being, and allow yourself to get lost in the meditation.

VERSE FOR WALKING MEDITATION: My mind can go in a thousand directions. Now I walk in peace. Each step creates a warm breeze. With each step, a lotus blooms.

Think that your life is as interesting and miraculous as the moon, the stars, and the universe.

Wherever you are, whatever you're doing, pay attention to the gap between the in-breath and the out-breath. Focus on the gap, but do not stop your activity. This meditation allows you to experience two layers of existence—doing and being—and to break your identification with the role you think you are playing.

While playing a sport, become fully involved with the flow and focus on every moment; this state of mindfulness is often called going into "the zone."

Serve the poor and needy.

If you lack motivation or energy, try meditating to the background of running water, such as that of a fountain or stream. Focus on the liveliness of the water and invite its effervescence into your spirit.

Through skillful effort, you become thoroughly fed up with your mind's clinging, whining, and grouching. You see the futility of trying to have things your own way. You let go more and more.

Spend an afternoon driving, eating, walking, or engaging in any other routine activity—but experience it as though for the first time.

Close your eyes and touch whatever is nearest you—whether it be your spouse or child, a tree or flower, or even the windowpanes in your house. Close your eyes and connect with that entity from the bottom of your heart.

Mindfulness takes effort but yields rich rewards.

Learn not to want what you want. Recognize desires, but do not be controlled by them.

Meditate on an evergreen tree, which symbolizes constancy.

Relax in a bathtub, hot tub, Jacuzzi, pool, or lake. Let the tension drain away. Be open and even a bit vulnerable. Drop your cares. Rest, relax, breathe slowly. Melt into the water. Rest in wholeness and completeness, simplicity and buoyancy.

One night a week, prepare a feast with awareness. Choose the menu and set out the ingredients with attentiveness. Make sure the space is clean and organized. Slowly and consciously begin cooking. Take your time and be aware of each step. Allow your efforts to flow smoothly and naturally. Eat slowly and savor every bite.

Writing, painting, singing, dancing, or engaging in any other creative endeavor opens you to a greater sense of spirit.

Use your conversations and interactions with people throughout the day to practice deep listening and mindful speaking.

Proclaim the good qualities of others, but do not boast of your own good qualities.

Whenever you feel bound or oppressed by external pressures, close your eyes and visualize a core of golden light in your body. Experience the light as a source of strength radiating through every fiber of your being.

Apply mindful breathing to stop your preoccupation with the sorrows of the past and your anxieties about the future.

Reality is perfect.

Meditate on the moon as it changes from new to full.

Whatever arises, welcome and let go.

Analyze your life closely, frequently. You will eventually find it difficult to misuse it.

The moment you notice you are lost in a story, you are no longer lost in a story. If you let go of the story, you will be right back in the present moment.

How can you learn to merely observe situations you cannot change, rather than react to them?

Act upon the inspirational words you read.

Joy is not in things; it is within us.

Light a candle and invite your guardian angel to join you. Sit by the candle and close your eyes. Breathe deeply. Feel the angel's comforting warmth, security, and strength.

Contemplate your past errors. What did you learn, and how have these lessons shaped your life?

Do you seek out meaningful, fulfilling relationships and connections? Or do you gravitate toward people who pull you away from your spiritual path?

If it is true, helpful, and pleasant, know when to say it.

Look at the things and people around you as already broken (for they will ultimately be gone)—and every moment you have with them will feel precious.

You have limited time and what is not reasonable is not to enjoy life. Let go of yourself so that you can remain happy.

Sit and listen to the music of silence.

When reading, stop every half hour. Close your eyes and bring your attention back to your breath.

Adhere to simple tasks with full attention, following through to the next moment, and the next, and the next.

Pretend that you are talking to the Buddha.

You cannot step twice in the same river, and you never meet the same person twice. Nothing remains the same. You, and everyone in this world, are constantly changing. Always meet someone as though for the first time. And always meet him or her as though for the last time.

Think good thoughts. As you think, so shall you become. Every thought affects the way you perceive and interact with the world around you.

Passage meditation: Choose a passage from a religious text, and trust that it is the seed of a spiritual experience. Memorize and continually repeat it in your mind, gradually absorbing its spiritual nature. Eventually, the meditation will slow and will even still your mind. Then you will perceive what lies in the space between your thoughts. In this interstice, you may experience a sudden flash that can illuminate your true nature and show you who you really are and have always been.

Do the necessary things—the essential things—but pour your energy into watchfulness and awareness.

Stop hanging on to what has been and longing for what might be.

Something as simple as eating a piece of fruit can bring you to awarenss. When you peel the fruit, know that you are peeling it. When you put a slice in your mouth, know that you are doing so. When you experience the fragrance and sweetness, be aware that you are experiencing them. Eat each morsel with awareness. See the fruit tree, the fruit blossom, and the sunlight and rain that nurtured the tree and the blossom. See ten thousand things that have made the fruit possible. See the wonders of the universe and the miraculous way in which all things interact.

Be aware of the sensation of the breath.

Empty your mind and fill it with dharma.

The more you think of others, the happier you will be.

If you let your upset mind settle, your course will become clear.

Sense the surrounding space that connects you to everything.

Silence can be a way of demonstrating love.

HEARTBEAT MEDITATION: Place your hand over your heart or wrist. Count each pulse, starting over each time you reach four, or simply label each pulse "beat," without numbers. If you lose count, start again. Relax, breathe, and try to get a longer pause between each pulse, slowing and soothing your heart.

VERSE FOR WAKING UP: As I wake up, I welcome a new day, smiling mindfully with each breath. May I live each moment with compassion and awareness.

Turn off machines when you are not using them. Buy the quietest appliances you can. Drive without the radio or other sounds, visit a park or walk in the woods and listen to the birds and other life forms, choose restaurants that don't overwhelm you with a soundtrack, watch television selectively and don't leave it on for background noise.

Let your breath quiet your mind and recenter you.

Start right now and make a brand-new ending.

See how the entire universe supports our existence.

Set aside some time each day to practice a guided meditation.

You see that the arrows shot at you come out of other people's pain. You do not feel injured by their arrows and actions; instead, you have only compassion. Your compassion transforms their speech and actions.

Increase your mental agility and complexity. Read the writings of great philosophers.

PRAYER MEDITATION: Do this at night in a darkened room right before you go to bed. Raise your hands toward the sky, palms up, head up. Feel energy flowing down into your arms and then into your body. You will feel at one with the earth. Now bend down and touch the earth. Repeat this six more times, so that each of your seven chakras becomes unblocked. Then go to sleep.

Close your eyes, stop their movement, and feel your inner being.

Meditate on love and compassion, and stabilize your awakening mind.

Subdue yourself and discover your inner master.

If a problem is consistently nagging at you, realize that it is a koan. Stop trying to figure or work it out, and take a different approach. Sit with it, be with it, make friends with it. Stop longing for a solution. Realize that this koan, as it is now, is part of your lifeblood.

Meditate on the North Star to help clarify your needs and experiences. Ask yourself what you're looking for, and let the answers come to you.

Relax exactly where you are instead of spinning best-case and worst-case scenarios. Just breathe and let strong emotions dissipate.

Keep the three doors—your body, your mouth, and your mind—as pure as possible.

Hear the laughter of children.

VERSE FOR PREPARING FOOD: Earth, water, sun, and air, all live in this food I prepare.

The only way to understand meditation is to meditate.

Stretch often. Welcome your impulse to move.

Use ordinary, repetitive, domestic events as opportunities to practice mindfulness. Whether answering the telephone, opening the refrigerator, or getting the laundry—just slow down a bit and be in touch with the present moment.

See the suffering of an angry person and breathe in. Feel compassion for this person and breathe out.

Make a habit of asking yourself, "Is this task or behavior really necessary, or is it just a way to be busy?" If you can reduce or eliminate some activities, you will achieve greater peace and quiet, which is essential to advancing in training.

If you make dietary changes, do so gradually, giving your body time to adjust.

Use a Native American totem to inspire and guide you during meditation.

Your work is to discover your work and then, with all your heart, to give yourself to it.—HINDU PRINCE SIDDHARTHA GAUTAMA, THE FOUNDER OF BUDDHISM, C. 563–483 BCE

As soon as you feel an impulse to do something, stop.

Become timeless.

Favor products that are durable, easy to repair, nonpolluting in manufacture and use, energy efficient, functional, and aesthetic.

Through reducing your cravings, you learn to keep your bowl small.

Mindfulness meditation is continuous, calm, focused attention through all activities, punctuated by periods of formal sitting and walking.

Concentrate on a single object and let your senses melt.

The thought manifests as the word; the word manifests as the deed. The deed develops into habit, and habit hardens into character. So watch your thoughts with care, letting them spring from love, born out of concern for all beings.

DIVINE-OM MUDRA: Form two circles representing the cycle of Divinity. Sit with your palms up, hands resting on your knees. Join the tip of your right thumb with the tip of your right index finger, and do the same with your left hand. Breathe and expand.

Observe the ways in which your feelings are merely creations of your mind's limited point of view. Your view may not be complete. Be patient, explore those feelings, and let them be. Don't be controlled by old, limiting views.

Join your inhalation and exhalation. Empty your lungs, inhale and exhale, and mentally count "one." Inhale, exhale, and count "two." Count up to "five" and down from "five" to "one." Repeat until your breathing becomes refined and quiet.

Let each in-breath calm your mind and body, and let each out-breath release any tension or thoughts you are holding.

Practice silence, and you will be able to look deeply and discover the truth. You will be free and in touch with the essence of things.

Consider joining a trusted friend in mutual self-exploration. As friends, you will be able to give each other some truly objective feedback, helping you to see your true natures and tendencies.

MEDITATE ON A CRYSTAL OR GEMSTONE: amethyst for healing, aventurine for chaotic thoughts, carnelian for energy and motivation, clear quartz for protection and strength, rose quartz for self-acceptance, sodalite for mental clarity and verbal expression, tiger's-eye for confidence and courage, and yellow calcite for peace and inner strength.

Use mindfulness to respond appropriately in the moment. It can even help you turn a stress reaction into a positive response.

UNIVERSAL POWER MUDRA: Practice this hand position to relax before sleeping. Sit comfortably, tucking your thumbs into your palms, and curl your index and middle fingers around them. Bring your hands together so the pinkies and ring fingers touch. Turn your attention inward for five to ten minutes.

Link all actions throughout the day into a meditation.

Experience your food as though for the first time. Really pay attention to what you see, smell, and taste. How many different details can you perceive in a piece of food? Try to eat with that degree of awareness at every meal.

Accept your feelings, even the ones you wish you did not have.

You are your child's compass and teacher. Just as you choose a middle path for yourself, you must also choose a middle path for your child.

If you have an awareness of your feelings as feelings, then it becomes possible to break out of the passive or hostile modes that you automatically fall into when feeling threatened or put upon.

When you take your time . . . you save time.

Meditate on the idea of a world soul. Think about your connection with the whole world. We are inextricably linked to one another and to our environment.

Express yourself freely.

When you meditate, you cannot clear your mind, stop thoughts, or get rid of emotions. You can, however, learn to move beyond these distractions and false responses.

Draw upon the color white to reinforce your sense of wholeness and purity.

Are you following your path with heart? Be still and listen deeply.

Respect everyone's right to happiness.

Communicate mindfully; be aware of what you say and use conscious, loving speech. Listen deeply to hear what is being said and to notice what is not being said.

Forgiveness meditation: There are many ways in which I have been wounded and hurt, abused, and abandoned by others in thought, word, or deed, knowingly or unknowingly. In many ways others have hurt or harmed me, out of fear, pain, confusion, or anger. I see this now. I have carried this pain in my heart for too long. For this reason, I offer you my forgiveness. To the extent to which I am ready and capable, I offer you forgiveness.

Give yourself wholeheartedly to any activity that you especially enjoy. Don't conserve energy or hold back. Don't look at your watch.

Reflect on a current difficulty: How have you dealt with this difficulty so far? How have you suffered by your own response and reaction? What should you let go of? What has to be accepted? What lesson might you learn from this? What is the hidden value of this situation?

Practice mindful breathing when you arrive at your workplace.

Set a stopwatch to beep on the hour, and take a moment to pay attention to your body every time it beeps.

Meditation is difficult because the mind is in the habit of attaching thoughts, feelings, ideas, opinions, and expectations.

Meditate on a wooden table's history. Imagine it as a tiny seed, then a young sapling, then a mature, stoic tree. See its felling and its processing. Picture a carpenter constructing the table. Give thanks to the table for its faithful service.

Look away from the screen, breathing out. Let your mind decompress. Simply be, relaxing in the moment's experience.

Remain mindful and awake; don't be carried away by thoughts and projections.

Practice the Buddha way.

Stop reading and simply notice how you are feeling. Take a deep breath. Rather than staying in the feeling, just step back. Observe and be aware.

Rest in openness, wherever you are.

Give yourself a chance to fall in love with breath.

Be fresh and pleasant.

KINHIN: Place your right fist, thumb inside, on your chest, and cover it with the left palm, making sure your forearms are parallel to the floor. Keep your arms in a straight line and your body erect, letting your eyes rest on a point about six feet in front of you. Begin walking with your left foot, letting it sink into the floor—first the heel and then the toes. Walk calmly and steadily, with poise and dignity. Practice this for at least five minutes after each sitting period. Think of your walk as *zazen* in motion. If you were counting breaths during *zazen,* continue during *kinhin*. If you were working on a koan, carry it with you.

While eating, working, or just moving around, see yourself as a source of light, as though your heart were a burning flame. Your body is nothing but the aura around the flame. Allow this feeling to sink deep into your mind and consciousness.

See how many times you can dribble a basketball before your mind wanders.

Shift your awareness away from the ordinary, and sense the infinite, invisible, vibrating energy within and around you.

Stop before making an impulse purchase. Is desire, greed, or discontent the reason you are buying?

Walk around for an hour, imagining that you have the power to bless anyone you choose. Bless everyone, including yourself.

MOUNTAIN MEDITATION: Sit with closed eyes. Inhale deeply through your nose, filling the lungs. Hold your breath for as long as possible, then exhale gently through your mouth and keep your lungs empty for as long as possible. Continue for ten minutes. Return to normal breathing, but this time, combine it with candle gazing or just being still. Then, with closed eyes, stand up and let your body be loose and receptive. You will feel a subtle flow of energy flowing through your body. Just stand and feel this energy for ten minutes. Finally, lie down with your eyes still closed, silent and still, for ten more minutes.

Use prompts to strengthen your mindfulness. Pick one simple everyday action and use it to remind yourself to remember what you are doing.

Know you are breathing in. Know you are breathing out. Ask if a thought, feeling, or perception is creating suffering or well-being. Explore it. Allow its true nature to be revealed. Ask who created it. Answer and smile. Ask if this is who you are. Answer and smile.

Imagine a safe, protected, peaceful place—maybe somewhere in a forest or on a beach. Experience this place fully and with all your senses. Note how calm and relaxed you feel throughout your body. Carry this feeling with you when you end the visualization exercise.

Be like the monk in the monastery who regards past and future as an illusion and knows that there is only this moment.

Listen to a CD of a whale song.

Practice perfect acceptance.

Meditation substitutes a more benign caretaker, watcher, or observer for the obsessively thinking mind.

Develop a joyous state of mind, and as you do, aversion will decrease.

Don't interpret your dreams immediately; let them simmer a little. Contemplate the symbols within. Look at your dreams from the different perspectives of each of the characters. Allow meaning to emerge from this contemplation.

Can you hear the sound of an instrument playing in your imagination?

Start your day with a ten-minute mindfulness walk. Be aware. Be present.

Each time you sign a document, pay attention to your signature. Gather yourself and take responsibility.

Be aware of your aloneness. You may be surprised at its beauty, and you will discover the joy of solitude.

The more you reflect on old age and death, the more you will see them simply as a natural process.

Mind illumination: Visualize a shining white letter *A*, glowing like a luminous moon. Concentrate on the white light. Focus on it and dissolve gradually into the light. Allow yourself to spontaneously awaken inside the dreamy light. See that everything is like a dream. Let it go as it will and be as it will.

Prepare your food with zest and attention.

What do you truly need to be happy?

The miracle of life is that the honey is always there, right under your nose. The calamity is blindness to the fact that life is miraculous.

With equanimity you can care for all things without trying to control them.

When you feel discouraged, help someone else.

Be aware of the preciousness of and the opportunities provided by your human birth.

Kinhin: Walk slowly and breathe normally. Measure your breath by counting the number of footsteps per exhalation and inhalation. Lengthen your breath by one footstep, for a total of ten to twenty breaths.

Time should be much more precious than money.

Reflect on your actions.

INNER-SMILE MEDITATION: Close your eyes, form a half smile, and smile into your eyes. When your eyes are filled with energy, send your smile down through the rest of your body. Smile into your jaw, tongue, neck, throat, heart, and internal organs. Then relax and soften. Now smile to the remaining parts of your body and again into your eyes. Smile as you swallow so that the energy goes through your digestive system. Smile from your eyes all the way down your spine. Let this energy propel you through your day.

Make keen use of your five senses.

Watch your character, for it will become your destiny.
—RABBI HILLEL, THE ELDER

It is always better to say something kind or encouraging than to speak sharply or derisively.

Work, serve, contribute.

An errand carries the same level of importance as a major project. Every mundane detail is an essential part of your time on earth.

Take time to be with nature, people, music, and children.

Let the areas that need healing reveal themselves. Bring careful, kind attention to these places, feeling and holding them with lovingkindness and soothing attention.

Find the silence that contains thoughts.

The more you listen, the more you will hear. The more you hear, the more deeply you will understand.

COSMIC-EGG MUDRA: This is a popular *Rinzai* Zen hand position. Keep both palms open, and let your left palm rest on your right palm. The thumbs should just barely touch.

Walk along a body of water and collect rocks, pebbles, or shells. When you are ready, toss a rock, pebble, or shell into the water and let it carry away a habit, fear, resentment, or belief that you are ready to let go of.

Try smiling and see what happens.

Sit in a chair and take a few moments to become aware of the way in which gravity acts on your body. Notice the weight of your legs and hips against the chair. Stand up and notice how gravity pulls you toward the earth. Begin walking and pay attention to the tug of gravity in each footstep. Notice how it holds in place everything around you. Move through the field of gravity like a fish swimming through water. Try to remain aware of this invisible force as you go through your day.

Be generous when you feel reluctant to give.

The best way to deal with delusions is to concentrate on your breath. It will help you wean yourself off disturbing influences.

Meditate on your spiritual ideal. Say a short prayer, followed by an affirmation that expresses your highest spiritual ideal. Repeat this affirmation until you begin to feel its meaning within your mind, body, and spirit. Then, focus on that meaning and hold it in silence. If your mind starts to wander, repeat the affirmation and return to the spirit behind the words. Conclude with a prayer for peace and healing, or meditate on sending love to people.

Wake up throughout the day.

If you listen carefully, you can learn from the most subtle as well as the most overwhelming thoughts and sensations.

Are you too easily distracted by cheap thrills, or are you able to keep your eye on the big picture?

See children as your teachers. Listen to them. Observe them. Be fully present and open to them.

VISUALIZATION MEDITATION: Imagine that you are a ball of light—clear, luminous, pure, and perfect. Envision a golden sun at your heart center, which opens like a sunflower. Give warmth and light to all who wander through the darkness of ignorance and delusion. Awaken spiritual awareness and joy like the dawn. Let go and see the afterglow. Simply relax in the joy and peace of this meditation.

Half-smile, inhaling and exhaling three times.

When you are confused, conflicted, or in trying circumstances, stop and ask yourself, "Where did this all come from? Who is in control?" When you find the source, rest and do nothing. It will take care of the situation.

When traveling by air, take advantage of the opportunity to meditate. The altitude, removal from the earth's pull, and clouds and space create a perfect environment for you to detach and focus. Close your eyes and feel yourself expanding and filling the plane. Then feel that you are bigger than the plane and that you have encompassed it. Finally, allow yourself to fill the entire sky. Feel the clouds, moon, and stars moving within you.

Accept the life that presents itself to you now.

Carry your inner light wherever you are.

SKY-GAZING MEDITATION: Relax into your posture. Drop your mind. Let it rest in simplicity and awareness. Chant *ah*. Raise your gaze. Elevate the scope of your awareness until it encompasses a full 360 degrees. Be mindful, be present. Rest in the natural state. Like a child lying in the grass, watch the clouds roll by and allow everything to simply pass through the sky.

Make your day precious.

Don't be annoyed by slow drivers; think of them as protecting you from driving too fast.

If you feel drowsy, do a quick scan of different touch points in your body and allow your mind to alight at each place for a brief moment. Do this until you feel more alert.

Master your words.

When you lose your focus and conscious attention, just stop for a moment. Smile to yourself. Chide yourself gently. Then breathe and move on.

Meditate on your posture. Concentrate on each of the seven points of sitting:

1) Legs in the chosen posture.

2) Arms hanging loosely, hands in chosen position.

3) Back straight, relaxed, lightly upright with vertebrae stacked like a pile of coins.

4) Eyes fully closed or slightly open.

5) Jaw and mouth relaxed, with teeth slightly apart.

6) Tip of tongue touching palate just behind upper teeth.

7) Neck bent forward slightly so gaze is directed naturally toward floor.

Affirmation: I believe, but I am not my beliefs.

Practice daily kindness.

Be aware of your reactions. Stop making so much effort, and simply see, for seeing is your very nature. When you are no longer criticizing, evaluating, concluding, or looking for results, you will perceive your tendency to react, and when you do that, you will no longer be an accomplice to it.

When you arrive at your destination, let yourself fully arrive. Take three deep breaths. Explore the moment. Notice the surroundings. Then take your place.

Are you awake? Where is your mind right now?

Meditate on the full moon. Let its whiteness fill your consciousness and flood you with strength and energy.

When you wash your hands, say: "Water flows over these hands. May I use them skillfully to preserve our precious planet."—THICH NHAT HANH

You are moving forward each time you remember your breath.

To help eliminate deeply ingrained habits, shift your attention to something other than those habits. Channel your energy toward another activity.

The night sky is a perfect koan. Consider that it goes on forever and that your mind can never fully grasp something of that magnitude. Just accept the awe and beauty without needing to understand it.

Think of something that makes you feel whole.

Smile more. Laugh more.

Develop a compassionate state of mind, for as your compassion increases, your vexations will decrease.

Try to act more skillfully, more appropriately, and with more consideration for all parties involved.

Your most meaningful relationships are a central part of your spiritual path. Use them to develop mindfulness and understanding. Keep before you the vision of your loved ones' true selves, especially when they are hidden from view.

NET-BEARER BOND OR *BANDHA*: Sit cross-legged and inhale deeply, slightly raising your chest. Hold in your breath, and place your chin gently into your chest to prevent the escape of *prana* from your upper body. Hold for a few seconds, then release this *bandha*, and lift your head before exhaling.

Breathe deeply, exhaling stress, agitation, and tension.

Whenever you find yourself ensnared in negative behavior, increase the amount of time, thought, and energy you direct toward positive behavior.

When you find yourself in an unpleasant situation, take a moment to look for the beauty in it. After a few minutes, shift your focus back to the situation and note whether your attitude has changed.

Practice each foundation of mindfulness for two weeks. Start with the First Foundation: the body. Focus on some specific practices, such as stretching, eating, or bathing. Move on to the Second Foundation: the feelings. Note any and all experiences of pleasure, displeasure, and indifference. In the Third Foundation, mind factors, notice your emotional patterns. Finally, move on to the Fourth Foundation: mind objects. Contemplate the subjects of your thoughts and explore whether they are making sense to you.

Water the seeds of positivity every day.

Prepare for sleep by focusing on calm thoughts and meditating away your worries.

Completely engage with the process unfolding in your life. Consciously live your everyday life.

Create a personal retreat. Choose a day that you can have all to yourself. Draw up a program for the day with the length and number of your meditation sessions. (Four twenty- to thirty-minute sessions should be enough.) Decide what you will do between sessions, such as reading, cleaning, or spending time outside. Prepare your food for the day beforehand, keeping it simple and frugal. Drink only water or juice. Enlist the cooperation of everyone who lives with you, so that you can stay silent for the whole day.

Don't do a job just to get it done. Do it with all your being.

Being in control of the mind means that literally anything that happens can be a source of joy.

Listen to the hum of your heart.

When your mind tries to dwell on negative things, sit in a quiet place and silently empty your mind. Think of a clear, flowing brook with fresh water that gently cleanses and refreshes you—until you feel calm.

At the gym, focus only on exercising and strengthening your body—not on eating, reading, or the music or television.

When you are feeling down or just not quite right, relax and stretch into a few slow and relaxing movements, such as tai chi poses.

FIRE BREATHING: Try this before a meditation session. Take a deep breath, filling your lungs, then exhale in quick snorts, rapidly contracting and releasing your stomach muscles. Do this for a minute or two to oxygenate your blood and raise *prana* in your system.

Speak gently to everyone and they will respond accordingly.

Pay attention to your thoughts. Notice what the voices in your head are telling you. What are the main themes? What is the emotional tone? Do this for ten minutes. Then, stop once in a while and pay attention to your inner dialogue. Watch the thoughts the way a tennis player watches the ball. Remember, you are not your thoughts and you do not have to believe them.

Are you consistently practicing self-examination? Do you see yourself realistically?

Zazen: Sit on the forward third of a cushion. Arrange your legs in a position you can maintain comfortably. If you choose the Half Lotus position, place one of your feet on the opposite thigh. If you choose the Full Lotus position, place both your feet on opposite thighs. You may also sit with your legs simply tucked in close to your body, but be sure your weight rests equally upon your knees on the ground and your bottom on the cushion. (You can also sit *zazen* on a chair: Keep your knees apart about the width of your shoulders, and plant your feet firmly on the floor.) Then straighten and extend your spine, keeping it naturally upright, and center your balance in the lower abdomen. Push your lower back a little forward, open your chest, and tuck your chin in slightly, keeping the head upright—not leaning forward, backward, or to the side. Sway your body gently left to right, until you come to a point of stillness on your cushion.

Work within your own mind.

Several times a day, tense your muscles, then relax them.

Don't depend on written texts alone for your spiritual enlightenment. Try to look beyond the words and to really understand what you are reading.

When you need to slow down and come back to yourself, you can breathe. Sit anywhere—in the office, in the car, in a line—and practice conscious breathing and smiling.

Refrain from acting upon any impulse until you have been compelled to do so twice. Notice that the impulses will flare out as quickly as they have flared up.

In an emotionally charged situation, focus your attention on your physical sensations rather than on your emotions, the situation itself, or the other people involved. Bring your attention to any tension you may feel. Breathe and relax. Open yourself to finding a creative solution to the challenge.

Practice compassion, and other virtues will come with little effort.

Be aware. Stay awake.

Refrain from speaking about anyone behind his or her back. For one week, do not gossip, even if it's positive.

Express your most positive thoughts and feelings. Tell others that you care about them.

Pranayama breath (breathing pattern for alertness): Inhale for six counts, hold for four, exhale for two, hold for two.

If you embrace a more natural, less wasteful way of living, even a single day each week, you give the planet a much-needed sabbatical from your constant demands.

Reflect on your journey so far and celebrate every step you have taken.

Serenity meditation: To let go of distractions, imagine that your mind is the trunk of a tree and that all your thoughts are branches. The strong branches with green leaves represent healthy mind states; withered, dying branches represent distracting emotions, feelings, and thoughts. Visualize yourself reaching up to the branches of distraction and cutting them off one by one. If you like, gently note or label each distraction as you do so. Then let go of the distractions. Promise yourself that from now on, whenever a distraction enters your mind, you will see it, acknowledge it, then let it go.

If someone behaves angrily toward you, do not respond with anger.

Be mindful of the position of your body and of the purpose of this position. Know where you are.

Skilled meditators take their world as they find it, without sunglasses, earplugs, or nose clips.

Do a nine-part breath each morning while you are waiting for coffee to brew or your car to warm up.

Take three mindful breaths before turning on your computer.

Cherish others, and the sun of real happiness will shine in your life.

Say to yourself, "No bitterness."

INFINITY-LIFE-DEATH-REBIRTH MEDITATION: To do this important Kundalini meditation, sit with your hands on your knees, palms up. Let your thumbs sequentially press each finger as you chant the mantra: *sa* (thumb and index finger), *ta* (thumb and middle finger), *na* (thumb and ring finger), *ma* (thumb and little finger). Continue this sequential pressing and chanting for two minutes. Then continue the finger movements, but whisper the mantra for two minutes. Finally, continue the finger movements, but chant the mantra silently, without moving your lips. Now reverse the process: silent, whisper, regular voice. Work up to five minutes for each part of the meditation. This practice clears the subconscious mind and allows access to the higher centers of the brain. More important, it teaches us to accept and appreciate the cycle of life.

The less you have, the more easily you can give.

Perform a meditation on your bodily sensations. Notice how, when, and where various sensations arise. Some may be external—head, arms, hands, or legs. Others may be internal—heart, lungs, stomach, or kidneys. Note each of them. Observe each sensation without interfering with or suppressing it. Allow your awareness to float freely where it will. Be like a camera, just observing and taking things in. This is the middle way.

During walking meditation, reflect on a question you have or a decision you must make. An answer may emerge.

When you feel a spontaneous rush of love or compassion, don't hurry on to the next moment or push the feeling away. Instead, close your eyes, meditate on the emotion, and allow it to deepen and open your heart. Gradually extend these meditations so that they fill your life.

See your body as a mandala. Through meditation, wind your way inside and discover the center.

Neither repressing nor wallowing in anger is healthy. The best antidote is lovingkindness—to yourself and to whoever made you angry. Lovingkindness develops from realizing that only someone who is unhappy or unenlightened would hurt someone else. Therefore, we should try to feel compassion rather than anger toward that person.

Find and pursue your passion.

Asking yourself, "What am I doing?" will help you overcome the habit of wanting to complete things quickly. Smile to yourself and say, "Washing this dish is the most important job in my life." If your thoughts are carrying you away, you need mindfulness to intervene.

Imagine talking to your alter ego (a mirror image of yourself) about a problem you have. Allow the words to come without judging. What would your alter ego say or do?

Eat with joy.

Tap into your compassion and lovingkindness by recalling all the times you have looked into the eyes of a loved one and seen the pain you caused. Remind yourself that you brought suffering to someone you loved. In admitting your faults, you will awaken your sense of concern for others, and compassion and lovingkindness will flow forth.

Set aside time for extended silent periods and retreats throughout the year to renew your spirit and deepen your practice. Participate in group meditation retreats or take personal retreats at a center or alone at home. Even hiking in the mountains or walking along the ocean can nurture your practice.

Zen is feeling life instead of feeling something about life.

Put up a sticky note or sign that says "Smile" so you can see it when you open your eyes in the morning. Before you get out of bed, inhale and exhale three gentle breaths while maintaining a half smile.

Close your eyes and imagine rowing down a river. You try to stay in the middle, but the river's crosscurrents make it very difficult. So instead you decide to let the boat drift, and the currents take it where they will. Just enjoy the experience. When you come out of the meditation, take this attitude into your daily life. Try to release your need for control.

You need to face one of your deepest anxieties: not knowing how you would define yourself or find meaning without your array of possessions, opinions, beliefs, roles, and achievements.

Read Zen books by Alan Watts—mystic, philosopher, writer, spiritual teacher, lecturer.

AFFIRMATION: I am here, now, in bliss.

Let go of your desire for the end of suffering. Instead, focus on this thought: Whatever difficulties life brings, I will not be anxious about them.

Let music transport you to higher planes.

Being grounded means having your attention completely inside your body no matter what you are doing.

Be both still and alert, physically and mentally.

Meditate on your speech.

If you sleep with a loved one, give him or her a cuddle when you wake up in the morning. Appreciate the gift that he or she is to you.

For good karma: Plant positive seeds. Have faith. Be good. Wait patiently.

Acknowledge emotions for what they are, and allow them to pass through you like wind through the leaves of a tree. Just let them exist, without judging or getting caught up in them.

In dwelling, live close to the ground. / In thinking, keep to the simple. / In conflict, be fair and generous. / In governing, do not try to control. / In work, do what you enjoy. / In family life, be completely present.
—*TAO TE CHING,* LAO TZU

Explore nature blindfolded, with the help of a partner.

Do you have a tendency to speculate? Catch yourself each time you do so, and come back to the experience of the breath.

Take a moment to settle yourself before the rush of the day begins. Let the profound calm act like an anchor, a reminder that there is silence under the chaos.

Overcome the habit of rushing things to completion. Ask yourself, "What am I doing?"

Enlightenment is intimacy with all things.
—JACK KORNFIELD

Every time you are able to restore even a small amount of peace within yourself, you are already having a positive effect on your family and society.

Do not feel guilty about taking time for yourself. If others become jealous of this time, ignore them!

Nurture your character by acting, speaking, and thinking as though the following virtues already existed fully within you: patience, appreciation, sympathetic joy, gratitude, love, compassion, fearlessness, humility, and tenderness.

Do you have a tendency to daydream? Feel the enticing quality of these fantasies, but label them as nothing more than daydreams. Gather the courage to come back to your breath.

Pick happy thoughts to meditate upon.

Embrace all animals with your compassion. Contemplate the suffering of farm animals, animals killed for sport, animals bred for fur, animals used in experiments, and animals that have lost their natural habitats. Wish for your compassion to ease their suffering.

Let go of the idea that you exist.

Find some time early in the day for simply being, without any agenda.

Even if someone slanders and criticizes you or spreads cruel rumors, speak of that person with kindness. Respond to negativity and harm with compassion.

Bring grace to all your endeavors. Before you do something, stop and feel the energy of the moment. Become completely present while performing the action; you might feel as though you were disappearing. When you have completed the action, stop and feel the energy of that moment.

Remember to serve living beings, but don't be enslaved by your work.

Meditate with great perseverance.

Recognize that you are a spiritual being having a physical experience, rather than a physical being having a spiritual experience.

Check your inner mirror every time you look into a regular mirror. Make sure you are a crystal-clear reflection of nature and its processes, and let this beauty shine through.

Talk only when necessary, using words that are sweet.

When your thoughts return to sticky, oft-visited places, ask yourself, "Where does simplicity lie in this moment?" Listen to the responses that arise within you.

Question everything. Take nothing for granted.

Relish the pauses and trust flowing within a conversation.

Reflect upon your inner life: where you can be more mindful, how you can learn to be wholeheartedly attentive, and what you need to let go of. You will discover the source of genuine happiness and freedom.

Lighten the burden of someone else.

VERSE FOR ARRIVING HOME: I have arrived, I am home, in the here and now. I am solid, I am free. In the ultimate, I dwell. My mind can go in a thousand directions. Now I walk in peace, each step a warm breeze. With each step, a lotus blooms.

Don't fixate your mind.

Listen to some music to balance yourself before sitting meditation. If you are agitated, choose something calming. If you are tired, choose something energetic.

Know when to speak.

Pay attention to what you are eating and how it affects you.

Accept periods of suffering with gratitude, knowing that suffering can teach you very important lessons.

Listen with a still and concentrating mind.

When troubled feelings threaten to blow you off course, meditate and be aware of the storm. Watch the waves of negative feelings and thoughts as they wash over you. Accept their presence rather than trying to avoid them. Observe the turbulence rather than identifying with it. Move into the eye of the storm, into your center. Watch the storm die down and be replaced by a calm mind.

Be as aware as possible of your thoughts and emotions so you can prevent harsh speech. When you are aware, you are able to notice any impulse to be cruel in your speech. You will also notice when you are preoccupied, which can cause your speech to become accidentally rude or hurtful.

Learn by listening.

What good does it do to brood on the past or to anticipate the future?

As your mindfulness grows sharper, you will begin to be aware of your actions before taking them.

Reflect on the emotions that hold the greatest power in your life, the places where you most easily lose yourself. Invite them into your heart. Observe their effects upon you. Do not look for answers; experience the freedom and simplicity within your heart from simply letting go.

Don't wait until tomorrow to be loving and compassionate. Begin right now.

Cleansing-breath meditation: Sit with closed eyes and take a few deep breaths. Focus on your lower abdomen, at a point about 2 inches below your navel and 1½ inches inside your body. This is a focal point of chi. Direct your breath to this area, expanding it on the inhale and contracting it on the exhale. Breathe into this point for at least five minutes. Then imagine that you are a tree with roots that go deep into the earth. Visualize these roots originating in the focal point and going through the base of your spine into the ground, far down into the soil. Upon each inhalation, visualize these roots drawing energy up from the earth into your focal point. With each exhalation, feel energy spreading down through the roots and into the earth. Meditate until your focal point feels charged and strong.

Make a list of everyday sounds you can use as mindfulness bells, such as the chiming of a clock, the ringing of a telephone or doorbell, the click of a stove or microwave timer, the arrival of an email or instant message, or even the sounds of cars and sirens. Each time you hear your chosen bells, pause, take three breaths, and reconnect with yourself and with what you are doing.

Pay attention to the thoughts, images, and memories that make you sad. Explore these feelings and experiences. Open yourself to your own suffering and hold your sadness with compassion and lovingkindness.

How would you feel if someone talked to you the way your inner voice does? How would you feel about a person who said everything your inner voice says? You would avoid that person or tell that person to go away.

When someone insults you or behaves violently toward you, you have to be intelligent enough to see that the person suffers from his or her own violence and anger.

Be as highly aware of your words and intentions as you can possibly be. It is especially important to do so with loved ones, for with them, your every utterance is listened to more closely and interpreted more quickly than with anyone else in your life. Let your words clearly and unequivocally express what you mean.

Contemplate a spiritual text. Start by sitting as usual. Take a favorite passage and read a few sentences or paragraphs, just enough to feel a spiritual truth, but not enough to trigger the process of literary analysis in your mind. Note how the passage affects you. You can read it again or just hold it in your heart. Don't think about it or analyze it. The passage is a box holding a precious treasure—you have discovered the treasure, and that is enough. Return to your usual way of meditation or just end the contemplation here.

The center of a healthy life lies in meditation.

Whenever you sense a judgment rising in your mind, exhale, and throw out the judgment with the exhalation.

HAND MASSAGE: Massage the web between your thumb and forefinger, using the opposite hand to press as close as possible to the point where the two bones meet. Continue for about a minute, then repeat on the other hand.

LAUGHING BUDDHA–SMILING YOGA MEDITATION: Sit and relax. Breathe and smile. Be happy and peaceful. Smile. Smile even more. Grin as though you were already enlightened. Be silly. Relax your mind. Be happy.

Chant the mantra *om* as a single attenuated note: "ahohhhhhhmmmmmm . . ." You can also combine it with other words at the beginning and end of a prayer, like *Om Shanti* (peace).

Regularly evaluate the negative and positive effects of feelings such as anger, hatred, jealousy, and lust. You will begin to see that they are usually harmful, and often senseless. This insight will cause such feelings to diminish gradually.

Wealth is measured by the number of things one can do without.

Bow humbly to the earth, bending over to touch your toes.

Affirmation: I am becoming happier. The core of my being is at peace. Each experience is an opportunity for greater growth. There are no mistakes, only lessons. I forgive all who have hurt me. I forgive myself for all whom I have hurt. I go forth in love and peace. I embrace the universe. I send loving thoughts to all living beings.

Accept all of your experiences, even the ones you hate.

Breathing meditation: Lie on your back. Breathe evenly and gently, focusing your attention on the movement of your belly. As you breathe in, let your belly rise, bringing air into the lower half of your lungs. As the upper half of your lungs fills with air, your chest will rise and your belly will lower. Do this for a total of ten breaths, making each exhalation longer than the inhalation.

Be like a carpenter. The carpenter does not focus on the teeth of the saw as it moves in and out of the board; rather, he focuses on the line he has drawn so that the cut will be straight. Similarly, keep your focus on your goals in life, rather than being distracted by the details.

When sadness or anger wells up within you, do something completely unexpected to break the pattern. If you feel angry with someone, give him or her a big hug! Be innovative and imaginative.

STANDING GOLDEN-FLOWER MEDITATION: Stand tall and allow any tension to drop away from you. Breathe naturally. Imagine that your spine is a stem. Feel it growing upward, from your lower back, to the point between your shoulders, up to the back of your neck. Let this stem continue up above your head, where a large golden flower blooms. Allow the flower head to travel upward a little farther, pulling your spine straighter. At the same time, imagine that your feet are the flower's roots. Feel your feet sink deeper into the earth. Between the flower above your head and the roots that are your feet, let your spine stretch and lengthen just a little more. Feel your arms and hands becoming leaves, light as air. Now imagine energy, in the form of golden-white light, traveling up from the roots that are your feet, through your spine, to the top of your head where the golden flower blooms. Let the light fill the flower with cleansing energy and revitalization. Hold this image. Then feel the light descend back into your body and into the earth. See the flower close and the stem relax. Come back to your own body and relax as well.

Look at the beauty of a single flower. Stop and smell. Smile.

Seeking happiness outside ourselves is like waiting for sunshine in a cave facing north.—TIBETAN SAYING

Can you wait until the mind settles and the water is clear?

If you are not a happy person inside, then nothing outside you will ever make you happy and able to feel love.

Form your own prayer group.

Notice that even in its regularity, your breath goes through subtle changes. The sensations that accompany the in-breath are somewhat different from the sensations that accompany the out-breath. As you relax and let the breath happen all by itself, you will be able to sharpen your attention by noticing how interesting and complex the simple act of breathing really is. Rest in the breath's regularity and notice its constant, subtle changes.

Before going to sleep, rejoice in the day's accomplishments.

Feel that you have enough, and your sense of hunger will diminish.

Softening-the-belly meditation: Sit and breathe deeply, allowing awareness to descend from the sensations in your head, down through your body, until you reach your belly. Soften the sensations in your belly. Feel your breath enter and leave the belly, and continue to soften it. (You might want to repeat the word *soften* aloud.) Whenever you encounter tension, gently breathe and soften your belly again. Notice how your heart responds to this exercise.

Acknowledge your feelings so that they can pass.

This particular breath will not come again—so pay attention.

Give spontaneously.

If you have to sit through a lot of tiresome or stressful meetings, make a card that says "Breathe" and put it somewhere where you can see it.

When you're in trouble, imagine that you're entering the gates of a walled town. Walk through a labyrinth of narrow streets, and eventually come to a peaceful meadow in the center of the town. Know that your difficulties will pass, and that you will eventually arrive at your green haven.

Minimize self-lecturing.

Volunteer at a hospital. Visit the sick and elderly. Give them your love and attention.

Are your thoughts directing you or are you directing your thoughts? Are you in charge? Can you say, "Stop"?

Constantly apply cheerfulness, if for no other reason than because you are on a spiritual path.

Notice that each moment carries its own task. When you are in the car, your task is to drive. When your child comes to you with a problem, your task is to listen. Just as you follow your breathing, direct yourself to the task of the moment.

Dynamic meditation: For ten minutes, breathe rapidly through your nose, letting your breath be intense and chaotic. Allow your body to move with this fast breath, especially your arms. Then, for the next ten minutes, give your body the freedom to express—to just explode! Sing, scream, laugh, shout, cry, jump, shake, dance, kick—do whatever you want. Do not hold back. Next, for ten minutes, let your neck and shoulders relax as you raise your arms and shout the mantra *hoo hoo hoo* while jumping up and down. Make sure you land on the flat part of your feet. In the next fifteen minutes, stop everything. Freeze right where you are. Just be. Finally, for the last fifteen minutes, celebrate with more dancing and singing, perhaps with some music in the background.

Be mindful of cause and effect. Notice how your actions, feelings, and thoughts influence others and your own state of mind.

Remember the peak experiences—moments when all your senses were deeply involved in a particular event or activity—in your life. As your mind sifts and categorizes these experiences, one in particular will strongly assert itself. Focus on it. Let go and relive this timeless moment. Do not try to change it. Open to it with calm awareness.

See opinions forming and melting away like snowflakes. See that each comment is like a bubble.

Basic listening meditation: Sit comfortably, in whatever position works best for you. Put on slow and gentle instrumental music. Let your eyes close gently. Invite your body to relax and release into the ground, cushion, or chair. Let go and accept the nondoing of meditation. Sense your breath, and listen closely. Breathe through your nose. Feel the air as it goes in and out of your nostrils. Feel the rise and fall of your chest and abdomen. Let your attention settle where you feel your breath most clearly. Do not control your breath—allow it to be what it is. Follow it. Sit for twenty minutes. Be aware of what is present. Listen to the music and relax. Subtly note the nuances of the music for twenty minutes. As you gently open your eyes, try to carry your mindfulness into your next activity.

Notice the immediate karma of your choices. For instance, when you eat something you enjoy, knowing that the food does not agree with you, you may experience feelings of discomfort. Acknowledge this; do not pretend that you feel fine. Try to avoid bringing bad karma on yourself in the future.

Imagine yourself standing at a crossroads. Mentally trace the path that you have taken. Do not judge or critique, for you cannot change the path. Just see it clearly. What matters is where you go from here. You can change direction now. You can choose your path in the present moment.

STRENGTH-CHALLENGE MEDITATION: Visualize yourself at the base of a mountain whose summit is wrapped in a thick cloud. Start on a long, difficult journey up the mountain, concentrating on the present moment and putting one foot in front of the other. Trust that the path will lead you to the summit, even though it is hidden in the clouds. Finally, as you near the summit, the clouds disperse and the way becomes clear.

Meditate on a large library—full of books containing knowledge and wisdom.

On a cold day, meditate in a sunbeam shining into a warm room.

How about refraining from saying anything about anyone who is not present? How about no talking about people who annoy you or excite you? How about no analyzing or dissecting anyone else's behavior or problems—good or bad—unless the person is actually there? When you stop talking about others, you discover how much time and energy you waste daily on conversations that serve no constructive purpose and take you away from the present moment.

Feel a sense of urgency in using every precious moment of each day.

Enter into your life. Don't just be an observer.

Walk in beauty, wherever you are.

CHAKRA SOUND MEDITATION: Using the scale *do re mi fa sol la ti do,* scan your body from the base chakra, which is at the bottom of your spine, to the chakra at the top of your head, singing one long note per chakra. Feel the differences in energy as your notes go higher and higher, and as you move from the base chakra to the top chakra. When you've reached the top, be absolutely still. Hear the sounds that the body makes from within.

ABDOMINAL BOND (*BANDHAS*): Sit cross-legged, exhale completely, then pull your navel up and back toward your spine. Then release. This works the diaphragm and forces *prana* up, intensifying its energy.

When you see the importance of having a quiet mind, you will have a quiet mind.

PEBBLE MEDITATION: Sit and breathe. Now think of yourself as a pebble falling through clear water. Sink through the water—without intention—toward a resting spot on the gentle sand at the water's bottom. Let your mind and body come to rest, like the pebble resting in the sand. Watch your breath and hold this image for a half hour.

Practice body awareness: Change your body position several times a day.

Letting go opens and frees you to receiving something new. You will lose pain and gain insight.

KNOWLEDGE MUDRA: Sit with your hands resting on your knees, palms up. Touch the middle of your left thumb with your left index finger, and the middle of your right thumb with your right index finger. This mudra will direct energy toward the higher chakras in your body. It also promotes harmony and opens you to the beauty of life.

When your mind begins to wander from what you are doing, be aware and gently bring it back.

YOGA MUDRA: Kneel on the floor and sit back on your heels. Place your hands or fingertips on your heels and keep your head and torso erect but relaxed. Exhale. On inhalation, raise your hands in front of you to the level of your waist, then fold your fingers over your thumbs to make a fist, and place both fists on either side of your navel. Exhale, keeping your bottom on your heels, and stretch your spine from your hips by slowly bringing your head toward the floor. Hold this position, with your forehead resting on the floor, and breathe for a minute, relaxing the abdomen. Come up and rest on your heels again, palms on your thighs.

Give up your expectations, even expecting results from practice.

Learn to see what's not important—which is most of it—and be willing to talk about the rest.

Examine the state of your mind each time you're waiting in line, walking to a destination, opening or closing a door, sitting down at a desk or table, or eating a meal. See if there is desire, aversion, or indifference.

Be happy where you are. Know that locked within the moments of each day are all the joy and peace you need.

Listen to the sounds of silence: Hear the wind murmuring, the leaves rustling, the birds flapping their wings, and your quiet breathing.

All of the dharma is about lessening one's self-absorption and ego clinging. This brings you, and all beings, happiness.

Choose or create an affirmation that is meaningful to you. Make sure it gives you a good feeling, is confident in tone, and is easy to say. For example: *I am very confident. I forgive myself. My body is beautiful. I am at peace. I am completely relaxed.* Write it down and put it where you will see it often.

Breathe out and send lovingkindness to everyone, including yourself.

Know what to overlook.

Note the impulses that tug at you as you meditate. Notice their quality, intensity, and frequency. Gently label and observe them.

Silently endure.

See yourself lying on a patch of thick, fragrant, green grass on a hillside, under an old elm tree. The sky is spotted with full, puffy white clouds that float slowly across the blue expanse. The temperature in the air is the same as that on your skin. You take many deep breaths, concentrating on how relaxing they are. See and feel yourself float into your surroundings, looking all around. Still floating, travel to a different place, such as a forest or a beach. Look. Smell. Feel. When you are ready to end this journey, imagine yourself back on the hillside, under the elm tree. It is now sunset. Take another deep breath and remember everything you felt during this meditation.

It is always possible to view your situation in a positive light. Find a way to change your outlook.

Make peace and forgive your parents. See your mother or father as a small child, fragile and vulnerable, and breathe in. See his or her suffering. Smile with love to the small child within your parent, and breathe out.

What kind of commitment can you make to your meditation? Make an honest, realistic agreement with yourself and stick to it.

Instead of letting every thought or feeling be the cause of action, let these impulses serve as energy by which to become aware.

Meditate on any hindrance—any irritation, aversion, craving, desire, doubt, restlessness, or sleepiness—that arises in your daily practice. Observe it, receive it, soften it, and let it go.

Learn confidence in the power of lovingkindness. It is not a state of weakness or complacency, but a source of tremendous strength that is more effective and powerful than anger.

In the bedroom, let go of the day and take your rest.

Say "no" when asked to do something you really do not want to do.

Coming back to the breath helps us discover the power of letting go, and deepens our ability to relinquish the mind's conditioned grasping.

Cease to be impelled by anything, and you will find that you are free.

In meditation, forget the whole world and turn inward. Tune in as if the world has disappeared.

Meetings can be very useful, but can also be a drain if executed improperly. If you are planning to call a meeting, contemplate whether it is necessary. If so, start and end on time, and stick with the agenda.

Love is the ultimate way to transform people, even when they are full of anger.

Draw upon the color green for a fresh start, to open up new opportunities, or to undertake personal growth.

Live it, don't plan it.

MANDALA MEDITATION: Place a mandala at eye level at a comfortable distance from your meditation seat. Illuminate the room with soft lighting. Sit and watch the breath as usual, beginning with the eyes closed. When you become still, open your eyes and focus on the image. Blink only when necessary. Notice the thoughts that come up and let them go. Sense the image, but do not attempt to analyze or decode it.

Have patience with all things, but mainly with yourself.

The most profound daily practice is whittling away your self-hatred through lovingkindness.

You do not need a teacher to be enlightened. Wisdom is innate.

If a mudra feels a little awkward, clasp your hands in your lap or rest them on your knees or thighs. Resting with palms up opens your awareness and makes you more receptive to surrounding energies. Resting with palms down calms your mind and balances your energy.

Perform sun salutations in the morning, facing east, toward the rising sun.

Grasp every minute, for time waits for no one.

Be empty of striving to become something, to be anything special, and free the mind from those kinds of ideas. Settle back and allow your nature to express itself simply and easily.

Running, jogging, and swimming make great meditations. Learn to meld your body, mind, and soul during these activities, whose movement allows you to generate awareness.

VERSE FOR THE FIRST STEPS OF THE DAY: As I take my first step, my foot kisses the floor. With gratitude to the earth, I walk in liberation.

Lie with your legs up against a wall to unkink your mind and body.

Bow to your desk before you sit down to work.

Take a habit you wish you could break and turn it into a meditation. When you find yourself indulging in this habit, pay close attention to every action, sensation, and feeling. Whenever your mind drifts off, gently bring it back to the present experience. Don't try to prevent or change the habit—just perform it with full awareness. The next time you indulge in it, see how you feel and what has changed.

Before you send an important email or letter, stop for a moment. Pause and be aware. Feel the grace of the present moment and bless your email (or letter). Then hit SEND (or place the letter in the mailbox) with a feeling of confidence and trust. Then pause again and turn your attention inward. Offer your gratitude. Feel that what is done is done.

Meditate on the fabric of life in a natural setting, like the woods or a park. Think of the role of each living organism in this universe.

Have faith in nature.

Do only what you will not regret.

The point is not to suppress thought, but rather to surpass it.

The world spins without your help, people do what they do, and your life will run its course one way or the other. Sometimes your plans don't work out. You can decide not to get upset, anxious, or angry about things over which you have no power. You can choose to do your job and live your life with integrity, compassion, mindful observance, and a healthy sense of humor.

Visit the trees and gardens. Walk through the woods. Learn the names of the flowers and plants. Take time to sit and reflect on nature.

Put the dough in the oven and watch it expand.

Walking along the path to enlightenment, connect with yourself by just doing what you are doing, 100 percent, one step at a time.

Call to mind the people or animals you love most. Visualize them and allow your feelings of love to rise. Imagine you are embracing them and protecting them with this love. Gradually widen this circle of love.

Sit quietly and take some slow, deep breaths. For five minutes, try to stop thinking. Do whatever you can to avoid generating thoughts. You will see that thinking cannot be stopped, but that it can be ignored.

Count up to ten, counting "one" while inhaling and "two" while exhaling, then "three" while inhaling and "four" while exhaling—until you reach "ten." Repeat this exercise as many times as necessary to focus your mind on the breath.

AFFIRMATION: My spirit is free.

In the autumn, as the days grow colder and the leaves change color and begin to fall, contemplate the laws of karma in your life. This meditation will help you to gain greater awareness into the nature of reality.

Meditation is an activity that helps you get to exactly where you are.

Think of hardships as spiritual training.

Develop an awareness of living things—people, animals, and plants—that you generally ignore, and cultivate a greater sense of care and reverence for them.

Don't let problems overwhelm you. Consider them within a larger context. Imagine you are looking at the problem from outer space, or that you have become a soaring bird, peering down at it from the height of the mountains. Your anxiety will diminish, and the problem will seem far less significant. Now return to earth, ready to face anything.

Stand in the middle of a room, close your eyes, and imagine that the source of one of your greatest fears is lying in front of you. Notice how you are feeling. Breathe deeply. Be with your feelings without fighting, judging, or getting caught up in them. Take a step toward the source of your fear. Repeat. Gradually, you will start to overcome this fear that has kept you from moving forward.

Become more aware of the room, the noise, and the silence.

Meditating is a new way of looking at things. You have to be willing to change. When you begin to tame the movements of your mind, it affects everything else. Once you start, it is hard to stop.

Enjoy the relaxation you feel when you retrain your mind and banish anger. Feel the inner spaciousness.

If you store mantras on your computer, think of the hard drive as a kind of prayer wheel, spinning the mantras and purifying the room.

Make a relaxation tape or CD of a piece of gentle, relaxing music. Choose something that lasts for at least ten minutes and that you associate with pleasant memories.

From the moment you wake up, pay attention each time you change your posture. Do you continually move in response to discomfort or pain, to relieve hunger, to scratch an itch, or to avoid boredom? Find the hidden source beneath your need to move.

Stay mindful even in the darkest moments. Your awareness will hold and understand the pain, helping you stay strong through the most difficult times.

If you have a busy schedule, prioritize your activities and do the most important ones first.

Serpent breath: Put your tongue between your lips and stick it out slightly. Inhale through your mouth while producing a hissing sound. When your lungs feel full, hold your breath as long as possible, then slowly exhale through both nostrils. Practice the serpent breath five times in the morning, five times at noon, and five times at night for a couple of weeks.

While breathing, concentrate on the rise and fall of your abdomen.

Identify feelings of loneliness whenever you experience them. Are they tied to certain times of day, places, or events? Hunger or fatigue? Something you see? If looking at your loneliness is painful, soften around the pain, but do not avoid facing these feelings.

Remember that your loved ones will one day be gone. Cherish every precious moment with them.

Each day holds possibilities for great discoveries and hidden joys. Enjoy everything.

Don't let your problems swell up inside you. Meditate and deflate the balloon!

Listen to a sound, from beginning to end.

Pretend that you have only one month to live. Who would you say good-bye to? Who would you thank? Who would you forgive or ask forgiveness of? What would you like to do?

Soften to minor annoyances. For instance, if your neighbor's barking dog bothers you, focus on the sound without judgment. Let the dog become your teacher rather than your tormentor.

The dharmas (truths) are boundless; vow to master them.

Take a mindful time-out: a coffee break, a visit to the bathroom, or a short walk down the hall. Pay attention to your surroundings. Smile.

HEALING-TEMPLE MEDITATION: Imagine that you're sitting at a temple—a place of great wisdom—and reflect on your spiritual journey. Breathe and be aware of whatever arises. Be open to pain. Be open to joy. Rest in the temple. Allow yourself to heal. Stay as long as you wish, and when you leave, remember that the temple is inside you and that you can always find healing there.

To stop rushing around, to sit quietly on the grass, to switch off the world and come back to earth, to allow the eye to see a willow, a bush, a cloud, a leaf, is an unforgettable experience.—FREDERICK FRANCK

Enrich your time with friends by being attentive, loving, open, and sympathetic.

Become the moment and put all else out of your mind.

Do you think that God likes to be around people who are happy or people who are miserable? What about other people? What about yourself?

Pick an object and look at it without thinking. Then slowly withdraw your eyes and remember its essence.

Imagine that you are a dancer with such a deep understanding of your body that you hear and feel the music within your soul. Let your body speak in movement and flow through life.

Make each move count. If you find yourself doing the same thing twice, you were not being mindful the first time.

Live with honesty and integrity.

Put out the welcome mat.

When facing a challenging situation, imagine that you are enveloped by blue light—the light of protection and tranquility. Imagine negative energy bouncing off the light and away from you.

Do what contributes to your awareness and refrain from what does not.

Be careful in all you think and do.

During the most difficult moments of your life, can you stay openhearted and maintain your commitment to the path of enlightenment?

If you are hungry, eat; if you are tired, sleep. These are also meditations.

Mindfulness helps you to accept life—without getting angry that it is not happening the way you want it to—and to enjoy pleasant experiences—without lamenting the fact that they will not last.

Yield to life.

Make sure your words create mutual understanding and love. Make them as beautiful as gems, as lovely as flowers.

Have the fearless attitude of a hero and the loving heart of a child.

Meditate on light to improve your concentration.

Knowing that others have conquered the same fears, venture bravely into your unknown.

Count up to ten for each inhalation and exhalation. Repeat as many times as necessary to focus on your breath.

Concentration is a necessary prelude to meditation. Focus on a single point and ignore everything else.

Run on the sand.

As you practice mindfulness during everyday activities, you will breathe more deeply and see more wonders. You will likely become more insightful, more content, and maybe more trusting.

Affirmation: Everything is perfect.

Breathe with daily life. Practice it every moment.

Even something as simple as wrapping a gift can be a meditation. Do everything with thought and precision, and meditate on the joy of giving.

Gently let go of distracting thoughts. Do not judge or try to figure out why you were thinking this way or that, or whether these thoughts will return. Always begin again.

Listen to the individual notes of a musical chord.

Rebirth every morning gives us the feeling of urgency, which is an important ingredient of spiritual life.

You are your only master. Straighten your crooked self.

Lovemaking should have a sacred dimension in addition to bringing physical pleasure. Let it come from the depths of your soul.

Accept responsibility for your situation, and you will have begun to change it.

See your life as a shaken snow dome; meditating helps the flakes settle down so that you can see more clearly.

Ease up.

You have to have the capacity to say things calmly. Don't get irritated too easily. Don't let sour or bitter speech leave your mouth. Build up your capacity for speaking with kindness.

Bring yourself into the flow beyond judgment, into the space of surrender.

As you breathe in and out, visualize yourself gently fading.

When the time is ripe—when you have entered into full concentration—stop counting your breath, observing and labeling, or anything else you have been doing to increase concentration.

Allow yourself to feel the self-esteem, the dignity, and the humility of the Buddha that you are.

Transcend your predicaments with laughter.

To be nobody but yourself in a world which is doing its best to make you everybody else, means to fight the hardest human battle ever and to never stop fighting.—E. E. CUMMINGS

Notice the different patterns you develop when you make a genuine effort to live well and when you do not. Practice one thing—protecting, supporting, nourishing, or maintaining—each week for four weeks.

Draw upon the strong, forceful qualities of the color red. Let it give you drive, energy, and courage.

Kindness is empowered by courage, and courage is empowered by kindness. Patience is empowered by strength, and strength is empowered by patience. All of these qualities increase love and peace.

When you wake up each morning, reaffirm your intention to practice lovingkindness and compassion. Remind yourself each day to let go of ego clinging, selfishness, controlling behaviors, negative thoughts, possessiveness, aggression, resentment, and confusion. Each day, find one small way in which you can change a negative pattern.

Direct all your energy in one direction.

Try to recall everything you did on this day a week ago.

Settle comfortably and take a few deep breaths. Bring to mind a modern convenience that you take for granted but find indispensable. Reflect for a few moments on how important this item is to you and what your life would be like without it. Think of all the people and hard work that contributed to creating this item. Take a few minutes to appreciate all of these people.

Consider a country or region currently suffering through war, oppression, or other injustice. See that every person is a victim. See that the opposing sides are really aspects of the same reality. Wish for them to find compassion and abandon the fight.

Let each action be just that action.

Recognize what you can control and let go of what you cannot.

TIME-AWARENESS MEDITATION: As you sit and relax, breathing deeply, check the time. Close your eyes and focus on your breath. Sit for as long as you feel comfortable. Before you open your eyes, guess how much time you had spent in meditation. When you look at your watch or clock, you may be surprised at your underestimation or overestimation. If you are correct, do not be pleased or disappointed with yourself; simply know you were right.

Magnify the good.

Eliminate the tendency to judge yourself as above, below, or equal to others. You are who you are—regardless of where anyone else is.

Each time you identify and acknowledge a state of mind without judgment—just noting—you weaken it and strengthen your ability to let it go.

Recognize the difference between awareness and interpretation.

Each person chooses his or her own path, just as your path is yours alone. Let them be.

Live your goals now.

Helping others is more virtuous than looking out only for yourself.

Prayer of refuge: Repeat this three times at the beginning of a meditation session: "I take refuge until I am enlightened in the Buddha, the Dharma, and the Sangha. Through the merit I create by practicing giving and the other perfections, may I attain Buddhahood for the sake of all sentient beings."

Remove your impurities little by little.

Don't let your actions, speech, and thoughts be controlled by greed, ill will, or delusion. It would only intensify your own and other people's suffering.

Commune with yourself.

Bubble meditation: Sit and visualize your thoughts as a mass of bubbles. Exhaling, imagine all those bubbles floating away. Redirect your attention to your breath at your nostrils. If your mind wanders or new thoughts arrive, visualize again the bubbles, and let them float away. Then refocus on your breath. Do this for as long as you need.

Verse for dealing with work problems: When things fall apart, I vow with all my being to use my unique energy to pick up and reassemble the pieces.

Remember that we are all in this together. We are everyone, and everyone is us.

To be happy, you must first see yourself as happy. Imagine yourself radiating with happiness from the core of your being. Rehearse this throughout the day. You can also do this exercise to cultivate other states of mind, such as love and peace.

See your desires as a group of wild horses, pulling you into a cart that is flying out of control. Take the reins and tighten them gently but firmly, slowing the horses and gaining control of the cart.

Do you make the practice of self-awareness a priority in your life?

Speak peacefully, walk peacefully, think peacefully, and you will radiate peace in all directions.

To love means to nourish another person with appropriate attention.

Concentrate on your everyday routine.

While driving, do a shoulder scan every once in a while. Notice exactly where your shoulders are. Take a deep breath and, as you exhale, lower your shoulders and feel the stretch in your neck.

Be awake and aware, without constantly readjusting your mind to what it perceives.

Never give up on yourself or anyone else.

Identify the most potent stressors in your life. Now blow up two balloons. Take a large pin and burst one balloon, imagining that your old response to the stress is gone. Now imagine that the second balloon is filled with positive energy. Think of a new response to the stressor, and write it on this balloon. Let it serve as a symbol of the new way in which you will handle the stress. Release the balloon into the air or tie it someplace in your home to serve as a reminder.

What really matters in meditation is not the sitting itself, but the state of mind you achieve after meditation. Prolong your calm and centered state of mind through everything you do.

Prepare yourself for prayer just as you would ready yourself for meditation.

Are you doing all you can to integrate your spiritual philosophy into your relationships with friends and family?

Sit like a frog on a lily pad. Be entirely at ease, yet entirely alert.

TREE-OF-LIFE MEDITATION: Watch your breath and focus on the concept of the natural, visible world. Stay with this concept. Focusing on only one concept at a time, move on to the concept of human consciousness, followed by the victory of the higher self over one's basic instincts, an awareness of the glory of the Divine, the beauty as one realizes the Divine in oneself, the Divine mercy and love, the Divine power, the Divine wisdom, the Divine understanding, and finally the Divine essence or crown. Beyond this lies the formless absolute. These ten concepts each represent a different aspect of the Divine on the Tree of Life. As you meditate on each of the *Sefirot*, you will sense its potential within yourself, representing the Divine immanence as well as the Divine transcendence.

Monitor your stress levels throughout the day. By consciously recognizing and reducing the "noise" in your life, you will allow the underlying harmony to naturally emerge.

Watch the watcher. Become the witness to the witnessing. You will find joy in the solitude of these roles.

Hold your coffee cup or milk glass and sip with mindfulness.

When you enter a meeting, keep an open mind and be patient. Do not allow your thoughts to wander; be exactly where you are, wait your turn, and contribute.

When you notice your mind wandering in the middle of an activity, make an effort to come back to what is happening and remain focused on the activity for as long as you are doing it. See if you can stay focused for increasingly longer periods each day.

Were you planning to wait for tomorrow to be alive?

You can't stop the waves, but you can learn to surf.
—JOSEPH GOLDSTEIN

Do something for a child.

Compassion will discourage attachment.

Sit comfortably and imagine an inner star centered between your eyebrows. Take a couple of deep breaths, and focus on the warmth of this spot, where the star radiates. Allow this star to renew your hope.

Read something uplifting, especially just before going to sleep.

You can walk *kinhin* briskly and energetically, or slowly and leisurely.

Will this action take you in the direction in which you want to go?

Focus your mind on something—and relax.

Only love can dispel hate. Only light can dispel darkness.

Lie on your back on a comfortable—but not too comfortable—surface. Be aware of your body as a whole unit and feel its connection to the surface. Now bring your attention to the toes of your right foot. Breathe into it for three to four counts. Shift your attention to all the other parts of your body—one at a time—focusing on each for three to four breaths. Take your time. Allow tense or painful areas to gently open and soften, and then move on. Be fully present in each part of your body. At the end of this exercise, go back to the awareness of your body as one mass. Stretch, and then open your eyes and slowly come back into the world.

One compassionate word, action, or thought can reduce another person's suffering and bring him or her joy. One word can give comfort and confidence, destroy doubt, help someone avoid a mistake, reconcile a conflict, and open the door to liberation. One action can save a person's life or help him or her take advantage of a rare opportunity. One thought can do the same, because thoughts always lead to words and actions. With compassion in your heart, every thought, word, and deed can bring a miracle.

Thinking is less interesting than looking.

Watch your mind while it is angry, while it envies, and while it is in conflict. Pay attention to the rise and fall of ten thousand thoughts and emotions.

During coffee breaks, meditate, rather than drink caffeine.

Surround yourself with art that evokes spiritual beauty, such as images of nature or people you love. Hang them up in your home or workplace.

If you have poor concentration, forgive yourself. Continue to make the effort, but do not force anything. Be gentle. Keep bringing your mind back to the meditation, over and over again.

Begin meditation by paying attention to your thoughts. Notice what your inner voices are telling you. Are the thoughts positive or negative? How do they make you feel? Try listening to your thoughts for ten minutes. Then stop and reflect on the experience.

BEACH-CHAIR MEDITATION: Lean back in a comfortable beach chair or chaise longue, legs outstretched, totally relaxed. Let go of body and mind; let yourself be guided by infinite goodness. When you're ready, open your eyes, raise your gaze, and broaden your heart and mind. Expand the scope of your perception to a panoramic 360 degrees. Watch the sun dance on the water and the clouds cross the sky. Let your mind unfurl, let your soul unfold, and receive the joy of meditation.

Now is the ideal time.

Joy comes not from possession or ownership, but through a wise and loving heart. Joy is inside you—not in attainment of things desired or in the achievement of goals, but in the simple feeling that lies within you.

If you feel panicky, make a conscious effort to calm down. Tell yourself to stop panicking, then close your eyes and breathe slowly and deeply. Feel yourself becoming more relaxed, notice your fears lessening, and feel your heartbeat slowing down.

Counting the breaths keeps the mind focused on something, so that it begins to calm itself.

DEDICATION OF MERIT: "Through this virtuous action, may I quickly attain the state of a guru-Buddha and lead every living being, without exception, into that pure world." (Say this at the end of a meditation session.)

When climbing the stairs, feel the pleasure of effort. Strain your thigh muscles, lifting yourself up. Let it serve as a useful exercise.

Meditating while walking is a pleasant, easy way to expand your powers of concentration. Just break your steps into slow, mindful movements, and breathe, counting your breaths as you walk, or repeating a favorite inspirational verse or affirmation. Notice how the ground rises up to meet your feet.

If you are hoping for new ideas to come to you, looking for someone to date, looking for someone in a crowd, or searching for something you lost—just stop and wait. Make yourself comfortable, stop, make room in your mind, listen. A new thought might come. The person appears within the crowd. You come upon your keys.

Spiritual writings are a kind of food for your brain.

If you're thinking about a pain in your body, notice the thought, and then return to the physical pain itself. Don't make it worse by letting it invade your mind.

Create positive thoughts that can boost your immune system. Surrender to healing and send your body loving thoughts. Imagine these thoughts penetrating all your cells, giving them strength to return to health.

Take care of your own behavior, and children will learn by example.

Visualize the earth as a small blue-and-green planet, orbiting an enormous sun. Feel love and gratitude for this living object, upon which you depend. Resolve to respect the planet on a daily basis.

Each day, remind yourself of all the good things you have: relationships, skills, health, children, or anything else that adds beauty to your life.

Meditation can be pared down to three points:

1) Bring your mind home and turn it inward.
2) Release the mind from its prison of constant grasping.
3) Relax the mind of its tensions.

AFFIRMATION: I am breathing freely.

When you wake up in the morning, aspire to keep a wide-open heart and mind.

Listen to the purposeful rhythm of your heart. Let it bring you courage and strength.

File things away as you deal with them.

Take the gentle path.

Breathing in, make your whole body calm and at peace. Breathing out, make your whole body calm and at peace.

INTERNAL MASSAGE MEDITATION: Massage the inside of your body with your mind. Sweep your attention through your body like a gentle breeze, moving from the inside out. Move your mind unobstructedly throughout your body, focusing on areas of discomfort or pain. Sweep your mind back and forth like a floodlight. Pay attention to your sensations, noting how they change under the focus of your mind.

When you put your keys down, you should be conscious of putting them down. When you pick them up, you should be conscious of picking them up. That's all there is to Zen.

Regard each day as a good day.

If you find yourself falling asleep during meditation, try standing up.

Plant good roots today.

Burn an essential oil while performing a healing meditation to relax your body and mind.

Cultivate the seeds of your life. Tend them lovingly.

COLOR MEDITATION: Think of the color red. Visualize a red bubble of energy all around you. Feel the bubble expanding and contracting as you breathe. What kind of energy is emanating from this bubble? Now think of the color pink. Visualize a pink bubble enveloping you, expanding and contracting. Exactly what shade of pink is this? What kind of energy does this bubble emanate? Do the same thing with orange, yellow, green, turquoise, indigo, violet, silver, gold, white, brown, and black. When you have finished, note any special feelings you had, especially any strong likes or dislikes.

Practice nonattachment.

When meditating, simply live in the moment. Don't look forward to future benefits.

Take care of something—a child, a pet, a plant, or even a material object, like a car—for one week. At the end of the week, notice whether you feel closer to the object. Realize that the act of taking care leads to real caring.

Face challenging situations like a warrior. Drop aggression and defensiveness, and open your heart. Let meditation show you the way.

During your lunch break, allow yourself some enjoyable time in addition to your meal.

Think about someone who has caused you great suffering. Try to examine that person's own suffering, perceptions, and motivations. Continue until you feel compassion replacing your anger and resentment.

Recognize loneliness, sorrow, emptiness, and loss of control—with mindfulness.

In moments of crisis, simply be present, without judgment or prejudice. See whatever is happening just as it is.

Life's most urgent question is, what are you doing for others?—MARTIN LUTHER KING JR.

HUMMING-BREATH EXERCISE: Sit with your eyes closed. Focus on your breath. Inhale long and deeply and, when you exhale, hum gently with your mouth closed, jaw relaxed. Do this for eight to twelve complete breaths. Let the sound vibrate in your head.

Take the middle route.

Identify the fundamental state of your mind, which is unsullied by thought. The mind is all luminosity, pure knowing. With mindfulness and introspection, remain in that state. If a thought arises, look into its very nature; it will lose power and dissolve of its own accord.

Develop an integrated awareness of your being, making your body, actions, feelings, relationships, work, and play all part of your meditation.

Find the universal in every particular.

Allow more things to unfold in your life. Don't force things to happen, and don't reject things that don't fit your idea of what should be happening.

Why are you reading this book?

Add contemplations to your actions. When sweeping, sweep away anger and fear; when mowing, cut down desire and greed.

The Third Way is the path of the yogi, the path of knowledge and consciousness. Follow this path, and you will develop your intellectual center.

Distinguish between the inevitable pain of the human condition and the optional, unnecessary suffering that comes from trying to avoid pain.

Think only what is right there, what is right under your nose to do. It's such a simple thing—that's why people can't do it.—HENRY MILLER

Before leaving for work, meditate on the day ahead and reflect on the idea of life as a gift. You are being given a new day. The day is a gift. How can you best use and experience it?

Acceptance of change is a deep spiritual insight that can transform your life.

Go within yourself. Close your eyes, then stop all eye movement, followed by all other bodily movement. Just remain there. You will suddenly find yourself looking inside your body. You can take this exercise even further by looking at your inner body in detail: every organ, every limb, every bone.

Be a lamp unto yourself.

When driving, perform a lovingkindness meditation. Say to the other drivers on the road, "May you safely reach your destination. May you find the happiness and fulfillment that you are seeking."

METTA MEDITATION: Send *metta* to the ten directions—east, southeast, south, southwest, west, northwest, north, northeast, above, and below. You can begin in any direction, and either perform the *metta* in your mind or speak the words aloud. Direct the *metta* to all beings in each direction.

Each time you bring your wandering mind back during meditation, you weaken the compulsive cycle and strengthen mindfulness.

Before you get out of bed each morning, lie very still for five minutes. Listen, see, smell, breathe. Do not judge.

When you feel overwhelmed by other people's pain, open your heart. Awaken genuine compassion.

Meditate on an acorn: See it grow into a big oak tree. Imagine how the world will change around it.

The best way to achieve your own goals is to back off from striving for results and instead to start focusing carefully on seeing and accepting things as they are, moment by moment. With patience and regular practice, movement toward your goals will take place by itself.

Don't let external noise distract you during meditation. If you can read a newspaper in a restaurant, you can handle external noise.

Eat each meal with gratitude, not greed. Let this harmony grow into a larger, all-encompassing harmony with all mankind.

Live with a sense of urgency and complete awareness.

BUBBLE OF PROTECTION MEDITATION: When you feel vulnerable, intimidated, or just in need of support and security, shake out all the tension from your body and relax into whatever position feels most comfortable. Breathe naturally. Imagine a bubble of blue-white light all around you, keeping you safe. The bubble is charged with sparkling, protective energy. It moves with you, and though it is soft and pliable, it is strong, shielding you from anything that worries you. Focus on your breathing. Visualize the blue-white light flowing in and out of your pores as you inhale and exhale. Feel the sparkling light fill you with strength and energy. Keep the bubble around you until the feelings of fear and vulnerability have subsided. Then let it melt away.

All problems are created by your own reactions. Absurdly, you blame the person who triggered the anger or sadness. It's impossible to get angry or sad unless it is a tendency inside you waiting to be triggered.

Happiness is a universal phenomenon. Trees, animals, birds, and plants all happily go about their day. It is not just for the lucky, the gifted, or the enlightened. Happiness is for everyone. Close your eyes and stay alert. Watch the way your mind responds to stimuli such as sounds, thoughts, and feelings. See how noticing its reactions restores its balance.

Spring-clean your brain.

Chew a single raisin for several minutes, experiencing every flavor and texture, and making it the sole focus of your attention.

For one day, no matter what happens around you, say, "This is miraculous." Notice how this outlook changes your relationship with everyday experiences.

Before starting work, say a brief prayer. Acknowledge the value of your tasks. Offer gratitude for the opportunity to contribute to the world. Ask for the skills and qualities you will need to perform your current tasks. Resolve to work out of love.

Mold clay and obey iron.

When shopping, pause before the entrance to each store and take three mindful breaths to calm and orient yourself.

When you desire something, watch the desire, consider it, and then let it go.

Be steadfastly open. Surrender.

Pay attention to every detail of your body when you wake up in the morning.

Listen to chants and other inspirational music.

Set down your baggage, every day, every minute.

Include everyone, everything, and every situation in your practice. They are the means by which you cultivate compassion and wisdom.

Affirmation: I am safe and at home in the world and in my body.

Write a haiku. It is a photograph in words; no emotion, judgment, or interpretation. Just a snapshot of a single moment.

Look at the interconnected nature of your breath. It is made possible by trees and plants, and shared by all other humans.

As you grow in mindfulness, you take back your life. You begin to see how much time you lose in empty consumption. When we are consuming, we are also being consumed.

Appreciate your clothes, which protect and beautify you. When getting dressed, say a note of thanks: "Putting on these clothes, I am grateful to those who made them, and to the materials from which they were made."

If you're butting heads with a colleague, search your subconscious for a color that describes this person. Try to figure out which chakra he or she is governed by. The seven chakras and their corresponding colors are base of spine (red), lower abdominal/genital region (orange), solar plexus (yellow), heart (green), throat (turquoise/blue), third eye/between the eyebrows (indigo), and crown/top of the head (violet). Understanding your colleague's temperament may help you forge a better relationship.

To do good means to share, to love, to serve, and to be compassionate.

Live in a simple, direct way—without cluttering your mind with hatred, judgment, worry, doubt, or want. Choose the experience of genuine happiness.

Give a thing your wholehearted attention.

Chanting mantras is not mechanically reciting words. It is praying. It is opening the heart to communicate with our true nature. The words serve to remind us of what we want to achieve, and the chanting helps us to transform the words and intentions into genuine thoughts and deeds.

Notice and encourage yourself to accept your wandering mind, and return to your breathing as peacefully as you can.

Give a heartfelt prayer of thanks for the gifts of sight, hearing, smell, taste, and touch.

Calm your emotions and nourish your joy.

Disappear into the moment.

Look at a bowl without seeing its sides or its contents: In a few moments, you will become aware of the entire bowl. Ordinarily, we look at parts, at details, at pieces. This practice will teach you to look at an object as a whole. You can practice this with any other object, or even with a person.

In insight meditation, bring your awareness to whatever arises within your mind and focus firmly upon it. Then deepen the focus and analyze your thoughts and feelings, but be careful not to identify with them. If you become distracted, bring your attention back to your breath and perform mindfulness meditation until your mind is calm again. It is a good idea to alternate between mindfulness meditation and insight meditation; they reinforce each other and protect the mind from becoming too agitated or too dull.

Bow gently. Close your eyes and imagine the Buddha in warm yellow robes, sitting under the spreading *bodhi* tree. Visualize him in meditation, radiating peace and joy. Dissolve into that vision.

Your peace of mind lies not in your individual circumstances, but in how you respond to them. Meditation helps you accept your circumstances just as they are.

Watch.

Cherish others, and your problems will become nonexistent.

Before a meal, fold your hands in mindfulness, and pray for all the people who do not have enough to eat.

Hike through a park.

Try to make decisions that will benefit others.

When you're under stress or in need of a pick-me-up, recite a mantra for strength and energy.

Are you so wrapped up with everyday things that your life is devoid of magic?

Be aware of your feelings. Know that you are breathing in. Know that you are breathing out. Now give yourself a pleasant feeling, and be aware of the presence of this feeling. Hold it as though it were your most precious child. Be aware that you like it. Smile with joy at your happiness. Then, give yourself an unpleasant feeling, and be aware of the presence of this feeling. Again, hold it as though it were your most precious child. But this time, be aware that you dislike it. Smile with compassion at your suffering. Be aware of both feelings rising and then passing away. Dwell in the present moment.

Forget achievement. Forget what others think of you. Just arrive in your body and mind, attending to the present moment.

Work with attention and joy, and you will receive genuine satisfaction.

For just a few moments, see the world in a different light. See everything around you as merely a dream. Recognize that everything is created by your consciousness. Maintain this awareness as you carry out your daily life—living on different levels of consciousness simultaneously.

Because meditative practice helps enlarge your perspective beyond identifying with thoughts and opinions, you are less likely to act from a tight, self-protected space. You have more patience and tolerance. You are better able to put yourself in someone else's shoes. Meditation matures you.

Watch the turning point between two breaths.

AFFIRMATION: My mind is now quiet.

If you want to be happy, just pay attention and be kind—unconditionally kind—at every moment. Everything else will work itself out.

Try assuming the attitude of nonstriving and simply engage with your current activities. You do not necessarily need to do more or strive for more in order to reach a more peaceful lifestyle. Enjoy just being.

Practice mindful breathing, careful listening, and deep looking.

Think of each meditation session as three major stages: arriving and centering, intensifying and focusing, releasing and allowing.

What good comes from letting something ruin your day? There is no benefit. If someone says something mean or someone cuts in front of you at the deli, let it go and stay open.

Let the body be aware of itself.

Resist your urge to grab another snack or cup of coffee. Focus on what you're doing at the moment.

Be a calm presence and conscious participant.

Imagine that your own self is seated in front of you. Regard this self, and become aware of your own stress, suffering, and dissatisfaction. Feel compassion for yourself. Breathe in suffering and take it into your heart's sphere of light. Breathe out soothing, compassionate energy.

Vital force meditation: For fifteen minutes, let loose and shake your whole body, feeling the surge of energy rising up from your feet. Fill every part of your body with this energy. Then, for the next fifteen minutes, just dance—any way you want, letting your whole body move as it wishes. In the following fifteen minutes, close your eyes and be still, either sitting or standing, witnessing whatever is happening both inside and out. In the final fifteen minutes, continue to keep your eyes closed, and lie down and be still.

One conscious breath can bring you back in contact with yourself and the world around you.

Put both hands over your closed eyes, allowing the palms to touch the eyelids with a very light pressure. Gradually reduce the pressure until you feel none at all—just a touch, light as a feather. Feel the energy moving within.

Stimulate your creativity and spirituality through journal writing. Begin each journal entry with a specific theme or focus, but allow your writing to flow from your own inspiration and uninhibited creative energy.

Notice all the layers of sound.

One by one, consider all the ideas you hold about yourself, and then discard them. Allow your choices to arise from the depths of your true nature, not from fabricated ideas about yourself or the way in which you should live.

Help others progress toward enlightenment.

Perform a meditation when listening to someone else. Still your mind and open your heart to fully hear the other person. Concentrate: Do not be distracted by your own thoughts and emotions. Hear the other person with acceptance and compassion.

Look deeply at a thought you are experiencing. Be with the thought.

What mundane concerns of the day can you drop to make room for more spiritual, timeless, and important values?

Feed your body and mind with natural, organic, unprocessed foods.

Watch the sunrise or sunset.

Just-sitting meditation: This meditation has two phases, just breathing and just sitting. First, become your breath. Merge completely with the inhalations and exhalations. Disappear as an observer, letting only your breath remain. In the second phase, just sitting, disappear into all of your sense experiences—seeing, smelling, hearing, touching, even thinking. Rather than being mindful, let only the experience remain.

Thank someone.

Mindfulness meditation: Choose an everyday task that does not normally require your full attention. As you go about this task, maintain an inner commentary on what you are doing, using the word "now" as frequently as possible. For instance: "I am *now* adding the detergent," or "*Now* I am putting the pillow in the pillowcase." Maintain this commentary and awareness for at least ten minutes. Analyze the effect that this mindfulness had upon the task, and how it has shaped the way you are currently viewing the world.

Affirmation: I am.

Find your center and stay there: It will allow you to live your life to its maximum.

Cultivate patience and perseverance. They are important for both meditation and everyday life.

Who-am-I meditation: Ask yourself, "Who am I?" Respond to each answer you provide. For instance, if you answer with your name, reply, "No, that is a name that my parents have given me. Who is the 'I' that the name is meant to signify?" Or, if your answer reflects your current mood or state of being (as in "I am tired"), reply, "No, the tiredness is merely a sensation that I'm experiencing. Who is the 'I' that experiences the sensation?" After each response negating the current answer, you will be engaged in an active, dynamic search for the next answer. Continue to reject and search for answers, ultimately moving beyond the need to define, deepening your understanding of the essence of nonself.

Are you consistently prioritizing what really matters?

Does each moment live and die? Does the act of breathing live and die? What are living and dying? Question whether life and death are opposites. Can you see beyond them? Can you see the eternal cycle of life, death, and rebirth, as shown by the breath? Try to carry this awareness into each moment of everyday life.

Visualization exercise: Picture a lemon, yellow as the sun, its thick skin just a bit oily. See yourself digging your fingernail into the peel, and see the rich citric oil well up. Pull off some of the peel to expose the white fibers of the pulp. Smell its tart scent as you bite deep into the lemon and taste the sour fruit.

Look lovingly at an object and find the beauty within.

Visualize yourself standing in a beautiful courtyard filled with exotic flowers. In the center stands a fountain of crystal-clear water, with several silver drinking cups spread around it. Step forward, choose a cup, and fill it from the fountain. Let the crystal-clear water fill your mind, body, and spirit with new life and vitality.

Give help unexpectedly. If you bump into someone on the street, offer to help them with an errand or buy them a cup of coffee.

Positive thoughts brighten your prospects.

During meals, refrain from discussing subjects that can destroy others' awareness of the present moment.

When you find your thoughts preoccupied with speculation about the future, don't berate yourself. Gently remind yourself that you exist only in the here and now.

Look and walk with love. Make a conscious effort to send love into the world.

If you can affirm something deeply, totally, and absolutely, it starts to become real. Happy people affirm happiness. Miserable people affirm misery. Stop affirming the negative and start affirming the positive. The law of affirmation is a magic key to a better life.

Simple mindfulness trick: Writing down what you want makes you think about not having it. You'll have to "admit" it in writing.

When you put something down, be conscious of putting it down. When you pick it up again, be conscious of picking it up.

Contemplate emptiness stretching away in every direction. Meditate on emptiness and be free.

Grocery cart bangs into you. You turn, see what has happened, move your own cart out of the way, and then return your full attention to shopping. The end.

How can you uproot confusion, anger, and restlessness? By acknowledging each state of mind, naming it, and giving it space. Shine the light of awareness on them, and they will lose their hold over you.

Recognize your inclinations, but resist the pull to be controlled by them.

Affirmation: My imagination is my spirit's vehicle.

Unclutter your inner space, so that the light that is hidden can expand and fill your being.

Smile often.

When you sit, know you are sitting. When you eat, know you are eating. When you walk, know you are walking.

Stop getting lost in your own movie. Go to a movie theater, buy a ticket, and find a seat about halfway back. Ten minutes into the movie, close your eyes and gently pull your awareness away from the movie. Take a moment to remember the real-life events that happened in the past hour or so—arriving at the theater, interacting with people, walking through the theater, and so forth. Now open your eyes and let your awareness return to the movie. Become absorbed in the movie for another fifteen to thirty minutes. Once again, pull your attention away from the movie, but this time, look around the theater, especially at the other moviegoers. Reaffirm your identity by using the power of your will to become aware of who and where you really are. Now go back to watching the movie, but remember that you are sitting in a theater watching a movie. Finally, when you leave the movie, retain the feeling of having two coexisting viewpoints. Apply that sensation to events in your own life. Place yourself in a seat of conscious awareness, watching the movie of your life as it unfolds.

Identify a situation where you feel limited and constricted. Today, walk right through this situation. Do not think about how—just do it. Do this every day for the entire week.

Meditate on someone you love deeply, such as your partner or spouse.

Follow the Buddha's instructions on how to meditate: Sit under a tree, cross your legs, and establish mindfulness.

Walk with fresh eyes. Let a walk be an unfolding surprise.

Imagine that your entire body is suspended in the air from a string attached to the crown of your head. Feel the string pulling up so that your spine lengthens, your pelvis tilts forward, your chin tucks down into your neck, and the back of your neck flattens slightly. Stretch and grow strong. Choose a word or phrase that means something to you. Sit quietly and repeat this mantra, allowing your mind to rest on the sounds of the words. Note the feelings it evokes.

Develop a mind that clings to nothing. Thoughts arise, sensations are felt, the senses are open and receiving, and preferences and opinions form in the spaciousness of mind, but there is no identification or interference.

WHISTLE BREATH: Perform this exercise outdoors or next to an open window. Purse your lips as though you were going to whistle, then inhale slowly through your mouth to the count of seven. Pause for one count, then softly exhale through both nostrils to the count of seven. Repeat six times. Practice whistle breathing in the morning and at noon.

Welcome mishaps, because they wake you up.

Your life is like a sailboat, and you are the captain. The captain cannot control the weather, the strength of the wind, or the condition of the sea. All he or she can do is deal—to the best of his or her ability—with the weather, the wind, and the sea, and keep moving forward.

Make a complete stop when you reach an intersection in your life. With full awareness, look to your left, your right, and the "crosswalk," and check your "rearview mirrors" before proceeding ahead.

When you meet someone who is suffering, take some time to imagine yourself in his or her position. It may give you a clearer sense of how to help this person.

Detach from your thoughts by saying, "The mind is now thinking" each time you notice a new thought pattern. It will help you see them apart from yourself, rather than identifying so strongly with them.

Attune your breathing to induce feelings of innocence and tenderness within your heart. Can you become like a newborn baby?

Watch your words; they become your actions.

When you are under pressure, think about an activity that induces calm, such as lying in the sun or taking a warm bath.

By setting aside time to meditate, you are programming yourself to experience more positive emotions and mind-states.

When you're reluctant to exercise, pay attention to the details of your preparation—tying your sneakers, carrying your gym bag, stretching as you warm up—to focus your mind. Through continued effort, you sweat out impurities and build a strong spirit.

Reflect on relationships in your life where you experience a tangible sense of trust, lovingkindness, and safety. Consider the ways in which those relationships allow you to deepen and open up. Be aware of the feelings of peace and well-being. Then reflect on relationships that may be scarred by mistrust, judgment, or alienation. Sense the fear or unease that may manifest in your body, and the agitation that may appear in your heart and mind. What can heal, nurture, and end these divisions and disconnections?

Follow your breath while listening to music—breathing long, light, and even, while remaining aware of the movement of the music.

Draw your own mandalas. Start with a circle, then add a design that is meaningful to you. Most mandalas contain symmetric, geometric designs, but feel free to draw yours according to your own artistic inclinations.

Examine everything as though you had just taken off blinders.

Probe the deeper nature of the mind to reveal its emptiness and lack of inherent existence. Reflect on its dependence upon perceived relationships and implied causes, particularly its limited understanding of time. The mind perceives any length of time—whether one minute, one hour, even the shortest instant—not as it truly is, but in relation to the moments that have preceded and the moments that will follow.

Every so often, stop what you are doing and breathe, noticing the world all around you. Open your senses to the environment. Experience the present moment in complete stillness.

When traveling, take a few mindful breaths to relax your body and mind. Do your best to step and act peacefully. Relax your shoulders, soften your face.

At some point midmorning, take a moment to meditate on the blessings you have received on that day. Consider how you can take those blessings into your heart and radiate them out toward others.

Be more mindful of the quality and quantity of food you eat.

Build a spiritual partnership with a teacher, mentor, or fellow spiritual seeker.

Bring your awareness to a small area of your body. Name the sensations you discover there.

It is better to meditate for a shorter period of time with enthusiasm and energy than to drag yourself through an hour with lethargy and discomfort.

Remain on your cushion without expecting anything.

Tend to your plants with care and interest.

Notice your feelings and thoughts. Question their truth.

Value the eloquence of silence.

Before moving or speaking, examine your mind, then act appropriately and with composure.

If you have hurt someone, see yourself plucking out the arrows you have fired. Break them in half. Send healing light to the other person and to yourself.

Nail biting is a mindless habit that allows you to remain engaged and to expend excess energy. If you live more energetically and intensely, however, taking up dancing, singing, or power-walking, your habit will gradually disappear.

Your treasure house is within you. It holds all you will ever need.—HUI HAI

Eat in silence, slowly and mindfully.

Write in stream of consciousness every day for ten to twenty minutes. Record anything that comes into your head, no matter how ridiculous, embarrassing, or unsophisticated it may seem. Don't judge, analyze, or interpret. Let the words flow.

Make your exhalations long and relaxed, and hold your breath at the end of each. See what it is like to move toward emptiness.

If you can name or feel something, you can be mindful of it.

If you drink alcohol, know your limits. If you abstain, do not judge those who partake. The path to truth lies in the middle way.

Take a few minutes, either at home or on your way to work, to notice something enjoyable about the morning.

Facing-wall meditation: Put your seat or cushion about twelve to eighteen inches from a blank wall and sit facing the wall. Concentrate on your breathing until you feel settled. Through half-closed eyes, look steadily at the wall. Avoid blinking. Try not to be distracted by any patterns you see on the wall's surface or objects in your peripheral vision, or by "projected" images from your imagination. As soon as you get distracted, bring yourself back to the wall.

Chew your food slowly so you can savor the flavors.

Observe yourself without judgment.

Visit ancient monuments, structures, and sites. They can help you understand your own connection to eternity.

Be grateful for every meal, no matter how simple.

Picture a lake during meditation. See the reflections of the sunset, the stars, or a blue sky. See the times of stillness. See the times of storm and turbulence, even though it remains calm beneath the surface. Use the image of this lake to carry you through difficult times.

If you have a strong habit that does not serve you well, consciously restrain yourself in that area. Start with a predetermined period of time, then gradually let go of the habit altogether. You will see that there is a direct relationship between restraint and freedom, and that the more you restrain yourself, the more freedom you create for yourself.

If you plant wheat, wheat will grow. If you act in a wholesome way, you will be happy. If you act in an unwholesome way, you water the seeds of craving, anger, and violence in yourself.

Minimize distortion by turning down the volume of your inner dialogue.

Visualize yourself as a natural, pastoral setting. Try to be the still pond at the center of the field.

Contemplate the positive qualities of each object or experience.

When you find yourself getting distracted by pictures in your mind, take note of this "imaging." Just observe it and move on.

Be natural.

Whenever your attention is on the here and now, perceiving your inner and outer reality without judgment, you are meditating.

Contemplate helping an angry person, and breathe in. Envision yourself as being able to help this person, and breathe out.

Use the act of eating to zone in on internal improvement: with the first taste, promise to offer joy. With the second taste, promise to help relieve the suffering of others. With the third taste, promise to see the joy of others as your own. With the fourth taste, promise to learn the ways of nonattachment and equanimity.

Can you share whatever you have, recognizing that nothing is really yours for very long?

Recognize the Buddha-light shining within everyone and everything.

Try to find time during the middle of your day to do a walking meditation, preferably outdoors.

Utilize every immediate circumstance for meditation.

When you are depressed, exercise.

The great opportunity is where you are. Look under your feet.

Feel now, act later.

Stop all of the "doing" by shifting into the "being" for a moment. Think of yourself as an eternal witness, as a timeless observer. Just watch this moment.

Notice the temperature and quality of the air and see if you can accept the air for what it is without resisting it or trying to make it different.

Be careful not to dwell on painful memories or indulge in pleasant ones. Remember that all thoughts and experiences are impermanent.

What is keeping you from being in the present? Find the hidden influence of your most ingrained emotional patterns.

When others act cruelly, remember that no one would act that way unless they were suffering themselves. The more quickly you can recognize and transform your reactions, the less likely you will be to hurt someone else.

Take stock of your current condition and see how you can balance it.

Draw upon the color blue when you feel tense or stressed.

Why should you believe and get involved in all the thinking that occurs in everyday life? When you see that you do not need to pay attention to your thoughts, it becomes easier to drop them.

Ask, "Am I accessing my inner wisdom and applying it? Am I understanding the emptiness and the interconnectedness of things?"

Notice all events equally.

Deep listening and loving speech can stop new anger and fear from arising as well as transform long-held misperceptions and suffering.

Forgetfulness is the opposite of mindfulness. It's drinking a cup of rose petal tea without knowing you are drinking. It's walking through an autumnal park without knowing you are walking. It's sitting with the person you love without knowing you're sitting together. Instead of appreciating the beauty of your present experience, you are someplace else, thinking about the past or the future, or lost in your imagination. You must refocus your mind in order to enjoy the day-to-day miracles of your life.

Dare and dare again.

Happy or sad, energetic or tired, just sit as the person you happen to be at the moment.

Imagine a golden mist all around you, filled with a subtle energy. Let the energy flow inside you.

Set up an altar so that you can make offerings on a daily basis. Appropriate offerings include candles, incense, or small bowls of water with a few flowers. Make sure, however, that the offering is not just a physical thing but is also an expression of your inner self.

Repeat a prayer you know by heart.

Breathing in, calm your mind. Breathing out, calm your mind.

If you want to receive love, be loving.

Talk to people as if they were doors, not walls. Feel that they will open, listen, and welcome your words.

Stop trying to understand what you are feeling and just feel. Just pay attention to everything exactly as it appears and don't judge it.

Be a part of life, not apart from life. Let it flow through you, and live in harmony with its ebb and flow. Ride the waves with equanimity, knowing that you are the whole sea.

Appreciate the time you have.

If you keep getting distracted, ask yourself, "What keeps pulling me away?"

Every meditative path encourages us to turn directly toward all that preoccupies and burdens us. Cultivating inner calmness, caring wholeheartedly for the moment we are in, and releasing anxiety and agitation are lessons we can learn only while living.

Make your trip home from work a relaxing transition time by slowing down and smiling.

When walking in *kinhin*, keep your mind totally focused on your environment, not on the thoughts that try to distract you.

Reflect and consider where your actions are leading you.

THOUGHT COUNTING: This exercise should give you a sense of your capacity for thought observation. Sit for five minutes, counting your thoughts as each one arises. Count each word or image as a single thought. Your awareness must be strong enough to withstand getting caught up in the content or story of each thought. When a thought crosses your mind, just observe and count it, and let it pass away.

Feel yourself participating in life.

Are you resisting the temptation to judge and talk about others?

Shovel some snow and jump into the pile.

Connect.

Visualize the image of a deity in your mind's eye.

Recognize that you are not your body.

As you grow old, be aware of what "old" really means, without deceiving yourself. See if you can enjoy life differently from how you did in your youth.

Learning to live is learning to let go.

Meditate on the water in a fish tank.

Always reflect on what provokes difficulties in your life.

TRANSCENDENTAL MEDITATION: Find a quiet place where you will not be disturbed. Take some deep breaths. Now choose a mantra. Slowly say your mantra to yourself, silently. Repeat the mantra at a comfortable pace. If you wander off, bring yourself back to the mantra.

Make the world your monastery. Wherever you are, whatever you encounter, know that it is meant to provide you with the exact teaching you need.

Mindfulness dramatically amplifies the probability that any activity in which you are engaged will result in an expansion of your perspective and understanding of who you are. It's a remembering, a reminding yourself to be awake.

Use moments throughout your day, when your mind is calm, to ponder these questions: What is happiness? What more do I need in this moment to be free? What is peace? What do I need to be at peace with a certain person, event, or memory? What am I clinging to? Listen to the responses that rise up within you, but let go of the need for answers; stay with the question. If your mind becomes agitated, let go of the question and focus on the breath or on external sounds. Return to the question when you are calm.

Mindfulness is a chance to be awake, and to respond consciously instead of reacting automatically.

Consider complementing your meditation practice by discussing any persistently troubling thoughts and feelings with a counselor, therapist, or mental health professional. They may be able to help you focus and direct your meditation to achieve some resolution, and may also contribute insights and suggestions you might not have considered on your own.

Choose ten memories, and imagine yourself pasting each of them into an album. Look at this scrapbook of your past. Tell yourself that it will be a long time before you revisit these memories. Imagine closing the album and putting it on a high shelf, in the back of a closet, in the least visited room of your home. Now visualize a new, empty album, which you are eagerly looking forward to filling.

Understand that Mind is no Mind, and you will understand Mind and its workings.—BODHIDHARMA

Approach people with curiosity, knowing that each person has something they can teach you. Seek the value in whatever they do or say. Acknowledge these teachings.

Be moderate and balanced. Open your mind to new ways of looking at things. Do not be too hard or too easy on yourself. Be disciplined yet open to guidance, loving yet self-contained. Take things one step at a time.

Practice will make it second nature to think of the positive things in life rather than the negative things.

Explore your chakras: Sit as usual. Rest your awareness gently on the first chakra, which is at the base of your spine. Set aside all thoughts and allow an image of the chakra to rise. If this chakra could speak, what would it say? Listen for an answer. If this chakra were an animal, what would it be? Wait for an image to unfold. Pose these questions to all of the other chakras. If you do not receive an image or response to every question, do not worry. It takes time to get in tune with each of the chakras.

Make it your way of life to stay awake, slow down, and take notice.

Pay attention to bodily sensations, such as itchiness or pain. Observe the feeling as it is; do not grasp or reject it. The sensation will disappear by itself.

Acknowledge inspirational thoughts with an exclamation such as "Eureka!"

Throw yourself into an adventure. Fear of the unknown will fade as you accustom yourself to exploration.

Standing–centering meditation: Lean forward a bit, then backward, then left, then right. Lean only an inch or two in each direction. Then rest in a position that feels balanced, in complete equilibrium.

Affirmation to quiet the mind and body and realize joy: I am breathing in and making the breath-body light and peaceful. I am breathing out and making the breath-body light and peaceful. I am breathing in and making my entire body light and peaceful and joyous. I am breathing out and making my entire body light and peaceful and joyous. I am breathing in while my mind and body embody peace and joy. I am breathing out while my mind and body embody peace and joy. (Use this affirmation for twenty to sixty minutes.)

If you feel pain, stop and allow yourself to feel the pain. Contemplate why it may be trying to get your attention. Look to the real source of your pain, and work to remove it.

Say "Good morning" to everyone around you, and really mean it.

View life as a game of chess. See yourself and others as pieces on the board. Let this viewpoint give you insight into the dynamics of your current situation.

Focus on what you can do, not on what you cannot.

Investigate the physical sensations and mental images related to your emotions. The mere act of investigating will cause their intensity to diminish. You will be able to calm and clear your mind and respond from a state of centered strength.

Before you start the car, reflect for a moment on what you are doing and where you are going.

Keep your attention focused within; at the same time, look around and allow yourself to be aware of the wonders that surround you.

Where you are is meditation.

Just do what you are doing without thinking about it. Just be where you are without holding on to it or running away from it. Dive into this moment.

PURE-LOVE MEDITATION: Picture a person or animal for whom you feel great love and affection, and imagine him or her giving you a look that melts your heart. Think about the things you love most about this special being. With each breath, let your heart fill with the love and affection you feel. Imagine your two souls connected by the caring you have for each other.

Awareness is key. It means acutely seeing, knowing, feeling, and sensing colors, contours, sounds, textures, and smells.

When you meditate, let your mind rest.

Are you inhaling and exhaling and following each from beginning to end?

Before speaking, examine your mind.

If something happy occurs, do not become too excited. If sorrow comes, do not be too depressed. Happiness and sorrow are not you. They are dependent upon your own mind, your own interpretation. Observe unattached.

Close your eyes and consider how your actions affect your own life and the lives of those around you. What would happen if you strove to be generous, kind, and thoughtful all the time? Release any thoughts of self-gain and remember that good karma depends on pure intentions. Resolve that from now on, you will make an effort to respond to all situations, easy or difficult, with generosity, kindness, and thoughtfulness.

Pay attention to the words you speak and the tone in which you speak. Let your words reflect compassion and concern for others.

Keep yourself as open and accepting as possible.

Value silence.

Go to bed when you are tired. Listen to gentle music, read a soothing book, or meditate just before sleeping. Try not to set an alarm; rather, work toward awakening naturally at the appropriate time.

Without self-blame, return to what is in front of your nose. Do this as gently as possible, and it will become natural and spontaneous.

The quieter you become, the more you can hear.
—RAM DASS

Close your eyes and turn your attention inward. Observe the pinpoints of light flickering on the backs of your eyelids. Go deeper within yourself, until the light recedes. This is your inner sanctuary of peace and stillness.

Mantras don't have to be spiritual phrases uttered during strictly meditative periods. Anything that is repeated over and over can be a mantra. For instance, at a baseball game, the constant repetition of a team or player's name functions like a mantra.

Listen to an instrument. Notice how it is capable of playing an infinite number of notes. Be alert and penetrate the music; listen to the core, the backbone of the instrument. Notes come and go, but the core flows on. Be aware of it.

The sooner you can identify and be mindful of a stressful situation, the sooner you can disentangle yourself from typical reactions and mind traps.

Make regular contact with sources of wisdom.

Habits are generally mindless, done on autopilot when the root cause triggers them. One of the best mindfulness practices is slowing down or pausing when you are about to carry out your usual reaction (like anger) or action (like overeating). Determine to increase your mindfulness from moment to moment.

Meditate on the profound power of the four elements: air, earth, fire, and water. Air is connected with purity and life force. Earth is associated with nourishing energy. Fire is connected with passion and purification. Water is associated with cleansing and life sustainment. Give thanks for all they give us.

Be still in mind and spirit.

EARTH GODDESS MEDITATION: Always seeking, seeing, and serving the Creator in all. Opening my mind, my body, my spirit, my heart, my soul, and my entire being to the infinite love, light, and healing energy of the one Creator. Feeling the infinite love, light, and healing energy of the one Creator moving through me, to Mother Earth, to heal Mother Earth. May every soul in pain on Earth feel infinite love, light, and healing energy. May there be peace and love in the hearts of men and women.

Let the Buddha speak through you with healing words of acceptance, love, and compassion.

When you learn to label your thoughts in meditation, you will be able to label them during your daily life as well.

Realization comes through the practice of surrendering.

Meditation is adventure, the greatest adventure the human mind can undertake. It is to take delight in simply being—delight that comes from nowhere and everywhere.

Dealing with negative mind states: Choose one of the most frequent and negative mind states that arise in your meditation practice, such as irritation, fear, boredom, lust, doubt, or restlessness. For one week, be particularly aware each time this state arises. Note how it begins and if there is a particular thought or image that triggers this state. Note how long it lasts and what follows when it ends. Become aware of physical or mental resistance to experiencing this state. Soften and receive even this resistance. Sit and be aware of the breath, watching and waiting for the mind state. Allow it to come, like an old friend, and just observe.

Meditation is more than just sitting by yourself in a quiet room. It is noticing the condition of your mind in any situation. It is becoming aware of the spontaneous rise of life in each moment.

Chew your drink and drink your food.

Withdraw in meditation from the pleasures of sense as a tortoise withdraws its limbs. Through this will you find peace.—BHAGAVAD GITA

What is the most important thing for you to do at this moment, knowing that death is certain, but time of death is uncertain?

The journey toward the center takes place within your own mind.

Perform every action artfully.

Take a walk to reconnect with the natural world.

When you drop the story you hide behind, you will find that everything is fresh and new, as if you were seeing everything for the first time, as it really is.

Hatred never ceases through hatred; by love alone it is healed.

Turn a bad habit into a meditation. Pay close attention to your every move. Notice how your body feels. Whenever your mind drifts off, bring it back to the experience. Do not try to stop or change this habit; go through the motions as usual, but do so with full awareness. Indulge in your habit with this high level of awareness over and over again. See how your attitude and feelings change.

Try to maintain the posture of *zazen*, letting go of thoughts. Open the hand of thought, which will try to grasp something, but refrain from grasping.

Pay attention to the taste, smell, and texture of every bite for an entire meal.

Discover the eternal within yourself.

Breath cuts through thinking, because you have to let go in order to breathe.

Realize that everyone is doing the best they possibly can. Judge no one.

Treat all beings with respect.

Some people take refuge in TV to evade the real issues in their lives. They cannot turn it off, because when they do, they have to go back to themselves, which is uncomfortable. They avoid the program running inside: confusion, conflict, and despair. They are turning away from suffering rather than dealing with the issues that really matter.

See the world as a dream. Enjoy its newness, its surprises, its beauty. Don't cling to anything.

Place a blank canvas in front of you, sit quietly until moved to action, then paint, guided by your soul.

Be mindful of everything you think, and learn to change your thoughts from unwholesome to wholesome.

When reading, be aware of reading.

Give thanks throughout the day. Be thankful for every blessing you receive. Say "thank you" with grace.

Each time you arrive at a destination, give thanks.

Picture yourself as a piece of bamboo, completely hollow and empty inside—just space. Suddenly, energy will start pouring into you. Become hollow again. You do not need to do anything else. The bamboo will disappear when the time has come.

Don't worry if you forget a dazzling solution or plan that arises during meditation—it will come up again.

Make a list of all that you have received today, even the smallest things. Then make a list of any pain you may have caused today. This activity reverses your usual thinking: We tend to think that we give all day and get very little, and that we are the ones who get hurt and disappointed, rather than the ones causing the hurt or disappointment.

Draw upon the colors indigo and violet to renew your dedication to a spiritual path, shedding your personal needs and wants in favor of universal peace.

Practice eating mindfully, driving mindfully, even taking out the garbage mindfully.

Allow your eyes to relax and focus on nothing while maintaining a general awareness of everything.

Focus on the spot between your eyebrows, putting all your attention on the third eye area. Observe your *prana*, the very essence of breath.

Concentrate on one thing, yet be mindful of all things.

MINDFULNESS VOW: I am committed to cultivating responsibility and to protecting the safety and integrity of individuals, couples, family, and society. I am determined to respect my own commitments and the commitments of others.

Let go of the thought that "I am this body," "I live in this particular time and place," or "I am I." Dive into the awareness of being everything all the time.

Zen is simple: Just sit and experience, without attachment, attitude, or opinion.

Spend a day or a substantial part of the day doing absolutely nothing: not speaking, not watching television, not listening to music, not reading, and not even eating much. Watch the restlessness of the mind. Soften and surrender to emptiness.

CHAKRA MEDITATION: Sit cross-legged, take three deep breaths, then breathe naturally. Starting with the chakra at the base of your spine, imagine each chakra as a lotus flower or spinning wheel. Breathe energy into the chakra, revitalizing it. Now move up to the chakra in the lower abdomen, just above your genital area. Again, breathe energy into this chakra. Continue for the rest of the chakras: in the solar plexus/navel, the heart, the throat, between the eyes, and finally the chakra at the top of your head. What does the energy of each chakra feel like? Where was additional energy required? Relax and take some deep breaths to finish.

As you grow older, ask yourself what you can do to continue to contribute to society. It shouldn't be hard, with the knowledge and insights that you have gained through the years.

Bring your mind back home and rest right here, in the present moment, with unbiased awareness.

Listen for the quietest sound.

Recognize your emotional states. Accept that all emotions are a natural part of being human. Take interest in your emotional experiences while remaining detached from them. Learn to take them less personally.

When you're angry, see yourself in a fire of rage, and breathe in. Feel compassion for yourself burning with anger, and breathe out.

After you ask for guidance—listen!

Gather a handful of different leaves. Sit and study them, noticing the variety of shapes, colors, and textures. Trace the veins with your fingers. Meditate on the patterns you see. Close your eyes and smell the leaves. Become completely absorbed in them with all of your senses.

What makes you human? Reflect on this question over and over again. Build on the answers that develop, to gain unwavering trust in your own nature and to find your self-confidence.

Abandon artificial words and silences and live your own Zen.

Practice awareness. Go for a walk. Listen to music. Eat a meal. Read. Stay single-mindedly, wholeheartedly focused on what you are doing.

Listen to a symphony, paying attention to the sounds of each of the different instruments and to the way in which they work together to form a coherent whole. If it is summer, try to attend an outdoor concert in a park or garden, so that you can experience nature and music together.

Meditate on your hair: It is always growing and ever-changing, a microcosm of nature's great cycles played out on the top of your head.

Mindfulness helps you see desire and its effects, and eventually, you will find a way to stop desiring.

In times of crisis, try to see difficult circumstances and events as bad-tasting medicine: You won't enjoy it, but it will eventually make you better. Embrace the reality of the situation without resistance, struggle, aversion, or avoidance. Try the lovingkindness practice of breathing in, and willingly assume the burden. Remember that everything is grist for the mill of awareness.

Seize this very minute; / What you do, or dream you can do, begin it; / Boldness has genius, power and magic in it.—GOETHE'S *FAUST*, TRANSLATED BY JOHN ANSTER

Train yourself to listen with compassion.

Each morning, stand in front of the mirror and take three deep breaths. Brush your teeth mindfully. Pay attention as you wash your face. Give yourself a little smile to start the day.

Learn from every person, every thing, and every situation in your life.

Instead of trying to stop judging, practice the simplest form of awareness: Notice your thoughts and beliefs as they arise, and inquire into their truth.

Feel a cloud of bliss around you. Relax into it. Become part of that cloud.

If you are so angry that you're starting a personal attack, stop immediately. Come back to the discussion when you feel calmer.

Acknowledge that everything that rises shall pass away. Acknowledge that all beings are heirs to their own karma. Acceptance of these truths will help you find balance, equanimity, and peace.

Observe and experience without reacting.

WALKING-BACKWARD MEDITATION: Breathe and walk backward as slowly as you need to. You will find your steps much less sure, and your usual paths unfamiliar. Learn to trust yourself and your surroundings.

Relax into what you are.

Pretend you are dying and there is nothing to be done. Rather than judging it, take no position in your mind. Stop leaning into circumstances and rest in your own awareness.

Don't sit around and ask, "What is the meaning of life?" The meaning of life can be found only in living life to its fullest.

The more compassionate you are, the more generous you will be. The more generous you are, the more lovingkindness you will be able to shine into the world.

Substitute an hour of meditation for an hour of watching television.

MEDITATION DEDICATION: May everyone I meet abide in happiness forever. May each person find peace and happiness. (Offer this dedication after your meditation practice.)

REQUEST FOR THE THREE REFUGES: I pay homage to the Blessed One, the Worthy One, the Fully Enlightened One. I go to the Buddha for refuge. I go to the Dharma for refuge. I go to the Sangha for refuge. A second time I go to the Buddha for refuge. A second time I go to the Dharma for refuge. A second time I go to the Sangha for refuge. A third time I go to the Buddha for refuge. A third time I go to the Dharma for refuge. A third time I go to the Sangha for refuge.

Enjoy the magic show called life, but do not be fooled by the illusions.

Can you stop clinging to others, trying to shape and control them, and instead allow them more space, freedom, and time? From possessiveness comes conflict; letting go gives satisfaction.

Restrain yourself from acting on small desires. This will give you the strength to restrain yourself from more powerful and harmful ones.

Ride the waves of your emotions. As waves change, so your emotions will change. Stay steady and centered through it all.

Find something or someone that can help you stay true to your highest spiritual aspirations.

MANTRA EXERCISE: Choose a mantra. Now close your eyes and start repeating it, either silently or out loud. Follow the rhythm of your natural breathing, letting the cadence and sound of the mantra lift you up and away. When your mind wanders, bring it back to the mantra gently but firmly, and try repeating it with more emphasis. Come out of the meditation slowly and open your eyes.

Let things be as they are, and accept all that you like and dislike with equanimity. Be at peace, neither pushing anything from you nor pulling anything toward you. When you no longer need things to be a particular way, what difficulties are there?

Look deeply into things and see their true natures.

After your workday, eat a good meal, have a cup of tea, read a book, play a family game, share stories with loved ones, and relax before you go to bed.

The only thing you need to begin and continue on your spiritual journey is a commitment to regular meditation practice.

Work with what you have and make your efforts worthy.

Use the act of writing to peel away layers of defenses and reactions, and to access the depths of your soul. Unmask yourself and give shape to your unique experience.

The Seven Factors of Enlightenment are mindfulness, effort and energy, investigation, rapture, concentration, tranquility, and equanimity. Halfway through your daily meditation, look for whether these factors are present in your life, and, if they are, whether they are strong or weak. Repeat this exercise for two or three weeks, pausing halfway through your meditation, at a point where you feel most attentive. Think of ways to nourish these factors in your practice and your life. Sometimes just being aware of them leads to naturally developing them.

Prepare a meal with your family and practice eating meditation together in a loving, relaxed manner.

Provide a peaceful atmosphere in your home.

You cannot do anything about the past, but you can make the present great.

DEEP-BELLY BREATHE: When you sit down to meditate, notice how you are breathing. Make a conscious effort to expand your belly. Breathe deeply and slowly into your belly. Continue for five minutes, then return to breathing normally. Practice deep-belly breathing regularly.

Explore areas of your life in which you are not as productive as you would like to be. How might the practice of mindfulness enhance your concentration and productivity?

When you take a walk, you may see, hear, or smell something that you want to savor. Stop and enjoy it, breathing fully in the present.

Clean up and pick up your belongings.

Watching is meditation. What you watch is irrelevant. You can watch the trees, the rain, the clouds, a river, or even children playing.

Take periods of mental and physical relaxation throughout the day to maintain long-term stress relief and optimal well-being.

Focus on just one spiritual teaching. Even if you do not understand the exact meaning, you may still be receiving it on a deeper level.

Befriend your emotions, particularly confused or negative ones. Smile and note to yourself, "There comes the angry dragon again!" or "It looks like the crazy cockatoo is at it again!"

Bring your attention to a pain or ache as if you were comforting a child—and hold it with soothing, loving attention.

Consider the changing seasons, noticing how there could never be new growth without death and decay.

Meditate on your spiritual riches, which matter far more than material ones.

Are you following your deepest intuitions, or others' intuitions?

When you conclude your formal meditation practice, carry your mindful presence into whatever activities follow. Throughout the day, pause from time to time for a minimeditation to renew these connections, continuing to infuse your life with the mindful presence, insight, creativity, and compassion that flow from your formal practice.

Use your own distress to become more patient, caring, and compassionate.

When you finish a meditation, realize that everything is open, pliable, and possible.

Before going to sleep, imagine that you are in a wild, mountainous region. It is a very dark night, there is no moon in the sky, and it is so cloudy that you cannot see a single star. You are lost and it is dark. Surrounded by danger, you are fully alert; you can hear every sound. Suddenly, you find yourself at a precipice. You throw a rock into the abyss to gauge its depth, and listen for the rock below. You listen, and listen, and listen. But the rock never hits bottom. It is utterly silent. Fall asleep in the silence.

Can you feel compassion even for those who wish you ill? Can you remember that they are actually harming themselves?

Divide housekeeping into stages or sections. Allow plenty of time for each task. Move slowly—much more slowly than usual. Focus your full attention on each task. Perform every movement with total awareness and involvement.

A Zen attitude toward family can have the curious effect of eliminating your buttons that are often pushed. Practice mindfulness and nonattachment when you are with family.

Observe your thoughts without following them.

Remove the layer of concept that sits between you and the reality of the present moment. Stop both your body and your mind. Allow yourself to be in just one place: the here and now.

Zen teaches perfect freedom to accept or reject without compulsion or remorse. As subconscious fears and compulsive habits disappear, your built-in wisdom will naturally select the food necessary for physical, mental, and spiritual growth.

Appreciate everything.

Learn to communicate skillfully.

If you behaved badly toward someone, recognize your mistakes and feel regret. Do not be depressed or wallow in remorse, but do not be indifferent or ignore what you did either. Forgive yourself, then apologize and ask for forgiveness.

When you trust, you become centered.

When breathing, focus on the nostrils, right where the breath goes in and out, and note the shift between warm and cool sensations.

Before you tell someone what they should or shouldn't do, think about what you're going to say, and make sure that it will be genuinely helpful, that it's definitely true, and that the right time has come. The right time is when the other person is peaceful and open to listening, and you are coming from a position of love, not negativity.

Learning to go with the flow rather than resist what you have to do can help you be more productive and enjoy your work more.

Mindfulness comes from beginning again, and again, and again.

Control the amount of time you spend on the telephone.

Listen to music with both your heart and your head.

BORN-AGAIN MEDITATION: For one hour, behave like a young child. No behavior, unless harmful, is prohibited. Then sit silently for twenty to sixty minutes. Reawaken into your current life.

After you have learned to simply be in the stillness of slow motion, learn how to simply be in the midst of great action. Become like the center of a cyclone or hurricane. Your personal practice benefits not only you but expands beyond you, helping you serve and be useful to others.

Invest 100 percent in making yourself and the people around you happy.

Take a walk, your whole body attentive to the experience. Feel your skin respond to the air. Feel the breezes press against you. Smell the air. Hear the wind. Listen to the sounds around you. Open your eyes like a wide-angle camera lens. Feel your whole body moving through space. Notice how all the parts of the body are naturally, unself-consciously involved. No planning is needed for walking; it just happens. Feel the walk with your whole body. Attend to the sensations. Stay awake.

When engaging in harsh, abusive, or sarcastic speech, you do not invite another to trust or listen to what you are trying to say. When faced with insults, sarcasm, or accusation, your first response is to protect yourself, avoid the abuser, or respond with equal aggression.

If you had only an hour to live, who would you call and what would you say? Why not make that call now?

Sit and become silent. Review major areas of your life—work, home, relationships, leisure activities, finances, possessions, spirituality—and see if you can simplify any of those areas. Just let the images or answers appear. After you have reflected on each of these areas, ask, "If this area became simpler, would I be happier?"

Morning meditation: Today I will avoid causing harm through my physical activity; I will avoid causing harm through my speech; I will avoid causing harm through my thoughts. Today I will do my best to engage in beneficial physical activity; I will do my best to speak useful and pleasant words; I will do my best to nourish well-wishing thoughts for all beings.

Visualize your path through life as a staircase that goes on forever and that has no end point. Continue up the steps; the process of climbing is all that matters.

Honor your needs for formal meditation, relaxation, exercise, sleep, intimacy, humor, and a healthy diet.

Before you speak, ask if what you're about to say is kind, necessary, true, and better than silence.

Confront challenges through inner strength and courage.

Focus on an object of meditation, trying to achieve and maintain stability and intensity. Avoid both laxity and excitement.

Label your moment-to-moment sensations. You will become more present, and will grow quiet and still.

Breathe in the lessons of life and death, and of the unity of the elements, by observing trees, plants, and other green growing things.

You are one person among billions on one planet among billions. In perspective, why let meaningless things cause you suffering? Do you really need to care what people think about your car or house? Do you really need to feel embarrassed that you made a mistake at work? You can be free, just having fun, being comfortable with whatever happens, enjoying whatever your experiences are.

Rest in the center. Reflect on how everything rises and passes away.

Give thanks and appreciation for the transportation your car provides you.

Small deeds really do matter. One by one, they fill a giant pot.

SANCTUARY MEDITATION: Picture yourself standing in a serene woodland setting, feeling comfortable and relaxed. Walk toward a clearing in the distance, and lie down and relax in the sun. You are safe here. Rest for as long as you need. When you are ready, move on to a glade of trees at the center of the clearing, where you meet your guide. Talk to him or her; see your guide listening to you with absolute attention and understanding. When you're finished, thank your guide and make your way out of the trees, the clearing, and finally the woodland setting. Open your eyes.

Sit quietly, close your eyes, and breathe. Imagine people, places, and objects as though you were seeing them for the very last time. See the beauty and preciousness of this moment, the only moment you have left. Recognize that every moment is like this one.

Look for work that suits your personality, knowledge, skills, and interests.

In the kitchen, prepare your food with zest and attention.

Imagine sitting beneath a rainbow. Gradually, the rainbow expands throughout your body, filling every pore and dissolving all obstacles. Your body shines like a lamp, and light streams from you in all directions. Your light dissolves suffering everywhere, and the world now shines with joy and meaning. Emanate this light for as long as it feels natural.

Let the process of thinking stop by itself. If a thought crosses your mind, let it come in, and let it go out. It will not stay long. When you try to stop your thinking, it means you are bothered by it. Do not let yourself be bothered by anything. Your thoughts will gradually grow calmer. In five or ten minutes, your mind will become completely serene.

All you have to do to begin is pay attention.

We must learn to reawaken and keep ourselves awake, not by mechanical aids, but by an infinite expectation of the dawn.—HENRY DAVID THOREAU

Align yourself with nature and accept today's weather. Whatever today's weather may be, it is a necessary part of the cycle of life.

Drop the head game. Cast out the person in your head who goes on talking and talking, asking questions, judging everything, calculating everything.

View each and every location as a temple—a place to discover that which is sacred.

Take a few mindful breaths before you get out of bed each morning.

Listen to yourself objectively.

Whenever you need to come back to yourself, breathe and smile. Sit in the office, in your car, on a bench in a public area, and practice conscious breathing and smiling.

The spiritual path means making a path rather than following one.

Keep your mouth closed. You do not *need* to say anything.

Pay close attention to every word you speak. Respect the power of each word. Your words will become increasingly powerful.

Bring a recurring self-judging thought into your mind, letting it become the object of your attention. Then intersperse it with a few moments of clearing your mind. After you have cleared your mind a few times, you may find that the self-judging thought feels less painful. Soften around the pain of that thought.

Feelings are as ephemeral as the weather. Meditation allows us to ride out the storms gracefully.

Think loving thoughts and perform loving deeds—they are beneficial to your physical and mental health.

Throughout the day, know the position of your body and the state of your mind.

Limit your daily intake of news and periodically go on a news fast.

Meditate on the delicate veins of a leaf, a symbol of the various paths one can take in life.

Exhale deeply—the longer, the better.

True success is about satisfying your spirit with spirit things. Your spirit doesn't want money for toys for your ego. It wants joy, happiness, love.

Before you eat, say three times, "Breathing in, I calm my body. Breathing out, I smile."

During the spring, do a flower-arranging meditation. Choose the blossoms carefully. Look at each flower or piece of greenery. Get a sense of where it was grown and how it blossomed. Cut off the bottom of each stem—carefully, attentively, lovingly. Find a vase that is suitable for the arrangement. Pour water into it. Arrange the flowers one by one. Remain in the moment and do not rush. When you have completed your arrangement, place the flowers where they can be viewed.

Approach a problem obliquely rather than head-on. Sometimes looking at a problem head-on can paralyze you. So shift your perspective, bringing the background into the foreground and vice versa. Try seeing it in a new light, at a different angle, or from someone else's viewpoint.

The essence of mindfulness is to make every moment your own. Even if you are hurrying, hurry mindfully. If you find your mind compelling you to get every last thing done, remind yourself that some of the tasks can probably wait. Or stop completely and ask, "Is this worth it?"

Use your energy positively.

Can you think of any pain in your life that was not caused by change?

Be patient toward bullies.

Peel an onion as a meditation. Increase your attention layer by layer.

Let nature enhance your meditation.

AFFIRMATION: I can do it.

Walk as if your feet were kissing the earth.

MEDITATION ON THE PLATFORM SUTRA OF THE SIXTH PATRIARCH: Awaken to this dharma of no-thought: You will penetrate all things thoroughly and come into the realm of Buddha.

Each time your attention wanders, notice the thought that distracted you, then gently return to the activity. Notice the thought, return to the activity; notice the thought, return to the activity.

Acknowledge that your thoughts are not facts.

BURMESE-STYLE LEG POSTURE: Place both your legs flat along the floor, knee to foot, parallel, one in front of the other.

Give something of yourself.

Before putting your mouth into gear, make sure your mind is engaged.

Trust the simple process of meditation: Follow the instructions—breathe and pay attention—and let go of the results.

Verse for drinking a beverage: This drink is my cup of mindfulness. I hold the present moment in my hands.

Transform sorrow into compassion by meditating: May I [or someone else who is suffering] be free from pain and sorrow. May I [again, insert someone else's name if you wish] be happy and be at peace.

Observe the way a material item, such as a watch, appears to you in the store when you first notice it. Then observe the way its appearance changes and becomes more concrete as your interest in it grows. Finally, observe the way it appears to you after you have purchased it and consider it your own.

Grounding exercise: Sit comfortably and close your eyes. Focus on the root chakra at the base of your spine. On each inhalation, imagine you are drawing strength from the ground up into your spine and body. On each exhalation, feel your strength increase. Maintain an awareness of the connection between your chakra and the ground.

Don't let negative thoughts weigh you down. Imagine each as a bubble. Let them slowly float up and out of your head, each carrying away a bit of tension. Your spirit will soon feel lighter.

Always practice.

Find the sun behind the clouds.

Imagine you are a hermit in a cave, completely alone and free from the demands and limitations imposed by work, family, and the outside world. You tend to your basic needs of food, warmth, and cleanliness, and engage in quiet contemplation. You appreciate the joy of simply being alive. There is really nothing to keep you from living in the present moment. Try to incorporate some of the hermit's peace and freedom into your everyday life.

Lessen your need for control by allowing someone to lead you blindfolded around your home, yard, or even an unfamiliar location. Notice all your feelings of distrust and fear, and the fact that you are safe in spite of them. You can also do this exercise yourself—alone, blindfolded, in a dark house.

Try meditating on your third eye, the middle of your forehead, right between your eyebrows.

Metta PHRASES: May I be free from danger. May I enjoy mental happiness. May I enjoy physical happiness. May I enjoy ease of well-being. Repeat this for others you know.

When the mind calms, you step back a little from the forces of craving and aversion and turn your attention to this moment, discovering your capacity to be delighted by all that is before you.

See how the appearance of the mind and the emptiness of existence support each other.

STEP-COUNT MEDITATION: Notice how many steps you take for each inhale and each exhale. Then count those steps, chanting, "One, two, three . . . one, two, three . . ." or whatever the actual number is. You will soon feel more peaceful and alert.

Believe that life is worth living, and your belief will help create that fact.

Increase your awareness of the intentions that drive your actions. Sit with each intention before deciding to follow it. Sense your feelings. Consider the decision to follow or not follow as a separate moment unto itself. The more aware you are of the nature of your intentions, the more choice you have in acting on them.

Reflect on the fact that death is certain. Recall all the people that you know who have died. Recall all the people that you have heard about who have died.

You can alleviate your own suffering by alleviating the suffering of others. Stop thinking about your own problems: Go and do good for someone else.

Dedicate yourself to valuable goals.

Treat an unexpected person or situation as an opportunity to practice patience and nonaggression.

Cosmic mudra: Put your left hand (palm down) on top of your right hand (palm up), middle joints of your middle fingers together, and touch your thumbs lightly. Your hands will form a beautiful oval. Maintain the mudra with care, as if you were holding something very precious. Hold your hands against your body, thumbs about the height of your navel. Position your arms slightly away from your body, freely and easily—as if you were holding an egg under each arm and did not want to break them.

What matters is whether you are aware of your thoughts and feelings during meditation and how you handle them. Your thoughts are just thoughts—and they are not you or reality. Once you acknowledge that, you are able to step back and see reality more clearly, so you can prioritize and make sensible decisions.

Rest in places of harmony—the sky, the ocean, the breath.

Identify the luminous and knowing nature of the mind that is unclouded by thoughts and conceptual overlay.

Relaxation is not something that you "do." It is a natural response that you allow to "happen." Relaxation is what remains when you stop creating tension.

Maintain a half smile while breathing.

If you are feeling foggy, take a walk to clear your head. Imagine the clouds in your mind dissipating. At the end of your walk, gently shake your head and take three deep breaths.

FOUR-STEP MINDFULNESS PRACTICE FOR HANDLING EMOTIONS:

1) Notice and label each feeling.
2) Cradle your feelings with love and mindfulness.
3) Reflect upon, analyze, and examine what you are feeling.
4) React to your feelings in a wise and deliberate manner.

Remain centered in dignity.

Try to smile at the people you see, or at least look at them directly and acknowledge them as fellow human beings.

OM BREATH: Inhale, silently saying "*Om.*" Hold the breath in your mouth, visualizing life-force energy in the oxygen coming into your body. Force the air against your cheeks, letting them fill to capacity and bulge out. Do this for as long as you can without discomfort. Then discharge the breath quickly and forcefully through your mouth. As you exhale, imagine that your breath is revitalizing every cell in your body.

Even now you may be thinking it's time for another cup of coffee and one of those blueberry muffins. Seems it's always time to be doing something other than what you are doing at the moment.

Pay attention to the way all your muscles feel during a workout.

You can construct a spiritual life from the everyday stuff. Instead of feeling like you don't have time for spirituality, you make the business of everyday living into a spiritual life.

Notice the moment before it is gone.

Balance your feelings. Remember that opposing energies cancel each other out. So if you are overwhelmed with sadness, get angry. Just make sure the opposing energy is of the same magnitude as the first one. With practice, you will begin to free yourself from your feelings.

TEA CEREMONY: Boil the water and arrange your tea cups in a straight line. Scoop out the tea, present the leaves to your guests, then put the leaves in the teapot. Pour some hot water into the pot, quickly pouring it out (to clean the leaves). Now pour some more water into the pot and allow the tea to steep. In a continuous stream, pour the tea from one end of the line of cups to the other, until all are filled. Offer the tea by sweeping your hand across the cups.

Nod to every thing—the lamp, the floor, the chair, the table—showing your respect and appreciation.

Be like the water. Flow, don't fight. Be flexible, yet persistent. Rise and fall like a soothing lullaby.

Live beautifully: Forget about yourself and just go about your work.

See yourself as a small child, fragile and vulnerable, and breathe in. Smile with love to this small child within yourself, and breathe out.

When you are suffering, tell yourself that there is always a remedy and that you have a strong chance of recovering.

Leaving someone alone means allowing them to have their own experience.

Let your thoughts be as light as bubbles.

Commit to enlightenment for the sake of others. Recall again and again the infinite benefits of doing so.

Imagine that you are a wave with the power of the whole sea behind you. You are unstoppable. Feel the life force surging through you.

Remember that you are not in charge of anyone or anything other than yourself. When you finally realize this, you will be free to live.

Be still enough to listen for the answer.

Pass a rosary or worry beads rhythmically through your fingers.

Embrace every minute.

Become more and more conscious.

DEATH MEDITATION: This meditation has nine points, divided into three sections:

1) Inevitability of death: Everyone will die, including you. In the time it takes to read this sentence, you have come nearer to death; life flows on and cannot be stopped. Assess how you spend your life and how much time you spend on beneficial activities like meditation, as well as the pointless things you do.

2) Uncertainty of time of death: Life can end at any time; you cannot know when you will die, so make the most of each moment. There are many causes of death and you do not know what yours will be. Our bodies are fragile and prone to illness, so even if you are well now, this may not last.

3) Only spiritual insight is useful when you die; possessions cannot be taken with us, and friends and family can do nothing when we die. Death is only experienced alone. Even our own bodies cannot be relied upon, and they become useless when we die.

The point of each moment is to forget that there is a point. Be so busy saying "yes" that there is no time to say "no."

When you turn off the television, feel the sudden emptiness in a room now silent. What fills the space?

When performing a chore, focus all your attention on your hands. Note all the sensations in your fingers, your palms, and your wrists.

When you do something, you should burn yourself completely, like a good bonfire, leaving no trace of yourself.—SHUNRYU SUZUKI

Thinking is the speech of your mind. Right Thinking makes your speech clear and beneficial.

Learn the art of drinking tea with mindfulness.

Move and exercise your body to become more complete and vibrant. Your body is a vehicle for the expression of spirit.

Open from the heart. Give fully.

Start your awareness practice with objects. Look at things with more consciousness. When you see a tree, stop for a while. Look at it with more alertness. Suddenly, the tree will appear different—sharper and more meaningful. Expand this exercise to people as well.

Forget about big compassionate thoughts. Just be kind on this breath. Be kind to the one who breathes.

Find the words that lead toward happiness, earn the trust and respect of others, and foster lovingkindness.

Clear away the overwhelming trash and debris of self-imposed concerns, petty resentments and angers, the need to prove yourself right, mean competitiveness, little lies, taking advantage of people who are weak and defenseless, piling up money for its own sake, and all the other aids devised to puff up the ego.

Do nothing. Don't focus so much on keeping your life moving. How about a huge silence?

Right Diligence is breathing in and out and feeling joy and peace.

On a warm day, sit outside in the sun with your eyes closed. Bathe in the warmth. Visualize a warm yellow glow, fed by the energy of the sun, in the *manipura* chakra. Let it spread to fill the rest of your body.

Be like an island that no flood can engulf. Meditate, exercise self-control, remain patient, and live in awareness.

Just practicing meditation once erases countless accumulated sins.—HAKUIN EKAKU

Surround yourself with other brave souls traveling toward enlightenment. Accept their help.

If you are feeling anxious, first notice how anxiety spins its wheels: It expands and expands, eating up valuable time and draining you of productive energy. Then say, "I am sick of thinking about this. Instead of feeling anxious, here are three things I can do." Find three things and stick to them.

Eat mindfully.

Make a note of any images that pop up during meditation. They may form a picture whose meaning will resonate with you.

Use times of suffering or unhappiness as opportunities to pay particular attention.

SILENT PRAYER: Silence is truth, silence is grace, silence heals, silence is real. Silence is within me.

Remember, flowers grow on their own. Doing nothing is often more than enough.

When you are aware that you are caught by a problem, you are already freeing yourself.

Abandon your judgments and concentrate on healing yourself, so that you can become doctor instead of patient.

The mantra is useless when not chanted. The house decays when not repaired. The body deteriorates when not cared for. The guard fails when eyes are closed.

Do you have the inner strength to respond intelligently yet gently to the diversity of opinions in the world?

As you wake up this morning, smile. Twenty-four brand-new hours are before you. Vow to live fully in each moment and to look at all beings with eyes of compassion.

Tap into your deeper essence.

Each time you refocus your wandering mind, you weaken the compulsive cycle and strengthen mindfulness.

With meditation, you will find yourself moving away from habits, leisure pursuits, people, and work environments that stress you. You will gravitate toward people and situations that help you feel calm, supported, and relaxed.

Whenever you find yourself wanting to do something else while in the middle of something you should be doing, stop and exhale as deeply as you can for five minutes. During this time, you are in neutral gear. When the five minutes are over, continue with the work at hand. You will soon find you are finished, and now you can do the other thing you had wanted to do. Keep practicing this technique, and soon you will reach a point where just one exhalation will be enough to put you back on track.

Be like the mountain in the face of a strong wind: firm and steady.

AFFIRMATION: Say, "I am wide awake." Before you go to sleep, review your day, beginning with the evening and working backward toward the morning. Did you do, think, or say anything that you now regret? If so, think about what contributed to that situation and whether you need to make amends or changes. Commit to necessary actions. Give thanks for what you have learned. Then forgive yourself.

Replace thoughts about yourself with thoughts about life.

Engage in simple kindnesses.

Each time you take a mindful step, you are walking from the land of sorrow toward the land of joy.

Think of a cat, asleep much of the time, yet always acutely aware of what is going on around it. It is being itself wholeheartedly, in the present moment, open to whatever occurs.

Learn to quiet your mind at will. Look inward and watch your mental habits and processes, but do not judge. You will know the truth from the depths of stillness.

Wash your hands before an important activity—it is both a practical and symbolic act of preparation.

The more you are willing to just let the world be something you are aware of, the more it will let you be who you are: the awareness.

Adopt a positive attitude in the face of difficulties. Remember that by undergoing them with grace, you are preventing bad karma in the future.

Be less harsh with yourself and others.

Each moment is like a snowflake—unique, unspoiled, unrepeatable—and can be appreciated in its surprisingness.

Silence meditation: For three to five minutes, conceive of the masculine Mind of the Universe, the Mind that manages all things. For another three to five minutes, conceive of the feminine Intelligence of the Universe, the Intelligence that produces all things. Then visualize them joining within you. Discover that although Mind and Intelligence are distinct from each other, they are One. Let the images flow together, like streams converging into a river. Let this Power fill your body. When you are ready, open your eyes and break the silence by saying, "The Power is divided above and below. The One generates itself, makes itself grow, seeks itself, finds itself. It is the mother, father, sister, brother, wife, husband, daughter, son—the source of the entire circle of existence." Look for the Power of the One in your daily life.

Whenever you feel stuck, frustrated, or limited, become aware of where your thoughts are dwelling. Then focus on something else. Do this over and over. Then focus on the breath and dwell upon nothing at all.

Transcend your ego and sense your oneness with life. You will then naturally act for the best.

Experience the wavelike motion of thinking—rising and falling, rising and falling. Riding the wave of your thoughts, you can be perfectly still, even though your mind is still thinking. Focus on the space between thoughts.

Bow by slightly lowering your head and holding your hands directly underneath it in prayer position. Then kneel, sitting on your buttocks. Lay your palms on the ground about four inches apart. Touch your forehead to the ground between your hands.

You are already complete, whole, perfect. All this action and effort to become special is just making you very unspecial and creating tremendous pain and suffering. You are already who you are, and you are already everything you need to be.

Lock into the natural rhythm of your walk, setting the rhythm for your breath like a metronome.

Invite the child you once were to sit on your lap. Place your hands palms up. Invite this child to place its hands on your hands. Feel the warm and trusting fingers nestled within your hands. You are a child of the universe, but inside you the Universal Mother resides. You are sitting in a sacred lap just as the child sits on your lap. Be your breath and be filled with the knowledge and the light.

For a youth, be present even in silence—ready to listen without judgment and with an open mind.

Before you begin cooking, wash and bless your hands. Clear your mind with three deep breaths. As you prepare the meal, think of the people you are feeding, transmitting love from your heart to the food.

When you wake up in the morning, see everything as a miracle, a mystery.

Before filling a bowl with food, see the empty bowl as a pair of hands cupped together.

When experiencing the sadness of loss, look at the root of the emotion. What did you have with that person that you do not have now? Visualize the memories you once shared. Try to re-create the feelings. You will see that you have not lost those things after all.

HIGHER KNOWLEDGE VISUALIZATION: Sit in a quiet, darkened room with a candle lit a few feet in front of you. Concentrate on the flame. Do not blink. When you feel your eyes getting heavy or starting to water, close them. Continue to see the flame through your closed eyelids. If the flame vanishes, try to refocus on it with your eyes still closed. If you cannot, then open your eyes again and look at the flame. Repeat the process. Eventually, you will be able to retain the image of the flame without having to reopen your eyes.

Learn a variety of relaxation techniques and practice at least one technique regularly.

Before spending time and money on unnecessary indulgences, ask yourself, "Do I really need this?"

Do you hear the sounds outside? This is meditation.

Let go of labels.

When washing clothes by hand, scrub them in a relaxed way. Pay attention to every movement—to the sensations of soap and water. When you finish, you should feel as clean as your clothes.

Overcome fear by shifting your concern from yourself to others. When you see the difficulties that they are facing, your own difficulties will seem less important.

If you hurry, you waste precious time—the time for being alive.

EXPANDING BREATH: Exhale completely by flattening your stomach. Now close your right nostril with your right thumb, and slowly inhale through the left nostril. Fill your lungs to a comfortable capacity, and close your left nostril with any finger. Keep holding your breath for as long as possible. Then open the right nostril while keeping the left side closed, and slowly exhale. Repeat this cycle five times, gradually increasing the cycles to twelve.

If you are suffering from confusion or dissatisfaction, take an hour, an afternoon, or several days to reflect on what will truly bring happiness.

You can use sacred words of any language as mantras.

You are in charge of what enters your mind.

Realize that though struggling is exhausting, it can be exhilarating. Making contact, standing up for yourself, and letting feelings out feels good. You get addicted to it. But perpetual struggle is not a good model for communication or growth or change.

The more your mind immerses itself in whatever you are doing, the less you will be plagued by distractions, desires, and self-fragmentation—and the more satisfying your daily existence will become.

Keep the radio or music off while you are driving. Each time you stop at a stoplight, Stop sign, or in traffic, check your awareness level. However, never listen to a guided meditation while driving: Your focus needs to be on the road ahead.

Contemplate the ways in which life depends upon variety—and resolve not to let others' differences disturb your tranquility.

See yourself as a strong warrior, drawing courage from your immense store of power and knowledge.

MEDITATION ON MEETING YOURSELF FOR THE FIRST TIME: Close your eyes and imagine that you are attending a party. A friend comes over and introduces you to . . . yourself. What are your first impressions? How does the conversation go? What behaviors and mannerisms do you observe? From this neutral viewpoint, locate your strengths and weaknesses. Use the awareness you have gained as a basis for personal change.

Be grateful even for difficult emotions, because they have the potential to wake you up.

"SEEING THE BIGGER PICTURE" VISUALIZATION: Take a few moments to stop and become aware of yourself, then broaden your perspective to include everything around you. After a while, let your awareness expand to include everything within a couple of miles around you. Then expand to include everything in the whole country. Finally, let your awareness expand yet further, taking in the entire planet, moving through the solar system. Be aware that you are a part of this planet, but that you are so small, you are essentially invisible. In light of this expansive view of the world, feel how insignificant your worries are. Try to maintain this perspective as you zero back in on yourself. Tell yourself that your worries and concerns are so small that you will have no trouble handling them.

When you meditate, sit down quietly so that you will not generate additional disturbances. As you seat yourself, let your body and mind be mindfulness itself, free from distraction.

Let what you think pass through your consciousness like clouds through the sky.

Create a vision and hold it in your heart. Write it down or describe it out loud. Picture the outcome and include it in your description. Feed this vision by empowering your heart through spiritual effort.

Mindfulness teaches you to calm down and dwell in deep relaxation.

Live in joy and peace, even among the troubled.

During walking meditation, raise your right foot (lifting the heel first), move it forward, and place it on the ground on the in-breath. Then exhale as you shift your weight onto that foot.

Special blessings come to us when we learn to informally meditate while communicating with those we love.

Children, especially young ones, can help us enter into "beginner's mind": the state of pure existence before concepts, conditioning, and defenses insulated us from directly experiencing the world. Be inspired by their joyfulness, and encourage them to expand their love and wonder.

Listen to audio meditations.

Meditation helps you to create a subtle shift from the spinning world inside your head to being here now. Moment by moment, your practice presents you with a fork in the road, a choice between the world you want to set up and the world that really is.

MEDITATION FOR A MEETING: Make this meeting your object of awareness. Open fully to the experience. Focus on the speaker, but be equally aware of the overall significance of everything going on around you. If you find yourself drifting off, simply note these feelings and bring your attention back to the meeting. Sit up straighter and open your eyes wider. If you are called upon to speak, pause for a long breath before responding. After the meeting, go over everything you have learned, no matter how trivial.

If you do not cling, whatever arises naturally disappears.

Whenever you can, be interested in doing one very simple thing in the moment. Think of each moment as a one-pointed concentration.

It's all funny.

Examine your impatience and anger. Eliminate these emotions by believing that everything will unfold in its own time.

Breathing in, feel happy. Breathing out, feel happy.

Tranquility meditation is the basis of all meditation because it stabilizes the mind for concentration. Pay attention to the breath, noticing the sensation at the tip of the nostrils as you inhale and exhale, and count each complete breath if you like.

When you drink water, remember its source.

Once a day, get down on the floor and stretch mindfully. Feel the breath moving in your body. Pay attention to what your body is telling you.

See all beings as enlightened, providing you with the education you need to awaken. Thank them.

Watch television mindfully. When you turn it off, be aware of what you are doing and why.

Stand still. Listen.

Mind and self-existing awareness are present when you abandon all conceptions of ownership and approval—accepting and rejecting, keeping and sending, judging and evaluating.

Ask for nothing and give everything.

Our words are our thoughts with wings. We open our mouths, and our minds fly out.

Gently direct your awareness from one focus to another. Try to focus on one object for as long as you can. Expand to another area when you have stabilized concentration.

Basic breathing meditation: Sit in a comfortable position and let your eyes close gently. Invite your body to relax and ease into the ground or cushion. Let go and accept the nondoing of meditation. Sense and listen to your breath. Feel the air as it goes in and out of your nostrils. Feel the rise and fall of your chest and abdomen. Allow your attention to settle where you feel your breath most clearly. Keep following the breath. Allow it to be exactly as it is; do not control it. See the pause between breaths. Out of sheer habit, thoughts will arise. Just watch them as you would the cars of a train going by. See them, acknowledge them, let them go, and come back to the breath. It does not matter how many times you get caught up in a thought, or for how long. Begin again and bring awareness back to the breath. If a physical sensation arises, watch it the same way that you would watch your thoughts. This is your practice. You are strengthening mindfulness. Awareness of one whole in-breath and one whole out-breath is a big accomplishment. For twenty minutes, follow your breath with singular attention. As you gently open your eyes, try to carry the momentum of your mindfulness into your next activity.

Do you have a genuine passion for truth and enlightenment—or are you just going through the motions?

Be a mentor.

Sit, following your breath. Concentrate on the beginning of your life. Know that it was also the beginning of your death. See that both life and death are manifested at the same time. You are both life and death—two aspects of the same reality—simultaneously.

Just before dawn, go outside and sit where you can watch the sun rise. As it emerges, be aware of the brightening hues of the sky. Rejoice in the beauty of a new day. Feel the sun warm your body and refresh your spirit.

Upon retiring, sleep as if you are entering your last sleep. Upon awakening, leave your bed behind you instantly, as if you are casting off a pair of old shoes.

Meditate on a pentacle (five-pointed star) to align yourself with the cosmos and harmonize the male and female aspects of your nature.

Affirmation: I commit myself to my divine destiny.

Think about areas in your family, your community, and the entire world in which you can contribute time, energy, money, or love.

Find harmony by following the Tao, by accepting the ever-changing patterns of life without judgment or resistance. Let go and trust in the natural flow of events.

When faced with a problem, take a walk in a natural setting and focus on your footsteps. It can give you a fresh perspective.

What is this really?

Rest in openness, consciously do nothing, take it easy while staying alert, repose in wide-awakeness.

Each crackling leaf beneath your feet is a personal invitation to come to your senses.

When driving, cultivate and inhabit your own peaceful atmosphere inside your car.

Write a haiku outdoors. Enter a calm, meditative state of mind and be aware of your surroundings. A haiku usually consists of seventeen syllables, but you can start with eight to twelve words, regardless of the number of syllables. Wait for your haiku to present itself. Once you have written it down, do not try to improve it. Leave it just as it is.

Navigate through life's ups and downs and the storms of the mind and body.

Be mindful of what is feeding your attention. Be conscious of what you read, what you listen to, and what you watch on TV and at the movies. Bring together a high-quality mixture of ingredients to make a yummy life stew.

Welcome sensations of relaxation.

Meditate on the clarity of the mind. Your mind is whatever you are experiencing at this moment—there is no form, shape, or color—just awareness. Try not to reflect on what the mind is; simply experience its pure nature.

You are where you are at this moment because of all the conditions that have created you and sustained you. The entire history of the earth and the cosmos needed to be exactly as it was for you to be exactly where you are. Appreciate the miracle of the life you have been given.

Look deeply at just one sensation in your body. Be with this sensation.

Pursue a livelihood that directly contributes to the well-being of the world and enables you to more fully use your competitive capacities for good ends.

Pay attention to the beauty of the sky just before you get into your car, a bus, or a train, and do so again when you get to your destination.

Delve deeply into the pain of life, pierce its barrier, and transcend beyond suffering.

Five minutes of practice with the sincere desire to wake up to the present moment is worth more than a lifetime of practice without it.

Water wholesome seeds of life through mindful living each moment of your day.

As you sort through fruits and vegetables at the market, recognize that they bear the blessings of life and that all things have a divine radiance.

Express your unique creative spirit.

Spiritual study and contemplation will allow you to see more of the big picture, and will help you gain greater knowledge and power in creating your karma.

Zen paintings capture the essence of objects. Close your eyes and picture a specific object, like a cat or a tree. What are the qualities that makes this object this particular object? Gather together a brush, some black ink or paint, and rice paper or bamboo paper. When you sense a clear image, express it on paper with a few swift brushstrokes. Then study your painting.

View your spiritual teacher as a representative of the Buddha.

With a peaceful heart, whatever happens can be met with wisdom.

Acknowledge even an inkling of fear. Label this emotional response "fear." If you notice your mind dwelling on it and spinning out a story to cover it up, note this and label it as "fear" too.

Breathing strongly and deeply, feel your nostrils, chest, and lungs expanding and taking in more air. Pay attention to the change in your mood.

Love always eases pain.

Synchronize your breath with your mantra.

Active meditations range from tai chi and yoga to intensive cathartic processes. Movement can be either slow or vigorous.

Maintaining silence at mealtime makes you less distracted and more aware of such details as how quickly you eat, how well you chew your food, what foods you really desire, and how much you eat.

Let whatever happens, happen.

Revive the lost art of interesting, animated, meaningful conversation.

Put the Four Noble Truths into action by practicing mindful walking and deep listening all day long.

Choose a negative emotion, and be particularly aware each time this demon arises. Notice everything about it, including what triggers it and what causes it to fade away. Greet it like an old friend, and then let it go.

When you awake in the morning, stretch your arms to the sky and breathe deeply. Fill your insides with the emptiness around you.

Enjoy the indescribable joy and peace of meditation.

Is it possible that what you are complaining about is in reality a blessing? Are you mistakenly viewing as a weed something that is actually a great treasure—and vice versa?

Genuine compassion is based on the recognition that others have the right to happiness, just as you do.

Be aware of an imperfection without turning it into a big problem.

When you look into a mirror, love yourself.

You can always use a chair during meditation. Choose one with a flat, level seat, a straight back, and no arms. Do not lean against the back of the chair. Do not use a chair that is too soft or upholstered, which would induce you to fall asleep.

MEDITATION FOR THE FIRST CHAKRA: Sit quietly, close your eyes, and take a few slow, deep breaths, relaxing. Rest your awareness gently on your perineum, which is on your body about halfway between the anus and genitals. Accept the first image that comes into your mind and sit with it. Is the energy in the chakra healthy and strong, or is it weak, blocked, or struggling? Ask what the chakra would say if it could speak. Don't worry if you don't feel an answer; you are simply "touring" this chakra.

To get more from spiritual reading, read fewer pages at a sitting, but do so slowly and absorb every word. Highlight passages that are particularly meaningful to you.

Schedule a regular ten-minute breath-awareness practice during a quiet portion of your day.

Practice letting go, and you will cultivate inner peace.

Smile when you're angry. Meditate on love.

When you are frustrated or restless, ask, "What am I wishing for now? What is wrong with what I have?" Then say, "This suffices." Welcome what life is offering you in this moment. Accept what you have been given and be satisfied.

Imagine someone massaging your shoulders. Feel them release and relax. Continue the imaginary massage, moving to other parts of your body.

Do every little thing with mindful awareness, and you will be living Zen.

Think of your loved ones as flowers. Gather them into a bouquet.

Imagine taking a warm shower. As the water cascades along your body and down your legs, let it carry away all discomfort and distress, leaving you refreshed and invigorated.

Unlearn the habit of ignoring and regain the freshness of a child's perception.

Concentrate on the now, and the future will take care of itself.

Smile at both the good and the not-so-good inside you. Embrace both.

Releasing the mind, breathe in and out.

Perform a certain number of sit-ups every day, or at least every other day. It's okay if your muscles are not strong enough to do many at first. Just gradually increase them. Focus on your sit-ups as an exercise in building perseverance and character.

MEDITATION ON THE EXPANSION AND CONTRACTION OF THE BREATH: During the in-breath, focus exclusively on those parts of your body that are contracting, such as the tightening of your diaphragm. At the same time, let your thoughts, feelings, and perception of space contract inward and collapse. Let everything contract into an effortless nothingness. There should be no pressure during this contraction—no feeling of discomfort. Now bring your attention to your out-breath. Focus only on those body parts, sensations, feelings, and thoughts that are expansive. Continue to contract on the in-breath and expand on the out-breath. After several cycles, open your eyes. Try to bring this quality of calm awareness to your next activity.

When you speak meaningfully, people will listen. When you speak kindly, people will be joyful. When you speak politely, you will gain friends. When you speak truthfully, you will be trusted.

Inhale negative karma, difficulties, and conflicting emotions. Exhale, turning it into happiness and joy.

Use a half smile to radiate well-being to yourself and to the people around you. Establish contact with others in a warm, kind, and friendly way.

Dance to express your gratitude for living.

When executing a yoga pose, pay attention to your breath. It will help you stretch far and long.

Imagine that the universe is about to whisper the answer to your deepest questions—you do not want to miss it.

Carry with you a small item of meditation, such as a meaningful quote or a pebble. Find calm wherever you go.

Koan meditation: Begin by calming the mind for five minutes, watching or counting the breath. When your mind is calm, try to awaken your true nature by asking, "What is this?" Do not look for an answer. Keep asking the question silently. Reflect that although you could be asking "Who is this?" your question remains "What is this?" because you are shaking off your usual identity and trying to discover the mystery of what you are underneath. Do not speculate; stay with the question and continue to repeat it. Be aware that irritation may arise, but that it will also pass. Keep the question with you as you go about your day.

Scooping the stream qigong exercise: Stand, feet together, hands loosely at your sides, eyes fixed on a point ahead. Inhale slowly as you raise your arms above your head and interlace your fingers, palms up. Stretch your body to its full extent, heels on the ground. Exhale slowly as you lower your arms to your sides. Pause and repeat. Then, bring your hands in front of your navel, palms up, and interlace your fingers to form a scoop. Slowly inhale while raising your arms to bring the scoop up to your lips as if you were drinking water, with your elbows held as high as possible. Hold this position for three counts. Then turn your palms down and lower your arms again, exhaling slowly. Repeat the entire sequence six times.

Meditation for releasing fear: Close your eyes and bring to mind one of your deepest fears. Acknowledge the presence of your fear. Be aware of its existence without getting caught up in it, and observe it without judging yourself for having it. Now imagine the fear as a caged bird, and visualize its appearance in detail. Then imagine opening the cage door and setting the bird free. As you watch the bird fly away, feel that you are releasing the fear from your consciousness.

Learn to appreciate the gift of simplicity.

When you eat, stop every few minutes to check how full you feel.

Inhale the scent of lavender for a quick hit of relaxation. Fresh lavender works best, but real dried lavender or lavender essential oil work well too.

CHANT: *In the early morning the dharma body shines radiantly. / Sitting in meditation, I smile with joy. / This is a brand new day. / I vow to walk through it in mindfulness.*—THICH NHAT HANH

Every thing you do, no matter how small, attaches itself to a larger whole. Live in a loving manner, and pay attention to every action.

Light a candle, turn off the lights, and sit one to two feet away, staring at it for several minutes. When your mind wanders, simply note this and bring your attention back to the flame. Become the flame. Now blow out the candle and close your eyes. Let the afterimage of the flame form on the inside of your eyelids. Watch the flame. Go into the flame. Be flame. Let go and dissolve into the clear light of the natural mind. Meditate.

Walk in a straight line, very slowly and silently, with lowered eyes. Take one step with the left foot while breathing in, and one step with the right foot while breathing out. Be aware of all the parts of your body. When you reach a turnaround point, pause, becoming aware of the fact that you are standing. Then slowly walk again.

Travel meditation: Let your whole body go loose, relaxing any tension, and take some deep breaths. Accept that there is nothing you can do to get to your destination faster. Focus on your breathing and visualize anxiety and worry floating away with each exhalation. Each time an anxiety or worry tries to come back, bring your focus back to the breath and let go. If you want, repeat the mantra "peace" with each exhalation.

Constellation mudra: Lie on your back with your knees bent. Breathe rhythmically for about twenty seconds. Now contract the sphincter muscles (at the opening of the rectum). Hold the tension for a count of five while continuing to breathe rhythmically, and then relax. Repeat six times. Pull the anus sphincter muscle and all the pelvic-floor muscles inward and upward. Hold the tension for a count of three, breathing rhythmically while you do so, and relax again. Practice this mudra for up to thirty seconds.

When talking on the telephone, stay connected with your breath and pay attention to the way the conversation affects you.

Walk around a beautiful flower bed, a garden, your yard, or a park.

The horse in the field knows nothing of breakfast, lunch, and dinner. It eats when hungry. The point of Zen is to follow that same kind of naturalness.

Do you genuinely understand the value of humility?

Wink at your stress. You know you aren't that important.

Imagine a perfect place in which you are completely safe. Take stock of your senses in this safe haven.

When your mind is completely empty, you have achieved purity. Don't think about it . . . or you will lose it again.

Zazen is the experience of emptiness; it's about nothingness. Correct posture is paramount. Make sure your back is straight. Your nose should be in line with your navel, ears squared with your shoulders, chin tucked slightly, lips closed, teeth together, and the tip of your tongue should be resting peacefully at the roof of your mouth, just behind the front teeth. (This is the position the Buddha was in when he received enlightenment.) Start by counting your breaths. If a thought intrudes, go back to "one." This is why most beginners count "one, one, one . . . ,"— for they are always interrupted by thoughts. *Zazen* may sound difficult, but with practice, it will become deeply relaxing.

Bow to your friends.

Silence is a natural mindfulness practice. Silence, a form of inner fasting, is a time-honored way of hearing your own truth.

Follow the practice of nondoing or nonaction. This means allowing an action to accomplish its purpose in accordance with the nature of things and events.

Watch out for mental lists. Let the mind rest on the breath and on life itself, not on these thoughts.

Humming meditation: Sit in a relaxed position with your eyes and lips closed. Start humming loudly enough to be heard and to create a vibration throughout your body. Visualize your body as a hollow tube or an empty vessel, filled only with the vibrations of the humming. Eventually, the humming will continue by itself, and you will become the listener. If you like, alter the pitch and move your body smoothly and slowly. Now stop humming and move into the second stage of this meditation, which is divided into two 7½-minute sections. During the first half, move your hands, palms up, in an outward circular motion. Starting at the navel, move both hands forward and then separate them to make two large circles mirroring each other. The movement should be so slow that it is as though there is no movement at all. Feel that you are sending energy outward to the universe. After 7½ minutes, turn the hands palms down, and start moving them in the opposite direction. Let them come together toward the navel and separate outward to the sides of the body. Feel that you are taking in energy. Do this for 7½ minutes. Then, in the third and final stage of this meditation, sit and lie absolutely quiet and still.

Empty the mind.

BODHICITTA PRAYER: May the supreme jewel *bodhicitta* that has not arisen rise and grow. And may that which has arisen not diminish but increase, more and more. (Say this at the end of a meditation session.)

Learn what you can, act upon these lessons, and share what you have learned through personal example.

Be satisfied with doing well, and do not worry about what others say.

Drink a cup of tea. Taste it. Feel it. Enjoy it. Don't think about the act of drinking.

Monitor your intake of sugar, caffeine, salt, and alcohol.

Heart is what separates good cooking from the idea of food as mere fuel.

Let your integrity and character define you.

If you stop running and listen closely, you may hear the voice of your own inner wisdom.

Remain in a state of perpetual meditation—total awareness, mindfulness, and full immersion in the present moment—ultimate Zen living.

There is no profit in waiting for an event and overlooking the miracle of the present moment.

Giving to others helps you become more mindful of your inner wealth. Give mindfully and watch the effects of your generosity on others and on yourself. Your generosity will transform and purify you.

Make sense out of change by plunging into it, moving with it, and joining in the dance.

Imagine finding yourself alone in a room with someone who has hurt you, or with whom you have struggled for a long time. What would you say to this person? What would you need to let go of so that you could truly listen to his or her reply?

CHORE MEDITATION: Count the number of breaths it takes to complete a certain mundane task, such as vacuuming, folding the laundry, or watering the plants. Number each exhalation, and try not to control the speed or regularity of your breath.

The joy of life lies not in the destination but in the journey.

Do you understand the importance of patience? Do you cultivate forbearance in all situations?

After formal meditation, vow to take with you the benefits of mindfulness.

The body is a mirror of the mind: Your thoughts, emotions, and habits continually shape and mold your body.

Refrain from misuse of intoxicants that can cause loss of awareness.

Pray for humility. Kneel with your head bowed and hands clasped.

The next time you feel an urge to interrupt someone during a conversation, pause. Instead, really listen to the thoughts being expressed. Don't just wait for that person to finish talking so that you can interject. Listen.

AFFIRMATION: I am joyful and free.

Watch an inspirational movie.

Be choiceless.

HEART-CHAKRA *(ANHATA)* MEDITATION: Focus on the middle of your chest. As you inhale, visualize your heart expanding with the light of love. As you exhale, visualize this light radiating from your heart into the world.

Spend time with little children. Try to see the world through their eyes. When they ask questions, try to feel the wonder they must feel as they search for answers to the mysteries of life.

NAMASTE MUDRA: Place your palms together, fingers extending upward in prayer position. Bring your hands to your heart as a gesture of peace and respect, and honor the divinity within you.

Practice beginner's mind: Encounter each moment with fresh eyes and ears.

You may create suffering through the stories you tell yourself. Your mind barrels along with a running commentary on everything, a constant judging of everything and everyone. These stories create separation and a sense of self, and therefore, suffering.

Meditate on situations where you feel a need for control, especially those involving the people who are most important to you. Acknowledge your desire for control, and find the compassion to heal the pain of this desire. Become aware of and accept the world's uncontrollability. Free yourself and drop your need for control.

When you lie down at night, reflect on the day that was. Remember your accomplishments and your frustrations—things done as well as things undone. Examine your behavior and the quality of your life with an honest and unflinching assessment. Recognize repetitive patterns. Assess how fruitful they really are. Then rest.

Channel healing to a body part: Bring your awareness to your hands. Place them on the affected area and close your eyes. Visualize healing energy passing from the top of your head, down your arms, into your hands, and then through your palms into the affected area.

Listen with only one purpose: to allow the other person to express him- or herself and find relief from his or her suffering.

See the sacred and the divine in every being and every thing.

Stop reading or whatever you are doing and imagine that you are going to die in one minute. It brings you into the present moment. You stop fighting, you stop needing, you stop being concerned with physical comforts, you stop wanting, you stop achieving, and you stop maintaining.

When you're really upset, take the opportunity to have a good cry. Life is joy as well as suffering. There is always something bad to counter the good, and something good to counter the bad. So have a good cry. It is one of the best meditations you can have.

Sense the ever-changing waves around us, and breathe and relax. Rest in the eternal present. Learn that no matter what happens, you are home.

Mindfulness is loving all the details of your life.

Simply bring the mind back into the present moment. That's all there is to do.

Train the mind in the direction of having enough, in being free, and you realize that the sense of hunger that you used to cultivate is a major source of suffering. You are much better off without it.

Make every act count.

Labeling your feelings can lessen their impact. By acknowledging—but not indulging—in these negative emotions, you can find peace of mind.

Letting go is the only way out.

See the roots of anger in your body, and breathe in. See the roots of anger in your consciousness, and breathe out.

Accept the present moment. This does not mean resigning to it; it is simply an acknowledgment that what is happening is happening. If you clearly see the present moment, it will guide your actions and show you which choices you should make.

Think of a situation in which you acted badly or inappropriately. Consider how your actions affected the other people involved. Take full responsibility for your actions. Breathe in the responsibility, the pain, and all the negative emotions you feel in reflecting on the situation. Breathe out forgiveness, understanding, and compassion. Continue to breathe this way until you feel cleansed.

When watching television, mute the commercials and follow your breathing. Get up and walk around, look out the window, stretch, and relax your eyes.

Free your mind to be itself.

Open yourself to the whole universe.

Simplicity, patience, compassion are your greatest treasures. Simple in actions and thoughts, you return to the source of being. Patient with both friends and enemies, you accord with the way things are. Compassionate toward yourself, you reconcile all beings in the world.—TAO TE CHING

We are born with empty hands and we die with empty hands. What is the point of laying claim to so many possessions?

In falling asleep, focus on your breath. Then transfer your awareness to your heart. Be aware of its beating, or simply focus on the space in your chest where your heart lies. Visualize your heart, and try to sense the presence of a disk of still white light, its center aligned with the center of your heart, its circumference extending slightly beyond your heart. Spin this disk slowly, gradually increasing its speed. As it spins, visualize a rainbow of colors merging together to form this white light. Fall asleep with the heart disk still spinning.

Instead of acting and reacting impulsively—following your thoughts and feelings here, there, everywhere—watch your mind carefully, and try to deal skillfully with problems as they arise.

Breathe in and out with rapture.

Keep quiet and find out what you are thinking before you speak.

Understand that the journey is as important as the destination. Enjoy every moment and live life fully.

Corpse pose: Lie down and close your eyes. Let your legs relax and flop out naturally, feet about two feet apart. Spread your arms, palms up, away from your sides. Relax your feet, your calves, your thighs, your hips, your buttocks, your lower back, your abdomen, your middle and upper back, your chest, your shoulders, your arms, your hands, and your neck. Let your eyes relax into their sockets, and feel your facial muscles and scalp becoming soft and relaxed. Scan your body for tension, and when you find any, tighten that body part, then relax it. Allow yourself to melt into the floor. Breathe into your abdomen, and with each exhalation, feel the weight of your body sinking deeper into the floor. Focus on the breath. Enjoy being supported by the floor. If your mind wanders, come back to the breath. Stay in the corpse pose for at least five minutes (ten minutes after a yoga session), and then take a deep breath and open your eyes. Come up slowly to a sitting position.

Perform manual labor in a sacred manner, as if it were service to the divine.

Verse for driving the car: This car embodies my legs. It goes where I choose. When I drive with awareness, everyone lives in safety.

Be aware of the fragile and impermanent nature of life.

Reflect on the kindness of everyone you meet.

Sensual feelings and fantasies may come and go during meditation. Acknowledge them. Do not amplify them or get caught up in the details. Bring all your attention to the breath.

When engaging in a group effort, get off to a good start: Set the pace and spirit of the event.

Understand that your feelings are like television channels; if you don't like the channel you're on, switch to another one.

Recognize that the source of suffering is ignorance, which results in anger, hatred, jealousy—all negative emotions. Reflect that suffering can be removed through the practice of morality, meditation, and wisdom.

When you realize that you are irritated, make a half smile. Inhale and exhale quietly, maintaining the half smile for three breaths.

Bow to your food.

Explore your relationship to all the hinderances to a happy life: desire, ill will, sloth and torpor, restlessness, and doubt. Examine each of these hindrances for a day or even for a week.

Ride a Zen horse: Stand with your feet shoulder-width apart. Bring your fists to your sides, wrists facing up. Bend at the knees, keeping your back straight, and lower into a sitting position. Hold this position while breathing evenly. When the position becomes uncomfortable, note how your ego/self wants to be released from the discomfort. Observe this truth without condemning it or identifying with it. Keep your mind relaxed. Let your soul tell you when to end this meditation.

When engaged in activity, keep your attention on your breath.

Here and now you know your faults. Drop them and be done with it.

Strengthen your compassion by working with someone in pain. Take some time to be with that person. Observe your mind's and heart's reactions. Look directly at this person with warmth—as a fellow human being—with a deep sense of connection.

Study your thumb. With each breath, relax it a bit more. Then bring your focus to a single wrinkle or hair on the thumb. If you have trouble focusing that narrowly, go back to the thumb.

If you want to be more articulate, visualize a blue spinning disk at the front of your throat, the *vishuddha* chakra.

Put one foot in front of the other.

Appreciate small gifts and everyday treasures.

Kind words and actions are their own reward.

Do not open your mouth before your brain is in gear.

Act well in the moment.

In renunciation lies a delicious taste of simplicity and peace. Hope for little and have nothing to lose.

At the moment of death, the quality of consciousness influences the rebirth consciousness. Nothing is carried over, but the new consciousness depends on that last moment's level of consciousness.

Just listen. This precise moment contains the whole purpose and meaning for the existence of everything.

Stop, notice, and appreciate what is happening. Even if this is all you do, it is a revolutionary step.

Once in a while, throughout the day, stop, sit down, and become aware of your breathing for a few seconds or minutes. Fully accept the present moment and the way you are feeling. Do not try or wish for anything to change; just breathe and let go into what is happening.

Breathe to the rhythm of your heart.

Take a look at how beautiful you are right now.

VERSE FOR SITTING DOWN FOR MEDITATION: Sitting in the present moment, I breathe mindfully. Each in-breath nourishes love; each out-breath nourishes compassion.

SELF-MASSAGE: Shrug your shoulders and push them back as far as possible. Hold for five seconds and release. Repeat five times. Now put your hand at the top of your arm and knead the flesh firmly, moving slowly toward your neck. Repeat three times for each arm. Press your fingers into the back of your neck and move your fingertips in a circular motion toward the base of your skull. Repeat five times. Holding the back of your head, rotate your thumbs at the base of your skull until you have soothed all the sore spots.

Encourage others.

SPRING *QIGONG* EXERCISE: Bring your palms to your heart, then stretch them to the sides slowly and purposefully. Be like a budding seed opening its case in two halves. Stretch to allow the new growth to spring upward. Start each day with a spring of energy inside you.

Make two little piles of stones each day: one for your positive actions and one for your negative ones. At the end of each day, count up the positive stones and the negative ones. Assess and evaluate your life.

Draw a map of the potential paths available to you. Then meditate on this map with eyes half closed. Previously unseen paths may suddenly reveal themselves to you. Allow your meditation to guide you to the right path.

For ten minutes, notice the ways in which your mind says "no" to life—suppressing your feelings and impulses, judging or rejecting other people, and refusing to accept things as they are. Then, for another ten minutes, just say "*yes.*" Say "yes" to whatever you experience, whomever you meet, however life presents itself to you. Say "yes" to your partner, your kids, your feelings, your body, your face, your life. Repeat "yes" to get you started on life.

Is there a right way to meditate? The answer lies within yourself. Pick the meditation that resonates with you.

As you read this book, become very aware of your body. Take an inventory. You may notice that you are hunched over a little. Maybe you are squinting because of inadequate light. Get in touch with your body right now, exactly as it is. Notice what happens when you shift your position. Pay attention to every detail.

Pay attention to touch. Focus on the sensation of your hands touching each other, your clothes brushing against your skin, and the air moving across your face.

VERSE FOR WASHING DISHES: Each dish I wash is my most cherished child. Each movement contains boundless love.

The best remedy for those who are afraid, lonely or unhappy is to go outside, somewhere where they can be quiet, alone with the heavens, nature and God. Because only then does one feel that all is as it should be.—ANNE FRANK

Notice your fear. Pay attention to the thoughts and images that cause you to fear. Fear comes from anticipating the future and imagining that you won't be able to cope with it. When you see how faulty these expectations are, and come back to the present moment, your fear will start to disappear. Just label your fearful expectations and thoughts "fear, fear, fear," and thrust them aside. Be compassionate and trust yourself.

Take breaks for short meditations, affirmations, and offerings of gratitude. Light a candle, appreciate nature, and hug somebody.

Pause between swallowing one bite of food and picking up the next one.

Meditate on the sound of birds. It will guide you out of confusion and back onto the path.

If you seek revenge, first dig two graves!—CHINESE PROVERB

Meet each moment mindfully, with as much calmness and acceptance as you can muster, and with a sense of your own integrity and balance. Don't worry about problems: Harmonious solutions will appear as you need them.

Use your heart, soul, and senses to live.

You can nourish your mindfulness by doing anything you truly enjoy, like cooking or gardening.

Give thanks for the joy of living.

Sit. Focus on any doubts or worries you might have about meditation. Be completely open to them, not censoring any. Examine each one carefully. The absurdity of most of these worries will quickly manifest. Consciously let go of each doubt, like a balloon floating away and vanishing out of sight.

The more you open to others and show love and compassion, the less you will be obsessed with yourself, and the more confident you will become.

Bow to your tools. Respect the great potential that lies within them.

Smell and savor the aroma of freshly washed linens or brand-new clothes.

If you have no concepts and no anxiety, you will see the Buddha standing in front of you.

If you are overweight, why not accept it as a description of your body at this time? It is all right to love yourself at the weight you are now, because this is the only time you can love yourself. You have to accept yourself as you are before you can really change. When you start thinking this way, losing weight becomes less important—and also a lot easier. By intentionally cultivating acceptance, you are creating preconditions for healing. Acceptance doesn't mean you "like" everything, and it's not a passive attitude that abandons principles and values. Acceptance means simply coming around to a willingness to see things as they are. You are much more likely to know what to do and have the inner conviction to act when you have a clear picture of what is actually happening than when your vision is clouded by judgments, desires, fears, and prejudices.

Relax into the flow. Rest in the flow. Allow your awareness to become more refined with each breath.

Savor the most fleeting delights of your days.

Pick a symbol from your memory that represents something of great significance to you but that is easy to visualize. Make this symbol your lucidity object. Experience lucid dreaming by recognizing that you are dreaming when you see it in your dreams.

Light a candle and brighten the earth.

To gather wisdom, you must follow your own path.

Resting in openness and acting with kindness is the right answer.

Embrace obstacles.

Practice acceptance.

Do not automatically turn on the radio in your car or the television at home, or open a book while you are waiting for an appointment. Do not needlessly occupy your mind. Just be.

Place a teacup on the table in front of you and look down at it. Notice the form of the cup and the space into which the tea is poured. Now concentrate on the space outside the cup. Would the cup be a cup without both its outer form and its inner space? Focus on the direct experience of emptiness-form-emptiness. Allow this wordless experience to fill your mind. Look around the room and notice the subtle interplay between form and emptiness in everything around you.

Stop wishing for the toaster, the water dispenser, or the microwave to work faster. Instead, wake up! Breathe, smile, and settle into the present moment. Waiting for the toast, the water, or your food is an opportunity to experience peace.

Be generous, offer compliments, give accurate feedback, listen carefully.

Inhaling, count, "One, two, three, four, five." Exhaling, count, "One, two, three, four, five."

Enjoy the things you have to do.

Play a game of catch. Never take your eyes off the ball, not even for one second. See how long you can go before your eyes shift away.

When you enter a room, be in a continuous flow, mindful of what you are doing.

Ujjayi BREATHING: Inhale. Close the right nostril with the right thumb and, slowly and smoothly, exhale through the left nostril for a count of four. Continuing to keep the right nostril closed, inhale through the left nostril, again slowly and smoothly for a count of four. Stay centered and breathe slowly and deeply. Now close your left nostril with the ring finger of your right hand. Turn the first two fingers inward to touch the base of the thumb. Continuing to keep both of your nostrils closed, retain your breath in your lungs for as long as you can. Then release the right nostril and exhale slowly, with control, to a count of four. Inhale through the right nostril, close it with the thumb, hold for a count of four, and exhale through the left nostril. This completes one round of alternate-nostril breathing. Repeat this cycle ten times.

To meditate is to listen with a receptive heart.

Step out of your attachment to the past in order to discover who you are at this precise moment.

Meditate while in nature as often as you can, taking note of the state of your heart and your mind. Concentrate on your breath, or focus on the sounds of nature.

Ring a bell three times at the beginning and end of your meditation session. Listen to the sound as it fades, taking your mind deeper into itself at the beginning of the meditation, and bringing your focus back to everyday life at the end.

To eliminate physical discomfort during meditation, begin by sitting with your eyes closed. When you become aware of uncomfortable sensations, allow yourself to move and sit still again. When you begin to feel discomfort again, however, sit through the urge. Notice that it is possible to resist such distractions. Be aware of the restlessness in your mind and the way in which this restlessness is reflected physically. As you continue to sit, you may experience distracting mental visions. As with physical discomforts, do not allow yourself to become attached to them. Let them pass through your mind and float away. Keep coming back to your breath, again and again.

Find your way toward the practice of peace, until it becomes a way of life.

Why turn meditation into some holy and separate ritual when you can sit, stand, walk, and lie down in awareness?

Live as you will wish to have lived when you are dying.—CHRISTIAN FÜRCHTEGOTT GELLERT

Meditate with incense. Breathe and focus your awareness on the smell of the incense as it enters your nostrils during each inhalation.

Real meditation is spontaneous. It is welcoming without choice. In this openness, live in the now.

It is normal to experience moments of doubt when attention wanes and resolve weakens. Acknowledge the doubts and be alert to sabotaging thoughts. Sustain your attention on the breath.

Recognize your inherent oneness with all things—and begin the process of slowing down within.

Go on a gratitude walk for twenty to thirty minutes. Look around and appreciate the great, pleasing, beautiful, funny details in each and every thing.

Breathe in for a long time. Note that you are breathing in for a long time.

AFFIRMATION: I have a right to express my truth.

Stimulate your curiosity and sense of wonder.

Light a candle at dinner. Between bites, stop and concentrate on the flame.

Watch your habits; they become your character.

Let go of the unkindness you feel toward yourself. Say, "For all of the ways I have harmed or hurt myself, knowingly or unknowingly, I offer forgiveness." Make forgiveness part of your daily meditation, and let your intention to forgive yourself work over time.

You do not need perfect quiet to meditate. It isn't the noise that bothers you but rather your judgment about the noise.

If you have to make a decision, stop for a moment and close your eyes. Focus on your breath. Imagine that you are having a private meeting with your own spiritual guide. Listen with your heart for intuitive guidance on what to do next. Just sit and wait for the answer.

Take one step. Once you have taken that step, you can commit to taking another.

Contemplate every detail of eating a meal: looking at the food, arranging the food, bringing the food to your mouth, bending your neck forward, feeling the food touch your mouth, placing the food into your mouth, closing your mouth, withdrawing your hand, touching the plate again, straightening your neck, chewing, enjoying the food's taste and texture, swallowing the food, and feeling the food touch the sides of your throat as you swallow.

Meditate on whatever provokes resentment in you.

Give thanks.

Can you watch the movie of your life without being overwhelmed or taking it too seriously?

Bow to the ingredients of your life.

Note the position of your hands during formal meditation. Does their placement influence the meditation?

Spend as much time outside as you can.

Pay attention to the aroma, color, and texture of a flower.

Only by being fully present and cultivating gratitude, generosity, and kindness can we find the renewable source of happiness in ourselves at each moment.

When angry, practice mindful breathing and/or mindful walking to embrace and accept your anger.

Change a destructive emotional pattern. Every day for fifteen minutes, when you are feeling good, sit down and experience that destructive emotion—but do not release it. Go almost crazy with the emotion, but repress it in every way. When the fifteen minutes are up, relax. See if this exercise forces your pattern to change.

With each weed you pull up, you make room for fresh green grass. Prune the garden of your mind.

Meditate on a candle. Once you have stabilized your vision of the flame, visualize it rising from the candle and floating into your heart. See the flame's light growing within you, becoming a warm magenta color. Let this magenta-colored light surround your body like an aura, radiating peace and self-love. When the time feels right, watch the flame return to normal. As this visualization ends, keep the warmth and strength of that inner love and peace within you.

As soon as you notice that you are lost in a story, you are no longer lost in the story. Let go of the story, and you will be back in the present moment.

Hold a *mala* in your right hand. Move it bead by bead with the thumb and middle finger as you repeat a mantra. Pause between recitations. Rest in the moment of silence between each mantra. Once you have circled the strand and reached the *meru*, which represents wisdom, you can start again. But this time, move the beads in the opposite direction.

Neither praise nor blame moves the wise person.

PRAYER: Grant that I may be given appropriate difficulties and sufferings on this journey so that my heart may be truly awakened and my practice of total liberation and universal compassion may be truly fulfilled.

Laugh when you see yourself getting caught up in something minor.

Increase your sitting meditation by five to ten minutes each day. Finish each sitting period with a few minutes of *kinhin* walking.

Become your activity, and the "I" is forgotten. There is simply music—everywhere and in everything.

If you are not able to speak calmly, do not speak.

Whatever pleasure you feel, send it out to others.

Do you apply ethical principles to daily decisions?

If someone embarrasses or insults you, do not join in by answering back.

Every morning, affirm the primary in your own being. Start the day with a mindful jump.

Sit quietly. Watch your thoughts and feelings pass in front of you.

On a rainy day, sit in a sheltered place. Close your eyes and breathe deeply three times. Become present with the natural sounds of the water splashing down on the leaves, the grass, the roads, and the buildings.

VERSE FOR CALMING THE MIND: Chasing after the world brings chaos. Allowing it all to come to me brings peace.

When waiting, wait mindfully. Create a sacred moment. Breathe in and out three times, refreshing yourself through awareness.

Just let negative feelings settle. Trying to force calm will only create further agitation.

Prepare for meditation with *bandhas* and deep breathing. This intensifies the energy of *prana* in the body.

Join a talk forum online and answer someone's question.

Take a hot-cold shower. Start with hot water. Breathe in the smell of the shampoo and soap. Keep your head under the water for a long time. Be conscious of your breathing. Let the water massage you. When you are ready, switch to cool water. You may have to adjust gradually, but it will feel refreshing. Move with awareness when you finally turn off the shower and dry off.

Hold a bell in your hand. Become totally alert, as if your life depended on it. The sound is going to come, and you are not going to miss its beginning. When you feel that your mind is without thought and that you are totally alert, close your eyes. Ring the bell. Hear the sound the instant it's created, and move with it. The rings will grow slower and slower, subtler and subtler, and soon they will disappear. Continue to hear and move with the sound. Now ring the bell again. Again, be aware and alert. Keep ringing the bell each time the sound disappears. Move with the sound to the very end.

Each of us has experienced what happens when we do not communicate or when we have said something that is not true or genuine or beneficial. Relationships are weakened or disappear. Communication that is open, truthful, genuine, and compassionate creates a sense of communion.

When you are happy, meditate for a few moments and be grateful for that feeling.

The secret of the mountains is that the mountains simply exist, as you do. The mountains exist simply, which you do not. The mountains are. Their meaning cannot be expressed in words.

Don't worry about a good idea or solution getting lost during meditation; what is of value will become available at the proper moment.

Act with a deep understanding that "This is it."

To calm anxiety, begin by saying, "Stop," and pause from your current activity. Breathe slowly and deeply. As you exhale, imagine that time is expanding. Continue to breathe slowly and deeply, each time lengthening the out-breath. After a couple of minutes, resume what you were doing with a calmer mind.

CHALICE MUDRA: This is the mudra of blissful energy. Cup one hand within the other, forming an oval, and joining the thumbs tip to tip. Place your hands on your lap.

If you do something that creates suffering, acknowledge exactly what you are doing.

Pay attention to the movement of a child at play.

DIGESTION MEDITATION: Imagine the enzymes in your stomach breaking down the food you have eaten. See the nutrients being absorbed into your bloodstream and then being transported to every cell in your body. Picture the cells turning them into energy, keeping you healthy and strong.

Offer all wonderful things—including your body, your resources, your virtue—to the Buddhas and bodhisattvas.

Select a specific period of time in the day to be aware of the intentions behind your desire to speak. Use your observations to evaluate whether you should or should not speak.

Practice the four aspects of Right Speech for a week each: abstaining from lying, abstaining from telling tales, abstaining from harsh language, and abstaining from frivolous talk. How does each abstention feel? Work with patience and perseverance.

In walking meditation, notice the thought, return to the walking; notice the thought, return to the walking.

Start your day, every day, with the intention to be more mindful.

Perform concentration meditations to narrow and focus the flow of your attention.

Do everything with a mind that lets go.

First and foremost, awaken compassion and eliminate selfishness.

When asked a question, try to pause for sixty seconds before answering. It is likely that your answer will include reflection, examination of intention, preview of tone—all the things that make for wise response.

Savor this precious breath.

Whenever you find yourself just sitting, relax your lower jaw and open your mouth slightly. Try to make your breath very shallow and relax your whole body. Start feeling a smile in your inner being. Let this smile spread from inside your belly throughout your whole body.

MINDFULNESS VOW: Aware of the suffering caused by the destruction of life, I am committed to cultivating compassion and to protecting the lives of people, animals, plants, and the earth.

Meditate on the fact that only you can attain your own enlightenment; no one else can do it for you.

Dance under the full moon.

Paint the walls of your mind with many beautiful pictures.

Explore your awareness. Notice exactly what it feels like. What are you most aware of? Are they internal or external sensations? Thoughts and fantasies, or moment-to-moment sensory experiences? Your exploration of your awareness will tell you something about yourself.

Holding your focus on an object trains your patience so that when a moment of anger arises, you may be able to refrain from angry speech and actions. It may even help you generate love and compassion on the spot.

EMOTIONAL-BALANCE MEDITATION: Start by drinking a glass of pure, room-temperature water. Now sit cross-legged on the floor, or upon a bolster or blanket, so that your knees relax down and are comfortable. Relax your shoulders. Keep the chest lifted and place your arms across your chest, locking your hands under your armpits, palms open against the body. You can keep the thumbs outside the armpits. Now close your eyes. Raise your shoulders toward your earlobes as far as possible, and hold them there. Lock your neck by contracting your neck and throat back into your spine, chin pulled back toward the neck, without tipping the head forward. If you do this correctly, you will feel that the cervical vertebrae are in alignment with the spine. You are essentially applying a brake to your brain. Start by maintaining this position for three minutes and work up to eleven minutes.

Study simplicity.

Most of us find that when we eat mindfully, we eat less. Our food consumption goes down, but our satisfaction goes up.

Mindful communication means not only being as clear as possible, but as compassionate as possible. Refrain from engaging in any act that causes harm to yourself or others.

Spend at least five minutes of each meal in silence. If you engage in conversation, keep the topics light, uplifting, and supportive.

Be gentle and kind to yourself.

THREE-STAGE BREATHING: Sit comfortably, with your eyes closed. Put one palm on your belly and the other on your chest. Inhale into your belly for three counts, then into your chest for another three, and finally into your throat for a last three. Then exhale from the belly for three counts, from the chest for three counts, and from your throat for three counts. Repeat this cycle nine times.

Take a step toward inner peace by accepting whatever is happening in the present moment. Silently say "yes" to your feelings and thoughts, to the sensations within your body, the sights you see, and to the sounds you hear. Allow what is there to simply be there, without wishing for it to change in any way.

If you feel drowsy, open your eyes and either scan the body or follow the breath.

CONFIDENCE VISUALIZATION: Relax and let all the tension drain out of your body. Take three deep breaths, then breathe naturally. Visualize yourself entering into an upcoming challenging situation. See yourself exuding confidence. Keep this image for as long as possible. Reinforce the visualization by repeating an affirmation such as "I can handle this," or "I am very confident."

Live purely.

Each morning, before you go to work, reinforce your resolve to stay as calm and relaxed as possible. Meditate for a short while.

Instead of lamenting or wishing, just continue with the life you are already living.

DALAI LAMA'S PRAYER: For as long as space endures, and for as long as living beings remain, until then may I, too, abide to dispel the misery of the world.

When thoughts or images of another's suffering arises in your mind, bring your attention to your heart, letting yourself be touched by the pain, and feel lovingkindness and concern for that person. You may also want to repeat the phrase "May you be free of suffering" to further develop your compassion.

Seek and touch the silence underneath.

In walking meditation, focus your mind by silently repeating a mantra or meaningful phrase.

Be guided by principles instead of reacting to momentary conditions or temporary circumstances.

Each meal is a means of attaining enlightenment.

Let go of the layers of relentless need and the thirst to accumulate.

If you're constantly thinking about what you'd rather be doing—getting off work, driving a more expensive car, eating a decadent dessert—your mind is starving for mindfulness. Focus your attention on what you're doing. Don't miss out on your life.

Make every attempt to leave your mind in its present, natural state, without thinking about what happened in the past or what could happen in the future. Let your mind flow of its own accord, until it becomes like clear, still water.

Be grateful for the protection and security provided by your home.

When struggling with a difficult feeling, just sit with the feeling. Try to identify the source of this emotion. Pay attention to the sensations. Now gently let it go. Feel it gradually dissolve. If the thoughts that gave rise to this emotion still remain, do not try to push them away; simply distance yourself and observe them as if they did not belong to you. Let them fade away.

Close your eyes and see clearly. Stop trying to listen and hear the truth. Be silent and your heart sings. Seek no contact, and find union. Be still and move forward. Be gentle and need no strength. Be humble and remain whole.—PARAPHRASED TAOIST MEDITATION

Ask, "Is this item useful to me? If not, why do I want to keep it?"

The past is over. The future will never come. Now is the only moment that you will ever exist.

MINDFULNESS VOW: Aware of the suffering caused by unmindful speech and listening, I am committed to cultivating loving speech and deep listening in order to bring joy and happiness to others. Knowing that words can create happiness or suffering, I am committed to speaking truthfully with words that inspire confidence, joy, and hope. I am determined not to spread news that I do not know to be certain, and will not criticize or condemn things of which I am not sure. I will refrain from uttering words that could cause division or discord, and I will make every effort to reconcile and resolve all conflict.

For seven days, say, "*yaa boo*" softly a few times, then allow yourself to cry for twenty minutes, for no reason at all. When you are all cried out, just sit and let go.

The more you practice ethics, meditation, and wisdom, the more difficult it will be for you to act contrary to those qualities.

Be grateful that one more day has been given to you.

Focusing your effort on the present, you will experience a spaciousness and ease of mind which comes from letting go of attachments. Enjoy the satisfaction that comes from effort.

Say "no" to negativity. Negativity can be self-fulfilling. So if a negative thought crosses your mind, immediately change it into a positive one. Drop it immediately.

Through meditation, awareness, and effort, you can learn to keep your center open. You just relax and release. There is nothing worth closing your heart over.

DIVINE VOICE MEDITATION: Every night before you go to sleep, sit in your bed for fifteen minutes. Start making a monotonous, nonsense sound, such as *la la la*, and wait for your mind to supply new sounds. Do not speak any actual words; just utter unfamiliar sounds and syllables. Do this for fifteen minutes. (You want your unconscious to speak freely here. It may feel strange at first, but you will soon get the knack of it.) Then lie down, silent and still, for fifteen more minutes, before going off to sleep.

Every morning, pretend that your whole life has to be lived in this one day.

Practice contentment during meditation. Cultivate gratitude for what you have been.

Remember that you are on an adventure.

Purify your actions to prevent bad karma.

Being frugal means having a high joy-to-stuff ratio. If you get one unit of joy for each material possession, you're being frugal. But if you need ten possessions to even begin registering on the joy meter, you're missing the point of being alive.

Pay attention to your thoughts—but do not mistake them for who you are.

Paint or draw the Celtic cross. Place it at eye level and meditate on it.

Look for what you can give, not what you can get.

Everything hinges upon how you look at things. Learn to see not what you want to see but what is. What is is usually a thousand times better than what might be or ought to be.—HENRY MILLER

Be your own Zen master: When you catch yourself in a rut, do something absurd. It will feel very strange, but you will find that it will stop you from taking your habits so seriously. Find new ways to respond to each moment.

VERSE FOR FLUSHING THE TOILET: My body's waste is compost. Down the drain it goes, returning to the earth.

Intending, be aware of intending.

Cultivate a way of speaking that is simple and spare. Cultivate deep listening and loving speech.

Each time you open the blinds or curtains, think about lifting the veil over enlightenment.

Recognizing the emotion at the very moment it forms, understanding that it is but a thought, devoid of intrinsic existence, and allowing it to dissipate spontaneously so as to avoid the chain reaction it would normally unleash are all at the heart of Buddhist contemplative practice.—MATTHIEU RICARD

Let go of your battles and open your heart to what really is.

Pursue every activity with this single intention: Be gentle, kind, thoughtful, caring, compassionate, loving, fair, reasonable, and generous—to everyone, including yourself.

When washing the dishes, consider each dish and utensil to be sacred. Perform this task as if it were the most important duty in your life.

While breathing in, count, "One, one, one . . ." until your lungs are full of fresh air. While breathing out, count, "Two, two, two . . ." until your lungs are empty of air. Breathing in again, count, "Three, three, three . . ."; breathing out again, count, "Four, four, four . . ." Count up to ten, and repeat as many times as necessary to keep your mind focused on the breath.

Whenever possible, do just one thing at a time.

Take advantage of moments when you feel naturally meditative. Sit down and meditate.

Return to the breath with patient perseverance.

As mindfulness gets sharper, you begin to be aware before talking. The intention to speak arises, and you are mindful of it.

Acknowledge your place as part of a greater whole. Close your eyes and ask for help in understanding the universal spirit.

When you are grounded in calmness and moment-to-moment awareness, you are more likely to be creative, more likely to see new options and new solutions to problems, more likely to be aware of emotions and not get carried away by them, and more likely to be able to maintain your balance and perspective in trying circumstances.

Meditate or simply look at the open sky—anything that encourages you to stay on the brink and not solidify into a view.

Develop a friendly state of mind, for as your friendliness increases, your ill will will lessen.

AUTUMN WATER-GAZING MEDITATION: Sit by the water. Count your breaths as though they were waves, rising and falling. Let the water wash away your cares as water washes away dirt. Let it carry you home.

AFFIRMATION: I am loving and worthy of being loved.

Visualize diving into a warm, calm lake. It is perfectly clear and completely silent under the water. You are in awe of the beautiful lake bed. When you are ready, return to the surface and retain the silence, purity, and beauty of this experience.

Meditate on your greatest achievements and the conditions that led to your success. See that your success was dependent on other conditions that were not within your control.

Release the past to enter the present.

Explore the relationship between your body and mind, particularly that between your mental state and any physical pain.

Remember, only an unhappy person acts in a nasty way. A happy person acts and speaks in a happy way and doesn't make others angry. The person you are so angry with is suffering, experiencing unhappiness. Have some compassion for that person.

To talk a lot unnecessarily is like allowing thousands of weeds to grow in a garden. It would be better to have a flower.

The object of meditation is not to stop the mind, but to develop a healthy relationship with the act of thinking.

Melt. Flow. Evaporate into the bright sky.

Be aware of all the heat your body generates. Think of your essence as a flame, and rest in that flame.

Mindfulness is not clinging, not condemning, not identifying with anything. As you grow more mindful, your mind will become lighter and freer.

Let your worries go, if you want to fill your heart with love.

Consider a situation that has been troubling you. Think about it, but do nothing. Stop all unnecessary activities and thoughts. Just take a walk. Enjoy the moment. After a week, observe the changes that have taken place.

Turn the smallest detail—making a salad for dinner, arranging flowers in a vase, or washing windowpanes that gleam in the sunlight—into a masterpiece.

Refrain from harming others either physically or verbally, even if you are embarrassed, insulted, or reviled.

Live neither amid the entanglements and intrigues of other people, nor hidden away in a world of inner feelings. Be serene in the oneness of things.

Happiness is a process, not a destination. So work like you do not need money. Love like you have never been hurt. Dance as though no one is watching.—ANONYMOUS

Awareness is your true self; it's what you are. You need to notice how you block awareness with thoughts, judgments, and so on.

Objects of meditation:

- Physical: candle
- Anatomical: breathing, hearing, seeing
- Mental: thinking
- Movement: walking
- Process: eating
- Phrase: mantra, sound, chant

Remember that the truth is already inside you.

Wouldn't it be wonderful if children in school learned to calm and focus their minds a little and then practiced sitting opposite another person and really paying attention to that person for a few moments?

Even thirty seconds of meditation a few times a day can transform and improve your life. If you simply pause long enough to be aware of your breathing and say, "I am breathing freely," you will awaken your whole-body consciousness. Listen to nature.

Allow one hour every weekend for your mind to play; do some crossword or jigsaw puzzles, card or board games, or math problems.

Whatever situation you are in, you can stop long enough to allow yourself a steady grasp on what is going on and an understanding that you have a choice about what to do or not do.

Breathing in, smile; breathing out, let go.

Identify and water the positive seeds every day.

Empty the cup of the mind.

Emulate the Buddha.

Meditation is an oasis from doing—an opportunity to just be, without strategy or agenda. Play with a few different techniques, then stick with your favorite one.

Make your whole life a meditation. Watch the water in the bath or shower. Watch your breath while lying in bed. Analyze your thoughts while walking through the shopping mall.

NAME-OF-GOD MEDITATION: Start and end each day with a brief meditation on a divine name you have selected. The names most often used are Yod He Vav He (Jehovah, the Brilliant Name of Fire) and Ahavah (Love), but feel free to choose a name that best reflects your beliefs. Ask God to favor you with grace, love, and wisdom. Repeat the name over and over while visualizing its harmony, beauty, and splendor glowing in your heart. Feel the warmth in your heart area. Thank God for what you have received.

Breathe in, sensitive to pleasure; breathe out, sensitive to pleasure.

Understanding and loving are indivisible. Great understanding comes with great love.—TAO SHAN

Be aware of the needs of those around you, and express your natural compassion.

Every night, before you close your eyes, take a moment to offer thanks for a night of safety and a warm, dry place to sleep.

ROOT (*MULA*) *BANDHA*: Sit cross-legged, inhale deeply, and contract your perineal muscle (between the rectum and genitals). This lock prevents the escape of *prana* from the lower body.

Let yourself go, drop all the anxieties of the day, and allow yourself to sink into the peaceful pool of your quiet mind.

Use breaks during the day to fine-tune your meditation.

Always end your mantras with a period of silence. This allows the vibrational aspects of the mantra to settle within you, where they will resonate through the chakras, stimulating and awakening them.

Live in nonjudgmental consciousness, simply watching and understanding.

Write a poem about the beauty around you.

Practice mindful breathing in any situation—sitting, lying down, standing, driving, or working. It will bring you more awareness and concentration.

Focus on just one of your senses, and see if you can increase your perceptions. Experience your external presence.

Move your energy away from your head and into your heart. Your problems will start to disappear, for most are created by the head. Your heart will help clarify your situation.

When fear arises, let it grow, and then watch as it peaks and fades away.

Look into the meditation practices of other cultures. You may wish to adopt particular features.

EARTH MOTHER MUDRA: Join the index finger of each hand to the first joint of the thumbs, keeping the palms turned downward and either touching the ground or resting on the knees. This mudra represents oneness with the earth.

When you come to a kind of honesty, gentleness, and good-heartedness, combined with clarity about yourself, there's no obstacle to feeling lovingkindness for others as well.

Hell is created by your thoughts, and so is heaven.

Take a conscious nap.

Power breathing: Inhale powerfully through your nose while lifting your arms straight up over your shoulders. Now exhale powerfully through your nose, bringing your hands down and resting them upon your shoulders. Repeat this sequence as quickly and as intensely as possible for sixty seconds. The more powerfully and rapidly you breathe, the more you will feel. Finally, take one last deep breath and hold it until you exhale.

You can practice receiving violent words and actions aimed at you and transforming them into flowers, like the Buddha. The power of understanding and compassion will give you the ability to do this.

In warm weather, do a walking meditation in water.

Lie on your back, close your eyes, and let each part of your body settle, from foot to head.

Explore what length of meditation time works best for you.

Let your neck muscles go limp. Sit comfortably, putting your palm behind your head at the base of your skull. Let your head rest back upon your hand, staying in that position for a few breaths. Breathing in and out, feel the wavelike undulation up the spine into your skull. Then take your hand away and put it in your lap. Let your head gently flop backward. Now imagine your brain going limp for a minute. Savor the feeling of relief.

Whenever you feel restless, exhale deeply, throwing the air out of you. Then pull in your belly, holding for a few seconds without inhaling. When you can't hold any longer, inhale deeply. Then pause for three seconds. Repeat the entire cycle. Your disruptive mood will gradually disappear.

Laugh.

With amusement and great affection, patiently gather your mind back again and again as gently and lovingly as you would a puppy.

If you can cultivate wholesome mental states prior to sleep, and allow them to continue right into sleep without getting distracted, then sleep itself becomes wholesome.—DALAI LAMA

MINDFULNESS VOW: Until I reach enlightenment, I seek refuge in Buddha, the doctrine, and the supreme spiritual community. Through the collections of merit of my generosity, morality, patience, effort, concentration, and wisdom, may I achieve Buddhahood in order to help all beings.

Open the door to your heart.

Reflect upon the quality of effort you are bringing to your life and to your meditation.

Recognize your limits. Be gentle with yourself. Watch what happens as you either approach or withdraw from sources of suffering.

Dance with life. Don't try to control it or figure it out.

Verse for after a meal: My plate is empty. My hunger is satisfied and my body's strength is fully restored. I use my power for the benefit of all. May all beings have the nourishment they need.

Reward yourself with a fifteen-minute *savasana* break every day. Think of this deep relaxation practice as a gift to yourself, your family, and the world.

Mindful exercise means keeping the body and mind involved together in an exercise activity. No books, headphones, Web surfing, or any other distractions.

Give energy, get energy.

Create a "relaxation button." Practice using a particular breathing technique that works well for you, and in your mind, pair it with a regular event of daily life. You can then set this event as a special time when you will relax and practice using your preferred breathing technique.

By courageously exploring your pain, you can go through the doorway to expanded consciousness.

Mindfulness teaches you to temporarily suspend all concepts, images, value judgments, mental comments, opinions, and interpretations.

There are many levels on which you can strengthen and awaken compassion in your life. You can practice your compassion in silence as you sit.

When you realize you are stressed out or overwhelmed, simply remember to breathe.

By meditating on each of the four elements (earth, fire, water, air) within yourself, you can see the wholeness of the human body. Start by meditating on one element per meditation session, and eventually you will incorporate all four elements into a single meditation session. Begin with the element of earth. Focus on the solidity of your body as you sit, feeling yourself becoming heavy. Next, move on to the feeling of warmth—the element of fire—pervading every part of your body, starting at your toes and moving upward. Then focus on your blood—the element of water—flowing through each vein and artery. Finally, breathe deeply and feel the expansion of the abdomen and chest with the element of air. Return to focusing on your body. Extend your awareness so that it is united with the earth. Feel warmth and feel connected with fire. Feel moisture or blood flow and feel at one with water. Feel your breath and feel a deep bond with air.

Calm your monkey-mind by making it singular in its focus rather than scattered and distracted.

Sit next to a tree and make friends with it. Wait for the tree's responses to come to you.

Your vision will become clear only when you look into your heart. Who looks outside, dreams. Who looks inside, awakens.—CARL JUNG

Do not rush washing the dishes so you can do something afterward.

Engage your senses of hearing, sight, smell, touch, and taste as you prepare food. Listen to the sound of the knife hitting the chopping board. Open bottles of spices and smell their rich scents before using them. Whenever you can, use your hands to mix instead of utensils or machines.

Imagine that in front of you is a large open palm. Climb onto the cushioned palm and curl up. The hand closes in protection around you. The hand then gently rocks you and you feel loved, safe, and warm.

PRAYER: May I practice dharma from now until enlightenment is reached.

In the dining room, receive each meal prepared for you with gratitude and delight.

Finishing, be aware of finishing.

Think of yourself as totally complete, like a seed or a bulb. All that you seek lies within you. To live a life of peace, you need nothing more.

Meditative prayer approaches God with humility and devotion, contemplates His divine qualities, and invites His presence into the heart of the meditator. It is not the same as "ordinary" prayer, which includes complaints, confessions, and requests.

When you are practicing outer presence or flow, try stating a specific goal out loud such as "While washing the dishes, I am going to focus on the sound of the water and the dishes being scrubbed." This verbalization will help you know exactly what to return to when you find you have gotten lost in your thoughts.

As you inhale, pause to envision the billions of atoms of air soaking through your lungs into your bloodstream, being carried to nourish and energize every cell and fiber of your body. As you exhale, pause to envision that through the power of your intent and imagination, you are able to imbue the energy bundles of each atom and molecule that you exhale with your unique blessings. Envision that each breath is offered as a blessing to the countless beings who are breathing. Become a great cosmic air purifier.

Breathing in, observe the fading of everything. Breathing out, observe the fading of everything.

Learning to slow down the thought process is difficult. Be patient.

It is good to continually ask yourself why you meditate. It is also good to keep track of your values, to remember what is really important to you.

Whenever you are spending time with a person, always remember that it may be for the last time. Do not waste your time together with trivia, creating small troubles and conflicts that do not matter.

When you eat, eat slowly, and listen to your body. Let your stomach tell you when to stop eating, not your eyes or your tongue.

Sing, chant, or pray until you totally forget yourself and lose yourself in your actions. Then stop and drop into a moment of inexpressible being, completely beyond concepts, stories, and strategies.

Meditation for a person you know who is suffering: May you find peace. May you find healing. For whatever words or actions I have expressed that have harmed you, I ask your forgiveness. I forgive you for the words and actions you have expressed that have harmed me. May I be at peace. May I find the trust and openness to befriend my anger and fear and to soften the harshness I feel.

Whenever you want to change a pattern of the mind that has become a long-standing habit, breathing is the best way to introduce change.

Concentrate on an object—any object—resting in front of you. Close your eyes and draw your attention inward. What do you see in your mind's eye now? You can do this exercise with your other senses too, such as hearing.

Use a red traffic light as a signal of mindfulness, reminding you to stop and enjoy your breathing.

You can reduce stress only by getting out of your head and showing up for what is happening right now. Once you learn how to be present through your meditation, you need to keep being present again and again, moment by moment.

Read Sufi stories and meditate on them.

Devote each day to the good of all beings.

Can you eliminate some things you do, like reading Internet news sites more than once a day? Can you leave for work a little earlier so it won't be as stressful? Can you plan a few midweek meals so that the ingredients are at hand? How about slowing down when you wash the dishes or brush your teeth?

From the depths of your heart, admire your own virtues and the virtues of others. Take joy in the good things you have done in this life and in previous lives, thinking, "I really did something good." Take joy in the virtues of others, including those of Buddhas and bodhisattvas.

To create peace in the world, you must be unruffled within. Walk in stillness, and act in harmony. The serenity that emanates from you will create peace.

You are free when you let go: Nothing that arises can pull at you, because there's nowhere for it to stick.

Make offerings to religious organizations.

Let go of as much as you can before you sit to meditate.

Be willing to be present with whatever arises, no matter what it is.

Walking meditation leaves no time for grasping.

Stand before a mirror in your bathroom, first looking into your reflection. You are looking, and the reflection is the subject of your gaze. Then change the whole situation, reversing the process. Start feeling that you are the reflection, and the reflection is looking at you. You will immediately feel a fundamental change, a great energy moving toward you. If you repeat this exercise for a few days, you will be surprised at how much more alive you will feel. There is an energy circle taking place, and whenever the circle is complete, there is a great silence. Completing the energy circle makes you centered, and to be centered is to be powerful. You can also do this exercise with a flower, tree, stars, or another person.

Be a tree. Visualize yourself as a tree, with branches reaching up to the sky and roots extending into the earth. On every other inhalation, draw air and sunlight in and exhale them down into your roots. On the alternate inhalations, imagine gathering energy from the earth up through your roots and exhale this through your branches.

Learn to flow with all the changes that come up. Loosen up and relax.

Know you are breathing in. Know you are breathing out. Be aware of thoughts arising and passing away within your mind. Be aware of your judgments about these thoughts. Realize the suffering your judgments cause you, and smile with compassion. Dwell in the present moment.

Accept and express who you are. Live authentically.

Let go of greed.

Complete that which you have begun rather than dabbling in many things.

Cultivate your garden.

Live contented.

GLOSSARY

bandha: inner knots or locks to hold the pranic energy or psychic energy within certain areas in the body

bodhicitta: the motivation toward enlightenment; the mind of enlightenment

Bodhisattva: an enlightened being who, out of compassion, forgoes nirvana in order to save others

chakra: one of the seven centers of spiritual power in the human body: crown of the head; third eye/center of forehead; throat; heart/lung; solar plexus; sacrum; root/ anus and genitals

chi: the circulating life energy that is thought to be inherent in all things; also spelled ki or qi

dharma: the eternal law of the cosmos; the principle or law that orders the universe; capitalized, it indicates the body of teachings expounded by the Buddha

kinhin: walking meditation, practiced in Zen

koan: paradoxical anecdote or a riddle that has no solution, used in Zen Buddhism to show the inadequacy of logical reasoning

lovingkindness: tenderness and consideration toward others

mala: a string of beads used in meditation, especially for counting recitations, in various lengths, mainly in 108- and 27-bead strands

mandala: an intricate circular or geometric motif symbolizing the universe

mantra: a word or phrase repeated to aid concentration in meditation

metta: lovingkindness, the virtue of kindness

mindfulness: a mental state achieved by focusing one's awareness on the present moment while calmly acknowledging and accepting one's feelings, thoughts, and bodily sensations

mudra: a symbolic position in which the hands are held in meditation, dancing, or ritual

namaste: a bow and gesture of greeting or parting with the palms together in front of the chest; also, expressing respect through this gesture and bow; "homage" or "bowing to you"

nirvana: the ultimate goal, a state in which there is no suffering or desire, and no sense of self; a state of perfect happiness

prana: breathing or the breath; also, one of five vital breaths moving in the body

qigong: a type of ancient Chinese system of postures, exercises, breathing techniques, and meditations to improve one's chi

savasana/shavasana: the yoga pose of total relaxation; also called corpse pose

sutra: a rule or aphorism in Sanskrit literature; a Buddhist or Jainist scripture

tonglen: a compassion practice of taking the suffering of others and sending lovingkindness to them

zazen: sitting meditation, as practiced in Zen Buddhism

ABOUT THE AUTHOR

Barbara Ann Kipfer is a lexicographer and author. She holds doctorates in linguistics, archaeology, and Buddhist studies. Barbara is the author of **14,000 Things to Be Happy About**, and more than fifty other books, including thesauri, reference books, spiritually themed books, and list books. Her website is thingstobehappyabout.com.